PRAISE FOR SCHOOL DESEGREGATION AND U.S. PRESIDENTS: HOW THE ROLE OF THE BULLY PULPIT AFFECTED THEIR DECISIONS

"LaRuth Gray's new volume fills a gaping hole in the story of American school desegregation: what role did post–World War II American presidents play in dismantling or encouraging racial discrimination in the nation's schools? Historians of the future will find valuable new insights into presidential decision-making in the vivid portraits Gray provides of what was going on in the White House under presidents from Eisenhower to Reagan."
—James Harvey, founder of National Superintendents Roundtable

"Public education in America is a function of our politics, and few issues have been as controversial as school desegregation. Yet, politics is the art of the possible, and as LaRuth Gray shows in her new book, American presidents post-*Brown* used their positions differently to push for a new reality in our schools and communities. Language and leadership matter, and the unique bully pulpit of the president of the United States can further our collective vision for a better society or retrench from it. Dr. Gray's depiction of how our nation's top leaders used their positions to spur states and local communities to implement *Brown*, or allowed them to run from it, offers telling insight into why we're still fighting over the same issues so many years later. The valuable insight that this book provides into the highest levels of leadership of our past can hopefully spur today's leaders to use their positions to finally realize the values and ideals that our nation stands on." —Joshua P. Starr, former CEO of PDK International; managing partner of the International Center for Leadership and Education

"LaRuth Gray's history of U.S. presidents' views and voices on segregation offers a fascinating account of how the torturous path to integration—still unfinished—has been shaped by our highest elected leaders. She places their use of the bully pulpit in the context of their life-experiences and beliefs, as well as the politics of the times, and deepens our understanding of how pitfalls have emerged and how progress can be made. A must-read for everyone who cares about where America has been and where it is going with respect to racial equity and the creation of common ground on which we can all stand together." —Linda Darling-Hammond, president & CEO of Learning Policy Institute; professor emeritus, Stanford University

"Gray's book provides a fresh perspective and adds to the lens so frequently used by examining the perspective and actions of the most powerful and influential leader in the land, the individual elected by the people to reflect the values and soul of the nation, the president of the United States. What the writing confirms is that, while the 'voice' of that individual (the bully pulpit) is powerful and as critically important as the laws and the courts in promoting equality, they all too often succumb to the temptation of convenience, politics, and the egocentric need to sustain/retain power, regardless of the practical or moral consequences it has on the pursuit of equality for all. It underscored for me and confirmed two things: how little progress we have really made over the decades; and how tentative, frail, and vulnerable even those modest gains are today. They exist because of the perseverance and sacrifice of a few and because of luck or circumstance. They do not appear to be strongly embedded yet and growing more rooted with each succeeding administration or generation. The bully pulpit seems to be used more for personal ambition than it does for representing the moral conviction of a nation. As I read, I found myself simultaneously drifting back and reflecting on my personal experiences as a student, young educator, and later a professional engaged in 'improvement of public education' over the course of those presidential administrations from Eisenhower on. What had I done (or not done); what could I have done; why didn't I? The ride was emotional. The outcome, thanks to this book, is that I am much better informed, more aware, and more deeply committed going forward." —Everett Barnes

"Dr. LaRuth Gray, because of her new book, confirms that she is a scholar and master storyteller. In this carefully crafted study, she examines the role of each of the seven presidents following the Supreme Court's *Brown v. Board of Education* ruling. She shows how each considered whether to use, or not use, the 'bully pulpit' to influence acceptance of school desegregation. For career educators, this is a page-turner that spells out the contemporary factors influencing those decisions, as well as the impact on schoolchildren. By doing so, Dr. Gray has further clarified our understanding of this important period in our history." —C. Fred Bateman, EdD, executive director of Urban Superintendents Association of America

"What a gift my friend and colleague Dr. LaRuth Gray has given me in this scholarly, yet culturally sensitive treatise on an issue that has both paralleled my life and my career. *Brown* was decided as I was graduating from high school, and its importance followed me through my years in a teachers' college, and in my 35 years as a school superintendent in communities as diverse as the backgrounds of the presidents whose work is explored in these pages: as a superintendent in a midwestern farming community (Eisenhower and Ford), and in a New England coastal community (Kennedy), in a Southern multiracial community (Johnson and Carter), and in a metropolitan urban community (Nixon and Reagan). Speeches, policies, legislation, and legal decisions all come to life in this historical analysis of how these presidents used their bully pulpit to address the most significant public school issue of our time. Thank you, LaRuth." —Dr. Charles Fowler, president of School Leadership, LLC

"For over seven decades, Dr. LaRuth Gray has been an extraordinary educational leader and a committed advocate for education and civil rights. In this important new book, she shares the journey from segregation to local and national level through the lens of the bully pulpit of seven US presidents. Read this book and renew your commitment to using education as a vehicle for progress!" —Pedro Noguera

"As a student of history, I found LaRuth's Gray's presentation of the influence of the bully pulpit on race relations to be important and revelatory. It sheds important light on the impact of leadership and administration that was not presented to those of us raised during and after the 1980s." —Anthony Bienstock, founder and partner, private equity

"The story of racial integration and desegregation is not one that can be simplified to a person or a moment, but rather it is a collection of decisions and at times inactions of individuals and groups. This book very concisely highlights the relevance of how presidents used tools such as agencies to manage desegregation and integration. Creating a humanized narrative of these presidents that includes their background stories, and their discussions with staffers and agencies, is a welcomed discussion that will advance our thinking of educational equity." —Edward Fergus Arcia, PhD

"Gray's book is eye-opening and essential to understanding the power of the presidential bully pulpit, or lack thereof. It's an engrossing and expertly crafted breaking down of the boundaries of compartmentalized history. She illuminates the insights of these seven presidents toward school desegregation." —Doreen E. Barrett, PhD, CEO of D. E. Barrett & Associates Authentic Consulting Training Development

"Gray's book offers a compelling view of the power of the presidential 'bully pulpit' and its use over time to influence the course of school desegregation. Meticulously researched portraits of the Eisenhower through Reagan eras provide fascinating insights on how these presidents chose to use (or not use) words and actions to advance, stall, or impede progress on school desegregation. The book provides that rare combination . . . it both informs and challenges readers' knowledge and understanding of this complex subject." —Diana Clark, independent researcher and writer

School Desegregation and U.S. Presidents

How the Role of the Bully Pulpit Affected Their Decisions

LaRuth H. Gray

ROWMAN & LITTLEFIELD
Lanham • Boulder • New York • London

Published by Rowman & Littlefield
An imprint of The Rowman & Littlefield Publishing Group, Inc.
4501 Forbes Boulevard, Suite 200, Lanham, Maryland 20706
www.rowman.com

86-90 Paul Street, London EC2A 4NE, United Kingdom

Copyright © 2023 by LaRuth H. Gray

All rights reserved. No part of this book may be reproduced in any form or by any electronic or mechanical means, including information storage and retrieval systems, without written permission from the publisher, except by a reviewer who may quote passages in a review.

British Library Cataloguing in Publication Information Available

Library of Congress Cataloging-in-Publication Data

Names: Gray, LaRuth H., 1932– author.
Title: School desegregation and U.S. presidents : how the role of the bully pulpit affected their decisions / LaRuth H. Gray.
Description: Lanham, Maryland : Rowman & Littlefield, [2023] | Includes bibliographical references. | Summary: "This book provides an eye-opening look at the outsized role that seven presidents played in shaping the policies and practices relative to school desegregation through their bully pulpit"—Provided by publisher.
Identifiers: LCCN 2023001291 (print) | LCCN 2023001292 (ebook) | ISBN 9781475871357 (cloth) | ISBN 9781475871364 (paperback) | ISBN 9781475871371 (epub)
Subjects: LCSH: School integration—United States—History—20th century. | Executive power—United States—Case studies.
Classification: LCC LC214.2 .G73 2023 (print) | LCC LC214.2 (ebook) | DDC 379.2/630973—dc23/eng/20230207
LC record available at https://lccn.loc.gov/2023001291
LC ebook record available at https://lccn.loc.gov/2023001292

For my husband, Joseph Morgan

For my children, Dierdra and Phillip

For my grandchildren, Alexander, Christopher, Jenni, Kenya, Maya, Ryan, Tierney, Tyler, and Zachary

Contents

Preface	xi
Acknowledgments	xv
Chapter 1: Dwight David Eisenhower	1
Chapter 2: John Fitzgerald Kennedy	23
Chapter 3: Lyndon Baines Johnson	45
Chapter 4: Richard Milhous Nixon	63
Chapter 5: Gerald Rudolph Ford	79
Chapter 6: James Earl Carter	95
Chapter 7: Ronald Wilson Reagan	109
Chapter 8: Conclusion	127
Bibliography	133
Appendices	145

Preface

As the 70th anniversary of *Brown v. the Board of Education* of Topeka, Kansas, approaches, questions are still raised as to the impact and effect of *Brown*.

The rationale for the "broken promises" of *Brown* include poverty, White flight, middle-class Black flight, federally-sanctioned segregated housing, low expectations, and all the coded terms and "isms" we have used over the years to explain why our public schools are so segregated and in particular why a significant number of Black children are not achieving. For so long, we have looked to the courts and legislation at the federal and state level "to fix this."

The author believes that the school segregation/integration journey has also been shaped by the executive branch exerting the highest power through the presidential bully pulpit.

Lyman Abbott, a former Congregationalist minister, liberal theologian, and editor of *The Outlook*, a magazine of the progressive era, described a meeting with President Theodore Roosevelt:

> Half a dozen of us were with the president in his library. He was sitting at his desk reading to us his forthcoming Message. He had just finished reading a paragraph of a distinctly ethical character when he suddenly stopped, swung round in his swivel chair, and said, "I suppose my critics will call that preaching, but I have got such a bully pulpit."[1]

Ron Elving argues that the Roosevelt observation means the president could reach the country with high-minded ideals through his public pronouncements and command of press attention.[2]

Lia Epperson spends time in the introduction to *Undercover Power* describing the impact of the bully pulpit:

> We are conditioned to think of civil rights as litigation-oriented, molded and transformed through judicial law, but that is just a fraction of the story of civil rights advocacy. The Executive Branch has had a powerful and arguably

dominant role in directing the scope and meaning of civil rights law over the last halfcentury.³

Tom Wicker states:

But as much as Americans might wish the presidency to be a place of moral purity and disinterested public service, it is essentially a political office, functioning best in the hands of an astute politician—a place from which to persuade people (in Harry Truman's words) to do what they ought to do without persuasion. That sometimes may mean that the presidency must be a "bully pulpit" from which leadership is effectively preached.⁴

Other authors have commented as follows:

The President's bully pit correlates to direct power. Within that power construct, the President sets the tone of the nation leading by example. If a president does not believe in the equality of all races, how can she or he lead our nation to believe in equality? To be a truly great president, he or she must genuinely believe in equality and social justice for all and do anything in her or his power to uphold these ideals.⁵

The president can frame, implement, and transform the government.⁶ The office of the presidency has enormous, larger-than-life quality; it is at once the most powerful and the weakest executive office in the world. The great opportunity to do good is matched by the equally strong capacity to do great harm.⁷

Indeed, some will argue that the president is merely a figurehead and has very little impact on social justice issues. The author argues, instead, that presidential leadership and power are essential for progress regarding social justice issues. "The presidency is the chief engine of progress in American history; its leadership and power are central."⁸

During the time of the civil rights movement, rhetoric proved to be a formative tool in shaping the outcome of legislation once it was passed.⁹, ¹⁰

The book looks at the president's voice in shaping policy. It pays special attention to how different presidents allied themselves with different groups and examines the instances when presidents attempted to shift public opinion and the impact and aftermath of those attempts. During the modem American civil rights movement, the power of the American president was undergoing a period of growth. President Franklin Roosevelt proposed a new vision of the office of the president that goes beyond the position's constitutionally enumerated powers, stating that it was the president's duty to propose laws.¹¹ President Johnson further expanded on this sentiment, stating that the legislative process would move "at the speed of a glacier without continued presidential pressure."[12]

This book is *not* about discussing systemic racism within the school desegregation journey. Rather, the author intends to discuss a particular *aspect* of America's attempt to address the impact of a landmark decision on America's public schools. It addresses the role of the president's bully pulpit as the country sought to eliminate de jure segregation in public schools and correct years of violation of the civil rights of millions of Black schoolchildren.

NOTES

1. Dorris Kearns Goodwin, *The Bully Pulpit*, xi. Simon & Schuster.

2. Ron Elving (2017, July 4), "Trump puts a twist on the meaning of 'bully pulpit,'" WBUR NEWS.

3. Lia Epperson (2008), "Undercover Power: Examining the Role of the Executive Branch in Determining the Meaning and Scope of School Integration Jurisprudence," *Berkeley Journal of African-American Law & Policy 10*, no. 2: 146.

4. Tom Wicker (1991), *One of Us: Richard Nixon and the American Dream* (Random House), 506.

5. H. Prentice Baptiste and Blanca Araujo (Spring 2004), "American Presidents and Their Attitudes, Beliefs, and Actions Surrounding Education and Multiculturalism: A Series of Research Studies in Educational Policy. Second Installment: Examining Presidents Andrew Jackson, Woodrow Wilson, & Dwight D. Eisenhower," *Multicultural Education 11*, no. 3: 36–42.

6. A. Schlesinger (2002), *The American Presidents Series* (Henry Holt & Company); H. Prentice Baptiste & Rebecca Sanchez (Fall 2004), "American Presidents and Their Attitudes, Beliefs, and Actions Surrounding Education and Multiculturalism: A Series of Research Studies in Educational Policy. Fourth Installment: Examining Presidents George Washington, James K. Polk, and Franklin D. Roosevelt," *Multicultural Education 12*, no. 1: 33-40.

7. Michael A. Genovese (2001), *The Power of the American Presidency: 1789–2000* (Oxford University Press).

8. Sidney Blumenthal (2003), *The Clinton Wars* (Plume).

9. Jared Cohen (1995), *Accidental President* (Simon and Schuster).

10. Roger W. Cobb & Charles Elder (1971), *Participation in American Politics: The Dynamics of Agenda Building* (Allyn and Bacon).

11. Franklin D. Roosevelt (1937), press conference.

12. Lyndon B. Johnson (1971), *The Vantage Point* (Holt, Rinehart and Winston), 448.

Acknowledgments

My greatest debt is to my husband, Joseph Morgan, who provided unrelenting support and always encouraged me when it was most needed. He would not allow me to give up when, for example, I could not seem to come up with the next paragraph, nor did he allow me to lose balance during this process.

An immense debt of gratitude is owed to my colleague Edward Fergus, who planted the seed for framing this book. In our many conversations while we were both working in equity spaces at New York University, his questioning centered around: Why had school desegregation been so tough? Why had the attitude of *Not in My Backyard* been so palatable to so much of the nation's majority? These and other similar questions led me to explore, through another set of lenses, the country's leadership.

Bringing this book to a final product could not have happened without the assistance of Markysha Douglas. She began with me while completing her work as a graduate student at New York University. She continued to assist me as she entered her social work career, working late evenings and crowded weekends. She provided diligent and indefatigable support through careful attention to every aspect of the manuscript's preparation. There are not adequate words to thank her for her time, her loyalty, and her perseverance through all my constant revisions.

My son, Phillip Gray, read the first chapter of the book in its initial phase. He called and said, "I want to read more." That was the first sign that maybe I was on my way. He then said, "Mom, you can write." His observations suggested that maybe I had a shot.

My daughter, Dierdra Gray Clark, was unwavering in her faith and support. She constantly reminded me that the theme of the book would relate to her generation. I appreciated her cheerful advocacy.

I am blessed with many supportive friends who provided continuous encouragement. Those include Betty Himmel and Yvonne Pollack, who were always there, asking the right questions, listening carefully to the progress

I was making, and stimulating my decision-making through invaluable lunch meetings.

My colleague and friend Doreen Barrett took the time to read the very first rough, uneven, over-paged draft of the manuscript. My conversations with her afterward helped me to further scrutinize the range of my arguments.

Years of friendship with retired school superintendent Barbara Pulliam served as an anchor for just "getting it done."

My first conversation with Tom Koerner, acquisition editor at Rowman & Littlefield, provided me with the needed confidence to continue the development of a plausible manuscript. His gentle but firm prodding to remove extemporaneous noise was so valuable. I am grateful for his patient guidance.

Sincere thanks to Pedro Noguera during his tenure and leadership as executive director of New York University's Metropolitan Center for Research and the Transformation of Schools, for giving me the space and time to explore the issues this book addresses. Working with him as both deputy director and then as scholar-in-residence at the Metro Center provided the best "light bulb" moments of my career in the field of education. His friendship, belief in me, and unwavering support has been priceless.

It is difficult to articulate my immense sense of gratitude to Christopher Hoffmann, who provided stellar editorial guidance and skillful editing support. His keen eye enabled me to often reconsider "What am I really trying to say?"

Sharon Adams Taylor, retired associate director of AASA, thought that my treatment of school desegregation deserved a look. She shared her thinking with her colleague James Municello, who then shared my initial proposal with Rowman & Littlefield. Jim and Sharon paved the way, and for that I am much obliged.

Finally, to my mother, Hazel Mae, thank you. She championed family excellence and helped me see in my earlier years that in spite of the cruelties of Jim Crow, if I always kept my eye on the prize, ultimately I could control my path forward.

Chapter 1

Dwight David Eisenhower

History remembers Eisenhower as the beloved warrior and honest man from humble roots. But much of history does not chronicle the canny politician who refused to take a strong stand, either personally or as a leader, on *Brown v. Board of Education* and who dragged his feet on desegregation to appease Southern politicians.

Eisenhower came to the president's office as a national hero, never having been elected to anything previously and therefore having no experience with partisan politics. He had been heralded by Black leadership for following through on Truman's decision to end segregation in the United States Armed Forces. The Gallup polls found him the most admired man for 10 straight years.[1]

Not only was Eisenhower a storied persona, he was sworn in at a time when the Republican Party had claimed the White House, the Senate, and the House of Representatives for the first time in a quarter century. Throughout Ike's presidency, his public approval ratings averaged in the mid-60th percentile,[2] compared with Truman's average in the mid-40th percentile. This fact shaped one of the core elements in Ike's response to desegregation and thus impacted his bully pulpit.

Eisenhower disliked speech-making, and he particularly felt uncomfortable in using the words *discrimination* and *racial* in public addresses. Acutely aware of the political risks inherent in a public leadership role in civil rights, Ike preferred to limit his involvement in racial questions to the occasional assertion of general democratic principles. This is exemplified by his 1953 State of the Union address, when he stated that "discrimination against minorities exists despite our allegiance to this ideal. . . . Much of the answer lies in the power of fact, fully publicized; of persuasion, honestly pressed; and of conscience, justly aroused."[3]

It was during the first year of his first term that the Supreme Court was preparing to issue judgment on one of the most virulent and eviscerating social issues of the country. Further, it was on his watch that the Supreme Court issued instructions to the Justice Department to participate in the *Brown* case. On June 8, 1953, the Supreme Court "invited" the attorney general to file a brief in response to specific questions from the Court on the applicability of the Fourteenth Amendment to the school segregation issue.[4]

The country was firmly in the grip of segregation in most aspects of its citizens' daily lives, but most significant was segregation in its public schools. Seventeen states and the District of Columbia mandated segregated public education, and four other states made segregation optional.[5]

Illustrative of the driving force of Eisenhower's bully pulpit are in his initial State of the Union address, February 2, 1953, during his first term, and a conversation with Portia Washington Pittman, daughter of Booker T. Washington, on October 9, 1956.

The language of his first State of the Union address is extremely cagey on the question of segregation in general. From the beginning of Ike's tenure, this language and tone became his Memorandum of Understanding (MOU).

Eisenhower said:

> We know that discrimination against minorities persists despite our allegiance to this ideal. Such discrimination—confined to no one section of the Nation—is but the outward testimony to the persistence of distrust and of fear in the hearts of men. This fact makes all the more vital the fighting of these wrongs by each individual, in every station of life, in his every deed. Much of the answer lies in the power of fact, fully publicized; of persuasion, honestly pressed; and of conscience, justly aroused. These are methods familiar to our way of life, tested and proven wise.[6]

When Portia Washington Pittman visited the White House, Eisenhower stated that change to the condition of African Americans could not be enacted by law:

> Mrs. Pittman, the vital things that affect your race and others, where changes have to be made in the attitudes of mankind, cannot, in my opinion, be done by law. I like to feel that while we have to change the hearts of men, we cannot do it by cold lawmaking, but must make these changes by appealing to reason, by prayer, and by constantly working at it through our own efforts.[7]

Further clarifying the tone in his personal account, Eisenhower declared:

> A matter which needed Executive impetus in the early months of 1953 was civil rights. My philosophy on this subject had often been stated. I believe that political or economic power to enforce segregation based on race, color, or creed is morally wrong and should by all practicable and reasonable means be abolished

as soon as possible. My feelings could well be summed up by one sentence: There must be no second-class citizens in this country.

It seemed to me that much could be done by Executive power alone. . . . The very least the Executive could do would be to see first that the federal house itself was in order and that segregation in all installations where federal money was spent should become a thing of the past.[8]

FORMATIVE YEARS

Dwight David Eisenhower was born under an American system of lawful racial segregation, which was instantiated in Jim Crow laws of the South and practiced de facto in the North. Although his birthplace was in Denison, Texas, Eisenhower spent his boyhood in Abilene, Kansas. Of German descent, his ancestors had arrived in North America in 1741. Family members became ministers in the River Brethren, an offshoot of the Mennonite Church, and purchased large tracts of farmland to accommodate the church's flock.

Ike's grandfather moved his family west, possibly due to the climate of the Civil War and conflict with the Native American population.

Eisenhower's father was not enamored with rural farming life. Hoping to establish himself in business and freshly married, he entrenched himself in a dry-goods business. Losing interest after two years, he moved his family to Denison, Texas, and became strapped financially.[9] Moving back to Abilene allowed Eisenhower's dad to find employment among his kin in the extensive Mennonite community. Eisenhower's family was perceived as living on the "wrong side of the tracks."

In *At Ease: Stories I Tell to Friends*, Eisenhower writes extensively about his mother and father's influence on his formative years. Family life was intentionally structured with an emphasis on hard work and Bible study. "Ambition without arrogance was quietly instilled in us by both parents. Part of that ambition was self-dependence. My mother could recite from memory long passages of the Bible. . . . But these were not her only admonitions. Whenever any of us expressed a wish for something that seemed far beyond our reach, my mother often said, 'Sink or swim,' or 'Survive or perish.'"[10]

Although his academic performance was only average, Eisenhower was a gifted athlete. He formed a friendship with "a group of South Side boys defending the honor of his neighborhood against the wealthier and socially more prominent lads from north of the tracks." He became a strong boxer and developed a healthy appetite for outdoor sports, including fishing, hunting, and camping.[11] Sustaining an injury to his knee in high school, he repeated a grade, but the work ethic that had been instilled by his family structure sustained him.

Eisenhower's admission to West Point exemplifies this leitmotif of grit and resolve. He had started out with an attempt to gain acceptance at Annapolis, and though his examination placed him as the top candidate for Annapolis, his age rendered him ineligible for the Naval Academy. He was the second-place candidate for West Point and therefore considered an alternate. Eisenhower tells us, "The man who ranked above me in the West Point examinations failed to meet the physical requirements. I got the appointment from Senator Bristow in the spring of 1911."[12]

Eisenhower later reflected, "In the fall of 1896, I was . . . I was starting on a road in formal education which would not terminate until 1929. . . . In the third of a century between my first and last school was a series of revolutions—political and economic, social and scientific—which were to transform the human environment of the entire globe."[13] Indeed, this commentary by the 34th president of the United States is significant in illuminating the shape of Eisenhower's bully pulpit.

JOURNEY TO THE PRESIDENCY

As a result of his military career and successful role as commander-in-chief of NATO, Eisenhower became the Republican candidate of choice. The hallmark of his journey to the presidency was the force of his personal popularity. After the Truman years, the Republican Party, as noted by many of the party's kingmakers and especially those known as the Old Guard, needed someone who could mount an appeal strong enough to bring together Democrat and Independent support.

The nominee also needed to help the party achieve the perceived reversal toward centralization in government. In 1951, Henry Cabot Lodge visited Eisenhower at NATO headquarters in Paris and told the Supreme Allied Commander, "You are the only one who can be elected by the Republicans to the presidency. You must permit the use of your name in the upcoming primaries."[14]

Eisenhower, however, had always been opposed to "personal involvement" in politics. A year earlier, Eisenhower had confided in his secret diary:

> I do not want a political career; I do not want to be associated with any political party. . . . My basic purpose is to try, however feebly, to return to the country some portion of the debt I owe her. My family, my brothers and I, are examples of what this country with its system of individual rights and freedoms . . . can do for its citizens.[15]

Lodge was not the first to exhort Eisenhower to consider a presidential bid. Earlier in his career, Eisenhower had been often approached to enter politics:

> So far as I can now recall, the earliest serious suggestion that I might become a presidential candidate one day was made by Virgil Pinkley in 1943. Pinkley, then a newspaper correspondent in the North African theater of World War II . . . observed that in view of a practice that had all but become an American tradition, I would, as the wartime commander of large and successful military groups, inevitably be considered as a strong presidential possibility. . . . To say that I was astonished by Pinkley's suggestion is far from an exaggeration. . . . "Virgil," I said, "you've been standing out in the sun too long."[16]

Appeals to entertain a run for the presidency came from others than the political stalwarts, too:

> Douglas Southall Freeman . . . had become convinced that our system of government was being endangered by one-party domination and that a president should be elected who was dedicated to constitutional government and to sustaining and maintaining the checks and balances.
> This great historian urged that I change my wholly negative attitude toward politics. He saw it as my simple duty to the nation. . . . A number of people knew of my convictions about the need for balance among the several branches of government and the maintenance of the proper geographical distribution of political power. Those who held similar beliefs gave me little rest.[17]

Even President Truman, in 1945, told Eisenhower that he would aid him in seeking the presidency. Ike wrote, "While I thanked him for his flattering thought I had no ambition whatsoever along political lines and would not consider the possibility of seeking a political position. I added that I would never in my lifetime experience a moment of more intense personal satisfaction than that which saw the surrender of Hitler's remaining forces at Reims, France, on May 7, 1945."[18]

In 1948, Thomas J. Watson, IBM founder and a member of the Trustee Board of Columbia University, asked Ike (for the second time) to assume the presidency of the university. Ike writes fondly of his time there. However, as William Hitchcock points out in *The Age of Eisenhower*, that time was short-lived, as President Truman asked him to go to Washington to serve as senior advisor to the secretary of defense. In 1950, Eisenhower was named as Supreme Allied Commander of NATO.[19]

Pressure continued to mount. Strong grassroots action emerged in the form of national clubs, called "Citizens for Eisenhower."

In February 1952, at a New Hampshire pre-primary, over fifteen thousand people assembled in Madison Square Garden to enthusiastically call for Ike to run in response to the dilemma of the Republican Party, which had not been in power for years since the Great Depression, the New Deal, the Fair Deal, and World War II. Many saw Ike as a symbol of national unity, while others used persuasive arguments that Eisenhower alone could save both the Republican Party and the two-party system.

As the momentum for his nomination to the presidency grew, voices like those of Philip W. Porter of the Cleveland *Plain Dealer* swelled:

> There's something about the common sense of his remarks, the clarity of his English, the homely chain of his smile, and the national humility of the unaffected, un-swellheaded man who has had greatness thrust upon him, that would bowl over the workers and the young people, the very groups that the opposition to Truman must reach. I defy anyone to watch Eisenhower in action, to see him personally and not be convinced of this. He's got it. He can really sway the country.[20]

On February 11, 1952, Ike agreed after speaking to friends that after returning home from his assignment in Europe, if he were nominated by the convention, he would campaign for the presidency. "I was committed in my own mind to run if nominated, but not to seek the nomination."[21]

A month later, invited by Eisenhower to Paris, Republican strategist Herbert Brownell Jr. arrived at NATO headquarters to discuss a possible run for president. Brownell questioned Eisenhower regarding his position on civil rights. "The general recounted his efforts to abolish racial barriers in the army, and, as Brownell recalled, stated 'flatly' that if elected, his 'first order of business' would be 'to eliminate discrimination against Black citizens in every area under the jurisdiction of the federal government.'"[22]

In the days before the Republican convention in San Francisco, Eisenhower directly intervened in the drafting of the party platform. Ike had seen a draft put together by the chairman of the platform committee, Senator Prescott Bush of Connecticut. The draft stated that the Eisenhower administration "concurred" with the Supreme Court's *Brown* decision. The president insisted this was untrue. His administration merely "accepted" the ruling and would follow the law; the court's decision was its own.

On August 19th, Eisenhower called Herbert Brownell and expressed his frustration at being caught "between the compulsion of duty on the one side, and his firm conviction, on the other, that because of the Supreme Court's ruling, the whole issue had been set back badly." William Hitchcock observes that Eisenhower "felt that any direct link between himself and *Brown* would appear as an affront to the White South. If the platform drafters did not change the language to distance Eisenhower from *Brown*," Ike would decline to attend the Republican convention. "Needless to say," states Hitchcock,

"[Senator Prescott] Bush altered the language of the civil rights plan as directed by Eisenhower."[23]

Thus began the slippery slope of moral conviction, commitment, and implementation on school desegregation as addressed by the bully pulpit of the presidents of the United States.

Hitchcock observes that though Eisenhower earned the Republican nomination riding on a wave of popularity rather than "for any set of ideas or policies," Eisenhower did not rely on his reputation on the campaign trail. Rather, he directly confronted the Truman administration. He said the administration was "vehement, polemical, and partisan. He . . . heaped abuse on the New Deal and curried favor with the right wing of his party."[24]

Early on the campaign trail from Abilene, Eisenhower revealed the scale of his bully pulpit on segregation. In a clear pitch to the Southern White vote, when asked about civil rights legislation at a large press conference, Ike declared "his unalterable support of fairness and equality among all types of American citizens." He sidestepped the issue. "I do not believe we can cure all of the evils in men's hearts by law."[25]

In September of that same year, Ike did say he would eagerly abolish desegregation in the nation's capital and the armed services. But only a month later, in early October, at a Newark, New Jersey, campaign stop, Ike said his goal was to act "in [a] spirit of goodwill towards states where segregation still persisted," and that he wished "to enlist cooperation, not invite resistance."[26]

This perspective had been hinted at earlier; while still president of Columbia University, Ike made a speech at the convention of the American Bar Association where he spoke about "the middle way." "When the center weakens piecemeal, disintegration and annihilation are only steps away in a battle of arms or political philosophies. . . . We instinctively have greater faith in the counterbalancing effect of many social, philosophical, and economic forces than we do in arbitrary law."[27]

This philosophical stance framed Eisenhower's response to school desegregation and caused great concern among the civil rights leaders of the time: It was clear that Eisenhower was never going to use his bully pulpit to challenge segregationists. As the 1956 presidential campaign approached, Ike adopted what his speechwriter, Emmet Hughes, called "the most conservative caution" toward the subject of civil rights. Although Max Rabb, the minorities' officer in the White House, urged for a push on civil rights, the president remained wary. He did not think there was much to be gained politically by drawing attention to the *Brown* decision.

PLATFORM ON DESEGREGATION

When Eisenhower campaigned for a second term, he campaigned on what he perceived as a good civil rights effort. After all:

- It was on his watch that Blacks received voting-rights protection through the passage of legislation that became the Civil Rights Act of 1957.
- He had desegregated schools on army posts, shortly after he took office and before the *Brown* decision.
- Immediately after *Brown*, Ike had directed the commission of the District of Columbia to make Washington, DC, "a model for the nation,"[28] with DC schools moving toward full integration in 1955.
- He had implemented Truman's order requiring equal opportunity for African Americans in the U.S. military, thereby "achieving in two years what Truman failed to accomplish in seven."[29] In fact, Eisenhower had followed through on his campaign promises to desegregate all federal institutions in Washington, DC. When confronted by a reporter regarding certain schools on military bases that were still excluding Blacks, Eisenhower promised to look into the matter, saying, "Wherever federal funds are expended for anything, I do not see how any American can justify, legally or logically or morally, a discrimination in expenditure of those funds as among our citizens."[30]
- He had responded to a Southern governor's defiance of desegregation implementation by sending in federal troops to Little Rock, Arkansas.

In his 1952 campaign, Eisenhower had made a promise to "close the gap between promise and performance in civil rights." Indeed, in November of the next year, the public learned that Eisenhower's Justice Department would oppose school segregation before the Supreme Court. At the same time, South Carolina and Georgia had threatened to abolish their public schools if the Supreme Court ruled against them.[31] Ike was nervous about this stance, though, and did not want "education" to become the responsibility of the federal government. He asked Brownell, "What would happen if states would abandon public education?" Brownell reassured Ike, stating that any desegregation ruling would take years to implement and that states would work out any problems on their own.[32,33]

A month later, in December, Chief Justice Warren called the Court into oral argument on *Brown*. The Southern perspective was that "the Fourteenth Amendment did not contemplate the abolition of segregation in the public schools."[34] Thurgood Marshall, arguing for the plaintiffs, told the Court that segregated education was a "sorry heritage from slavery," and that separate schools could not be equal in their impact on "the Negro." The Justice Department had filed an amicus brief on behalf of the plaintiffs, and J. Lee Rankin, Eisenhower's assistant attorney general, concurred with Marshall, arguing against segregation in public schools.[35]

Black leadership had changed its perception of Eisenhower after the armed forces desegregation efforts and the establishment of an advisory committee (chaired by Vice President Richard Nixon) to review nondiscriminatory policies in the awarding of government contracts. They held out hope and began to praise Eisenhower and to believe he would "do the right thing."

The Southern wing of the Democratic Party became quite concerned. One of Eisenhower's great friends, former governor James Byrnes of South Carolina, suggested he might have gone too far. On the expected ruling of the Supreme Court banning segregation in public schools, Byrnes warned Ike that there would be "riots, resultant ill feelings and the like" and that the Southern states "would immediately cease support for public schools." Byrnes went on to say, "They are frightened of putting the children together." Eisenhower said, "Byrnes was afraid I would be carried away by the hopes of capturing the Negro vote in the country."[36]

It is at this point that one can begin to determine more of the construct of Eisenhower's bully pulpit on school desegregation. Ike "entertained serious doubts about the wisdom of administration involvement, and his doubts were reinforced by his friendships with southern political supporters and by his agreed goal of building the Republican Party in the South."[37] He responded to the Southern governors through a letter to Governor Byrnes, throwing his attorney general under the bus by separating himself from the attorney general's amicus brief in *Brown* and expressing an affinity with the South's position. Fredrick Burk writes that:

> Expressing sympathy with the South's position, Eisenhower held out the hope that measures could be found that would "progressively work toward the goals established by abstract principle, but which would not, at the same time, cause such disruption and mental anguish among great portions of our population that progress would actually be reversed." . . . He also suggested, in an early draft of the letter, that the attorney general could not ignore the precedents of recent Supreme Court cases that had "beclouded" the original *Plessy* decision on "separate but equal" facilities.

Adam Serwer argues that "Eisenhower opposed discrimination but seemed to sympathize far more with the White southerners whose lives would be disrupted by the end of Jim Crow than Blacks dwelling under its boot heel."[38]

Conversely, Susan Eisenhower, Ike's granddaughter, says that Eisenhower's early critics "presumed that his measured approach to civil rights was a sign of indifference."³⁹ She claims that only after decades could people understand that "laying the groundwork for progress was as critical a contribution as making impassioned speeches and taking sides." She argues that a middle-of-the-road approach was necessary to "keep the country united and to assure a civil dialogue that might avert open rebellion and bloodshed."⁴⁰

Thus Eisenhower chose not to buck the system of Jim Crow, the unconstitutional subjugation of Black schoolchildren, and most of all not to seriously disturb the Southern pattern of states' rights in desegregating schools. Though the Supreme Court had declared that state-ordered segregation in the schools was unconstitutional, Eisenhower would only act at the federal level, and he would not lead from a moral bully pulpit. As Kluger states, "Eisenhower's hands-off-the-South attitude would be on exhibit and reflected throughout his White House tenure."⁴¹

There are few educational policy and legal decisions that have impacted public schools in the United States more than *Brown v. Board of Education of Topeka*. The *Brown* Supreme Court decision brought forth critical questions about America's educational system. How should Black and White students be integrated in school districts as ordered by the *Brown* decision? What is the federal role in the "exposition of the law of the federal constitution, and (regarding) that the principle of desegregation of public schools is a permanent and indispensable feature of the constitutional system of the United States?"⁴²

Eisenhower was the first president post-Reconstruction, operating from a seat of power and thus commanding a bully pulpit, to enter his first term facing a civil rights crisis: the implementation, evasion, defiance, resistance, and insolence of state governors in the exposition of the federal law in *Brown*.

In 1950, the NAACP and Thurgood Marshall began to mount a legal challenge to the doctrine of *Plessy* in five separate cases, which would later be grouped together by the Supreme Court when it decided to hear the case of *Oliver Brown v. Board of Education of Topeka* in December 1952. In June 1953, after six months of mulling, the Court decided to postpone its decision in order to hear another round of arguments.

Hitchcock, in *The Age of Eisenhower*, proposes that a possible reason for the postponement was that Chief Justice Vinson "was looking for guidance from the newly installed Eisenhower administration."⁴³ The chief justice invited Attorney General Herbert Brownell to file a brief as "a friend of the court" stating the opinion of the administration on the matter of public school segregation.⁴⁴ Kenneth O'Reilly states that "Eisenhower saw the court's 'invitation' for what it was (a command) and condemned it as crude power play that interfered with his party's courtship of the White southern voter."⁴⁵

Although other members of the cabinet were also wary of taking a strong stand, Brownell convinced Eisenhower that the Justice Department could not remain silent. He would have to comply with the Supreme Court's request.

Brownell took the leeway that Eisenhower gave him to quietly work with a team of Justice Department lawyers to explore the origins and limits of the Fourteenth Amendment. As it related to distinctions of race or color, did the intent of the Fourteenth Amendment apply to public schools?[46]

During the time that Brownell was working on his brief, Chief Justice Vinson died of a heart attack, in the fall. Vinson's replacement was Earl Warren, a former GOP vice-presidential candidate and a challenger to Eisenhower for the GOP nomination in 1952. Warren's recess appointment had been recommended by Justice Felix Frankfurter. While there was opposition to the appointment, inclusive of five professors at Harvard Law School and Southerners, but there was also significant support.[47] The executive director of the NAACP endorsed Earl Warren's nomination, seeing that the nomination guaranteed a *Brown* ruling unfavorable to segregationist interests.[43]

How Eisenhower would use his bully pulpit is also reflected in the language of the letter Ike wrote to Governor Byrnes a month before the Warren Court opened. As mentioned above, Ike distanced himself from the *Brown* case. He indicated that because the question of legality of segregation in public schools was "a matter for lawyers and historians, he had been compelled to turn over to the attorney general and his associates full responsibility in the matter." Ike further indicated that Brownell, in writing his brief and advising the Court, "had acted according to his own convictions."[49]

After the visit from Governor Byrnes, Eisenhower wrote in his personal diary, "I do not believe that prejudices, even unjustified prejudices will succumb to compulsion . . . consequently, I believe that federal law imposed upon our states in such a way as to bring about a conflict of the police power of the state and of the nation would set back the course of progress in race relations for a long, long time."[50]

The administration's 600-page brief was submitted to the court in the fall of 1953. The document supported overturning *Plessy v Ferguson*. Brownell's brief argued that the intent of the Fourteenth Amendment was to secure full equality for Negroes before the law. The brief continued that the justices had the constitutional authority to end racial segregation in the schools. The Supreme Court had a duty to "enforce all rights arising under the Fourteenth Amendment without awaiting exercise of the independent enforcement power granted Congress." The brief further suggested a one-year transition period.[51] William T. Coleman, a Washington, DC, attorney who collaborated with Thurgood Marshall on the NAACP brief, insisted in a letter to Huston of the *New York Times*, August 24, 2006, that Rankin and Elman told him that President Eisenhower himself had edited the paper of the *Brown I* brief that stated the government's position on the issue of segregated schools. Elman confirmed that Eisenhower edited the *Brown I* brief.[52]

Burk reported:

> Despite the incidents in the fall of 1954 at border-state schools, both the Eisenhower administration and Southern state officials realized that the real showdowns over desegregation, if they developed, would take place in the Deep South and would occur only after the issuance of the Supreme Court's implementation order. Writing to his longtime friend, Swede Hazlett, on October 23, 1954, the President observed, "The segregation issue will, I think, become acute or tend to die out according to the character of the procedure orders that the Court will probably issue this winter. My own guess is this; they will be very moderate and secure a maximum of initiative to local courts."

Summarizing his attitude on November 23, one day before the Justice Department was to file its implementation brief, Eisenhower commented, "I am sure America wants to obey the Constitution, but there is a very great practical problem involved, and there are certainly deep-seated emotions." He added his assertion that the Supreme Court's duty was "to write its orders of procedure in such fashion as to take into consideration these great emotional strains and the practical problems, and try to devise a way where under some form of decentralized process we can bring this about."[53]

As its new term began in October 1954, five months after its May 17 decision, the Supreme Court requested briefs on the matters of implementation. The Justice Department argued that school boards should be given 90 days to submit plans to end segregation. Federal district courts would then supervise the implementation of those plans, and there would be no hard deadline by which those plans would have to be fulfilled.

Arguing that the Court had now decided that the rights of Black citizens were being violated, the Justice Department asserted, "Relief short of immediate admission to non-segregated schools necessarily implies the continuing deprivation of those rights." Desegregated public schooling was "a fundamental human right supported by morality as well as law."[54]

Anthony Lewis, a reporter, revealed that inserted in the brief was one section in Eisenhower's own handwriting, which urged "understanding and goodwill" in implementation because of the long-standing perception of segregation as a moral and legal institution. Again, Eisenhower's deference to the institutions and feelings of Southern Whites was shaping the way desegregation would be carried out.[55] Nichols suggests as well that Eisenhower toned down the Justice Department's rhetoric, which might have shamed the South.[56]

On May 31, 1955, the Supreme Court issued its decision on the remedy in the case known as *Brown II*. Eisenhower's grandson, David Eisenhower, writes that "Eisenhower's views, communicated to Brownell and others, primarily focused on his practical concerns about implementation and southern acceptance, over time, of unitary school systems and the end of Jim Crow."⁵⁷

In *Simple Justice*, Richard Kluger remarks, "Much of the nation remained in calculated disregard of *Brown* because neither the President nor Congress came to the aid of the Courts." Kluger's concludes, "To stand above the battle was to side with the legions of resistance and Dwight D. Eisenhower, either by design or by obtuseness, comforted or dignified those who were ranged against the Court. He refused ever to say whether he agreed with the *Brown* decision."⁵⁸

EISENHOWER'S RESPONSE TO LITTLE ROCK

The events surrounding the integration of Little Rock's public schools put on display the commander-in-chief's absolute disdain for Arkansas governor Faubus for undermining the rule of law and constitutional guarantees upheld by the Supreme Court. It is instructive to visit the timeline leading to the deployment of federal troops in the attempt to enroll nine Black students at Central High.

Since the 1920s, there had been two high schools in Little Rock attended by most of its students: the Little Rock Senior (renamed pre-*Brown* to Central High School), built in 1929 at a cost of $1.5 million and attended by White students; and Paul Laurence Dunbar High School, attended by Black students, which opened in 1929 at a cost of $400,000. Those costs were leveraged with a donation from the Rosenwald Foundation of $67,500 from the Rockefeller General Education Fund.

Five days after the *Brown* decision, the Little Rock School Board issued a policy statement saying it would comply with the Supreme Court's decision in May 1955. The superintendent, Virgil Blossom, developed an approved Court plan, to become known as the Blossom Plan, which would gradually integrate the schools. Central High School would be integrated first, followed by junior-high-school students, and finally elementary students. Three months later, the NAACP's Legal Redress Committee petitioned the Little Rock School for immediate integration. As the Court's ruling specified no specific deadline, most Southern school districts followed Little Rock's path of "deliberate speed."

On April 29, 1957, after moving *Aaron v. Cooper* to the appellate court, the Court upheld Judge Miller's lower court decision to allow the Little Rock School Board to implement the Blossom Plan, which stipulated a gradual implementation of the desegregation plan. Because the Court maintained jurisdiction over the case, eventual implementation of the plan became a Court mandate. Between July and August 1957, an active campaign led by the Capital Citizens' Council was developed to spread fear, angst, and indecision. It was designed to thwart Black students' registration at Central High in the beginning of the school year in September.

The Capital Citizens' Council filed a motion seeking a temporary reprieve from school integration and a clarification of "segregation laws." The reprieve was granted two days later on the grounds that school integration could lead to violence. Events unfolded as follows:

August 18, 1957: A district-court judge, Ronald Davies, nullified the reprieve and ordered the school board to proceed with its gradual integration plan. It did grant a thirty-day stay of its order during which an appeal could be made to the Supreme Court. The NAACP immediately asked the Supreme Court to vacate that stay, which prompted the Court to schedule a special session for August 28.[59]

Labor Day, 1957: Governor Faubus interrupted the *I Love Lucy Show* to announce that he had received reports describing "caravans" of White supremacists traveling to Little Rock for the purpose of preventing the integration of Central High. Faubus told the television audience that he had called out the Arkansas National Guard to preserve order at Central High. His real goal was to prevent the Black students from entering Central High on opening day, September 4th. He legitimized his action by saying: "Now that a federal court has ruled that no further litigation is possible . . . there is evidence of disorder and threats of disorder which would have but one inevitable result—that is, violence which can lead to injury and the doing of harm to persons and property."[60]

September 4, 1957: Nine Black students attempted to enter Central High for the first time. They were turned back by the commanding officer of the Arkansas National Guard on the orders of Governor Faubus. At a press conference later that day, Faubus justified his orders with another description of the likely violence and harm he said would follow the students' entrance.[61]

September 7, 1957: Federal District Judge Davies denied a petition from the school board to delay integration at Central High School. He ordered that desegregation begin on Monday, September 9th. Judge Davies stated, "The testimony and arguments this morning were, in my judgment, as anemic as the petition itself. In an organized society, there can be nothing but ultimate confusion and chaos if court decrees are flaunted, whatever the pretext."[62]

September 14, 1957: Faubus and Eisenhower met in Newport, Rhode Island, with no clear-cut resolve or straightforward explanation of what was to happen. Nichols reports, "No one, Eisenhower said, would benefit from a 'trial of strength between the President and a governor.' . . . If Arkansas opposed federal authority, the outcome would be that 'the State would lose.'"[63]

September 20, 1957: Davies again ruled against the governor's request for a delay. The very next day, after running into resistance from the Arkansas National Guard, the Eisenhower administration obtained an injunction against the governor, forcing Faubus to withdraw the National Guard.

On September 23, nine Black students were escorted inside Central High, protected by Little Rock police and state troopers armed with riot guns and tear gas. It is reported that over a thousand Whites gathered in front of Central High, working themselves into a hysterical frenzy. The mob beat up and chased reporters, broke windows, and chased the students before they were evacuated to safety by the police.[64] The mayor of Little Rock sent a telegram to the White House in which he said, "The mob that gathered was no spontaneous assembly. It was agitated, roused and assembled by a concerted plan of action."[65]

The news incensed Eisenhower, because Ike "was a military man and didn't want his orders undermined. He felt Faubus had been insubordinate."[66] The president was also concerned the riots compromised the credibility of the United States as a leader of democracy and a nation of laws.[67] John Foster Dulles told Attorney General Brownell that "this situation was ruining our foreign policy" and that its repercussions in "Asia and Africa will be worse for us than Hungary was for the Russians."[68]

Eisenhower addressed the "disgraceful occurrences" at Central High by issuing Presidential Proclamation 3204, which commanded that "all persons engaged in such obstruction of justice to cease and desist there from and to disperse forthwith." That proclamation fell on deaf ears.

September 24, 1957: Mayor Woodrow Mann telegrammed the president again, "pleading . . . in the interest of humanity, law, order, and the cause of democracy worldwide to provide the necessary federal troops. . . . The situation is out of control and police cannot disperse the mob."[69] Eisenhower immediately issued Executive Order 10730, placing the Arkansas National Guard under federal authority and sending a thousand U.S. Army soldiers from the 101st Airborne Division to Little Rock.

After one year of integration, Governor Faubus closed the public high schools in Little Rock to avoid further integration. The Supreme Court found the governor's actions to be illegal, as a result of *Cooper v. Aaron*. Little Rock's high schools reopened in 1959.

Eisenhower's use of federal troops to further desegregation in Little Rock received massive public scrutiny. In her book, *How Ike Led,* Susan Eisenhower describes the fallout:

Criticism for sending in federal troops, however, rained down on the President, most notably from Southern Democrats, who saw the use of the 101st Airborne as an "'illegal, ill-advised use of troops that makes the United States a military dictatorship." . . . And James Eastland, a Democrat for Mississippi, declared, "The President's move was an attempt to destroy the social order of the South."[70]

Sherman Adams, Eisenhower's chief of staff, later wrote of Ike's sending troops into Little Rock, "Of all his actions in his eight years in the White House, this was the most repugnant."[71] David Lawrence, the publisher of *U.S. News & World Report*, said, "The current administration is now dead in the South."[72] Eisenhower's hope of bringing White Southerners into the Republican Party was dashed. Even his civil-rights community was reluctant to give the president a resounding applause for the Little Rock intervention. They felt Eisenhower's emphasis on "order" and not civil rights was an emphasis that was hurtful.

Civil rights activist Roy Wilkins attributed the crisis to Eisenhower's neglect of the bully pulpit:

> Firm words and resolute action by him and his Administration would have rallied public opinion in 1955 when there was ample evidence that things were going badly. The White people in the South who could be called moderate were begging for some encouragement from the Chief Executive.[73]

One of Ike's speechwriters, Arthur Larson, shared illuminating perceptions of the core of Eisenhower's bully pulpit after his experience. His conclusion was also shared by the active Black civil rights leadership: "President Eisenhower, during his presidential tenure, was neither emotionally nor intellectually in favor of combating segregation in general."[74] There are disturbing stories illustrative of the precarious position of Blacks on the campaign prior to Eisenhower's first term of his presidency.

E. Franklin Morrow, a Black graduate of Bowdoin College and Rutgers Law School, was granted a leave from the TV press bureau at CBS to join the campaign. Kenneth O'Reilly reported that "Morrow's principal responsibility at each campaign stop was to wander around Black neighborhoods and get a feel for the common people."[75] Morrow's life on the Eisenhower campaign trail was one of lonely segregation from other members of the campaign entourage and hotel and restaurants that denied him access.

Once Eisenhower was installed, he was told to report to the White House. Upon arrival, there was no job assignment either in the White House or anywhere else. He received no return calls from the White House. "A very disturbing situation," he stated, "I had no communication whatsoever with the White House." He waited patiently, living off his savings, and adjusted to the environment of segregation in the nation's capital. He finally called Sherman Adams after seventeen months and was offered a job in the Commerce Department.[76]

As early as 1957, Black leadership under the new organization Southern Christian Leadership was becoming increasingly concerned about the administration's attitude toward their numerous requests. The Eisenhower administration did not respond to these requests and literally brushed the requests aside.[77]

E. Frederick Morrow wrote, "With the exception of our unsettled relations with the Russians, there is no problem that gives this administration more concerns or more anxious moments than civil rights."[78] Eisenhower admonished the civil rights leaders to be patient in an appearance at the Negro Publisher's Association meeting on May 12, 1958. As Morrow recalled, Eisenhower stuck to his familiar perspective, telling them, "While laws should not be ignored in bestowing citizenship rights . . . it had to be acknowledged that prejudice . . . is deeply rooted in the hearts of men and can only be changed by education and by constant work on the part of enlightened citizens."[79]

Six years after he became president, Eisenhower finally held his first face-to-face meeting with Black civil rights leadership.[80] Though Eisenhower could be credited with the first civil rights bill since reconstruction and recognized for voting rights, his administration never advocated the rapid implementation for racial integration. The public school system took a hit from his administration's allegiance to White Southerners. All of Ike's actions signaled to White Southerners that he was not going to speak directly from his bully pulpit of moderate leadership to confront the Jim Crow policies and practices of the South.

Justice William O. Douglas, one of nine justices on the *Brown* decision, blamed Eisenhower, for not using his bully pulpit to stop the violence that ensued after the Court's ruling and for failing to move the nation on a positive path after that ruling. "If he had gone to the nation on television and radio telling the people to obey the law and fall into line, the cause of desegregation would have been accelerated. . . . Ike's ominous silence on our 1954 decision gave courage to the racists who decided to rescind the decision, word by word, precinct by precinct, town by town, and county by county."[81]

LEGISLATIVE PROFILE AS PRESIDENT

One month after *Brown*, eight governors of the former Confederate union and government representatives of Arkansas, Tennessee, and Texas met and unanimously voted to refuse compliance with the decision.[82] Shortly after the *Brown* decision, every congressman and all but three senators from the states of the former Confederacy signed the Southern Manifesto, which pledged to overturn *Brown*.[83]

Publicly and from a leadership perspective, the Executive Branch provided almost no direction on implementing desegregation policies in the immediate wake of the *Brown* decision. On the contrary, President Dwight Eisenhower famously opined that "you can't change men's hearts with laws" and privately expressed support for states' rights. In criticizing the Supreme Court's desegregation decision, Eisenhower promised Southern leaders he would "make haste slowly."[84] Eisenhower allegedly believed in the practical purposes behind the separate-but-equal doctrine espoused in *Plessy v. Ferguson*.[85]

Four years later, on a reversal note, the Eisenhower administration recommended school desegregation legislation, which addressed the voting rights issue, even though near the end of his administration it opposed a measure prohibiting discrimination in schools that received federal funds.[86]

The NAACP chair goes on to say about the 1957 Eisenhower Bill, "I wanted to see the attorney general given power to use civil action to desegregate the schools; I wanted to submit desegregation plans no later than the 1961–1962 school year, and I wanted the federal government to cut off the funds if they failed to comply."

NOTES

1. *Washington Post*, December 25, 1960.
2. Susan Eisenhower (2020), "Essay," in *How Ike Led: The Principles behind Eisenhower's Biggest Decisions* (Thomas Dunne Books), 305.
3. Dwight D. Eisenhower (1953, February 2), 1953 State of the Union Address, Dwight D. Eisenhower Presidential Library, Museum & Boyhood Home online, https://www.eisenhowerlibrary.gov/sites/default/files/file/1953_state_of_the_union.pdf.
4. Richard Kluger (1975), *Simple Justice* (Alfred A. Knopf), 605–55.
5. Robert Fredrick Burk (1985), *The Eisenhower Administration and Black Civil Rights* (University of Tennessee Press), 132.
6. Eisenhower (1953, February 2), 1953 State of the Union Address, Dwight D. Eisenhower Presidential Library, Museum & Boyhood Home online, https://www.eisenhowerlibrary.gov/sites/default/files/file/1953_state_of_the_union.pdf.
7. Frederic E. Morrow (1963), *Black Man in the White House: A Diary of the Eisenhower Years by the Administrative Officer for Special Projects, the White House, 1955–1961* (Coward-McCann), 99.
8. Dwight D. Eisenhower (1963), *Mandate for Change, 1953–1956: The White House Years* (DoubleDay), 234–36.
9. William I. Hitchcock (2018), *The Age of Eisenhower: America and the World in the 1950s* (Simon & Schuster Paperbacks), 5.

10. Dwight D. Eisenhower (1981), *At Ease: Stories I Tell to Friends* (Eastern Acorn Press), 37–38.
11. Hitchcock (2018), *The Age of Eisenhower*, 7.
12. Eisenhower (1981), *At Ease*, 107.
13. Eisenhower (1981), *At Ease*, 86.
14. Eisenhower (1963), *Mandate for Change*, 18.
15. Robert H. Ferrell (1981), *The Eisenhower Diaries* (W.W. Norton & Company), 168.
16. Eisenhower (1963), *Mandate for Change*, 4–5.
17. Eisenhower (1981), *At Ease*, 334.
18. Eisenhower (1963), *Mandate for Change*, 5.
19. Hitchcock (2018), *The Age of Eisenhower*, 9.
20. *Cleveland Plain Dealer*, April 6, 1950.
21. Eisenhower (1963), *Mandate for Change*, 21.
22. David A. Nichols (2007), *A Matter of Justice: Eisenhower and the Beginning of the Civil Rights Revolution* (Simon & Schuster), 6.
23. Hitchcock (2018), *The Age of Eisenhower*, 299–300.
24. Hitchcock (2018), *The Age of Eisenhower*, 66.
25. *Washington Post*, June 6, 1952.
26. Hitchcock (2018), *The Age of Eisenhower*, 216.
27. Eisenhower (1963), *Mandate for Change*, 11.
28. Nichols (2007), *A Matter of Justice*, 66.
29. Harvard Sitkoff (2008), *The Struggle for Black Equality* (Hill and Wang), 5.
30. The president's news conference, The President's News Conference | The American Presidency Project, March 19, 1953, https://www.presidency.ucsb.edu/documents/the-presidents-news-conference-459.
31. W. H. Lawrence (1953, November 15), "Administration Expected to Fight School Segregation in High Court," *New York Times*; M. Robert Chalmers (1953, November 15), School cases force Brownell stand, *Washington Post*.
32. Nichols (2007), *A Matter of Justice*, 59.
33. Burk (1985), *The Eisenhower Administration and Black Civil Rights*, 137.
34. Frank R. Kent Jr (1953, December 8), "High Court Told It Has Duty to End School Segregation," *Washington Post*.
35. Nichols (2007), *A Matter of Justice*, 62.
36. Diary entry, July 24, 1953. PDDW, 14:418.
37. Burk (1985), *The Eisenhower Administration and Black Civil Rights*, 134–35.
38. Adam Serwer (2014, May 16), "Why Don't We Remember Ike as a Civil Rights Hero?," MSNBC, NBCUniversal News Group, https://www.msnbc.com/msnbc/why-dont-we-ike-civil-rights-msna329796.
39. Eisenhower (2020), "Essay," in *How Ike Led*, 244.
40. Eisenhower (2020), "Essay," in *How Ike Led*, 244.
41. Richard Kluger (1975), *Simple Justice* (Alfred A. Knopf), 727.
42. *Gonzaga Law Review*, 6, vol. 2.
43. Hitchcock (2018), *The Age of Eisenhower*, 22.
44. Hitchcock (2018), *The Age of Eisenhower*, 22.

45. Kenneth O'Reilly (1996), *Nixon's Piano: Presidents and Racial Politics from Washington to Clinton* (Free Press), 169.

46. Hitchcock (2018), *The Age of Eisenhower*, 222.

47. Arthur Krock (1953, December 10), "In the Nation," *New York Times*, https://www.nytimes.com/1953/12/10/archives/in-the-nation-the-power-of-the-office-and-the-man.html.

48. Nichols (2007), *A Matter of Justice*, 58.

49. Ann Whitman (1953, December 1), letter to Byrne, Ann Whitman Diary Series, Eisenhower Library. Name series box 3, DDEL.

50. Robert H. Ferrell (1981), *The Eisenhower Diaries* (W.W. Norton & Company), 245.

51. Luther A. Huston (1953, November 28), "High Court Urged to End School Bias; Justice Department Brief Tells Tribunal It Has the Power to Compel States to Act," *New York Times*, https://www.nytimes.com/1953/11/28/archives/high-court-urged-to-end-school-bias-justice-department-brief-tells.html.

52. Nichols (2007), *A Matter of Justice*, 297.

53. Ann Whitman (1954, November 23), *Ann Whitman Diary Series: Eisenhower to Swede Hazlett, Oct. 23, 1954*, Eisenhower Library. Name Series, Box 18; transcript of presidential press conference, Morrow Records, Box 11, DDEL.

54. Hitchcock (2018), *The Age of Eisenhower*, 231.

55. Burk (1985), *The Eisenhower Administration and Black Civil Rights*, 149.

56. Herbert Brownell and John P. Burke (1953), *Advising Ike: The Memoirs of Attorney General Herbert Brownell* (Press of Kansas), 179.

57. David D. Eisenhower and Julie Nixon Eisenhower (2011), *Going Home to Glory: A Memoir of Life with Dwight D Eisenhower* (Simon and Schuster), 103.

58. Kluger (1975), *Simple Justice*, 753.

59. Nichols (2007), *A Matter of Justice,* 224.

60. Governor Orval E. Faubus, Speech, September 2, 1957.

61. Governor Orval E. Faubus, September 4, 1957.

62. Crisis timeline, National Parks Service. U.S. Department of the Interior, https://www.nps.gov/chsc/learn/historyculture/timeline.htm.

63. Nichols (2007), *A Matter of Justice*, 181.

64. O'Reilly (1996), *Nixon's Piano*, 182.

65. "Crisis Timeline," National Parks Service.

66. John A. Kirk and Minnijean Brown Trickey (2007), *Beyond Little Rock the Origins and Legacies of the Central High Crisis* (University of Arkansas Press).

67. Kirk and Trickey (2007), *Beyond Little Rock the Origins and Legacies of the Central High Crisis.*

68. O'Reilly (1996), *Nixon's Piano*, 181.

69. Crisis timeline, National Parks Service.

70. Eisenhower (2020), "Essay," in *How Ike Led*, 261–62.

71. O'Reilly (1996), *Nixon's Piano*, 182.

72. O'Reilly (1996), *Nixon's Piano*, 182.

73. O'Reilly (1996), *Nixon's Piano*, 183.

74. Arthur Larson (1968), *Eisenhower: The President Nobody Knew* (Scribner's).

75. O'Reilly (1996), *Nixon's Piano*, 166–67.
76. Morrow (1963), *Black Man in the White House*, 11–13.
77. Morrow (1963), *Black Man in the White House*, 226–27.
78. Morrow (1963), *Black Man in the White House*, 216.
79. Morrow (1963), *Black Man in the White House*, 218.
80. Morrow (1963), *Black Man in the White House*, 228.
81. Jill Lepore (2018), *These Truths: A History of the United States* (W.W. Norton).
82. Lia Epperson (2008, April 4), "Undercover Power: Examining the Role of the Executive Branch in Determining the Meaning and Scope of School Integration Jurisprudence," *Berkeley Journal of African American Law and Policy, 10*(2), 153.
83. Numan V. Bartley (1969), *The Rise of Massive Resistance: Race and Politics in the South during the 1950s*, 77; Steven A. Shull (1999), *American Civil Rights Policy from Truman to Clinton: The Role of Presidential Leadership* (M.E. Sharpe).
84. O'Reilly (1996), *Nixon's Piano*, 170.
85. *Plessy v. Ferguson*, 163 U.S 537, 548–57 (1896), Id.
86. Shull (1999), *American Civil Rights Policy from Truman to Clinton*, 44.

Chapter 2

John Fitzgerald Kennedy

Kennedy arrived at his presidency at a time when the nation was "poised on the brink of a second reconstruction." The civil rights movement was moving toward a fever pitch, yet the federal government's legal force was unengaged.[1]

John Fitzgerald Kennedy's presidency was anchored in several pillars: an indestructible family bond; the role of his health patterns (extended hospital stays), giving him enormous time to read and write; respect for acts of courage, a passion for knowledge, and a keen interest in foreign affairs; and a philosophical bent that was encompassed by a pragmatic approach to reaching a goal—and the goal was always to win.

These pillars, in addition to others often cited by his biographers, helped shape his life's vision and resulted in a bully pulpit that was muted on civil rights, and thereby school desegregation, in the first two years of his presidency.

FORMATIVE YEARS

Jack Kennedy was born into a middle-class neighborhood in Brookline, Massachusetts, where, initially, he went to Brookline's public schools. His family later moved to the wealthy suburb of Bronxville, New York, where he transitioned to private schools. Kennedy recalled that "It was an easy, prosperous life, supervised by maids and nurses."[2]

Joseph Kennedy, Jack's dad, also grew up in a life of privilege, though he avoided talking about it. Fredrik Logevall states that Joseph Kennedy "was keen to hide the fact that he had grown . . . wanting for nothing and with advantages others did not have."[3] Though a multimillionaire by the time he was thirty-two, it was repeatedly made clear to Joe Kennedy that he and his Irish American family would never be fully accepted by the elite of Boston society. In 1922, in Cohasset, a summer enclave for Boston's Brahmin class,

Joe was denied acceptance at the country club, and Rose, his wife, was snubbed by the other society ladies. Years later, the prejudice they had faced still bothered him. "Goddamn it! I was born here [Boston]. My children were born here. What the hell do I have to do to be an American?"[4]

FAMILY BONDING

Much has been written to describe the Kennedy clan character. Words like *arrogance, ungrateful*, and phrases like *sense of superiority* abound in the pages of biographers, journalists, and self-described experts.

Ralph Martin, author of *A Hero for Our Time*, offers a different perspective: "The Kennedys were taught early they were a tribe. . . . Fight the common enemy, even if the enemy was right. It seemed true that they preferred each other's company to everyone else's." Martin attributes the fact that the Kennedy children devoted themselves to public service and responsibility in spite of their wealth and insular nature to the influence of their mother, Rose.[5]

Both parents valued the importance of education, the avoidance of idleness, and loyalty to family. However, a major anchor of that value system was winning. Joseph impressed on his children it was not about playing well or competing for the sake of competing but to defeat all they met; to secure the top prize. "We want no losers around here, only winners."[6]

At his father's funeral, Robert Kennedy recalled, "We were to try harder than anyone else. We might not be the best, and none of us were, but we were to make the effort to be the best. 'After you have done the best you can,' he used to say, 'the hell with it.'"[7]

Born sickly and frail, at two years old Kennedy contracted scarlet fever and was reported to have almost died. Rose Kennedy was unable to care for him as she went into labor with his sister Kathleen. Barbara Leaming tells us that Joe Kennedy, who had been almost entirely absent for the first years of Jack's life, "burst into (Jack's) life with all the focus and intensity the lonely little boy had missed. . . . Joe's intensely emotional reaction to his son's ordeal, combined with Rose's absence, bonded the boy to his father."[8]

After his hospital stay, he was sent away to a recuperative facility in Maine for three months. At age four, Jack was able to attend only ten weeks of a thirty-week term. At age thirteen, at Canterbury, a Catholic boarding school in Connecticut, he suffered one malaise after another. The school infirmary became a second home. By the time the young Kennedy was fifteen, his entire body had been racked with pain. Afflictions continued to follow him at the prep school, Choate. Throughout these many years, Jack would cover his pattern of illness with charm, wit, humor, and a robust zest for life.

Thirty years after his birth, Kennedy was diagnosed with the potentially fatal disorder Addison's disease. The family did not disclose this publicly until after his death. These continuous health issues during his youth and college years often landed him in bed, recuperating, for weeks and on occasion months at a time.

Jack used these times to read and write, encouraged by his mother. Rose's rallying cry was that reading constituted "the most important instrument of knowledge." His interests from age 10 included tales of heroes who protected the weak and died of worthy causes. His mother said, "He had a strong romantic and idealistic streak. In fact, he was inclined to be somewhat of a dreamer."[9]

JOURNEY TO THE PRESIDENCY

At age 29, John Fitzgerald Kennedy entered the House of Representatives from the 11th Congressional district, where he would serve three terms in one of the most populous states in the nation, Massachusetts. He took the same seat his grandfather, Honey Fitz, had held 50 years earlier.

As a young Congressman, Jack's views were those of a liberal on eliminating racial prejudices; but he had no interest in challenging the intractably systematized place of Blacks in the fabric of American life. He circumvented the national debate over the "Negro" question by approaching the subject as a local matter.

Robert Kennedy explained, "We weren't thinking of the Negroes of Mississippi or Alabama—what should be done for them. . . . By keeping the focus local, Jack was free to accord his constituent Blacks the respect any human deserved without having to perform a political dance to justify it."[10]

Living in Washington, the young freshman got a firsthand look at the deplorable complexities of segregation—separate and often unequal public parks, hotels, theaters, restaurants, and public school facilities.

Compounding these factors, Jim Crow loomed large in the halls of Congress itself as a matter of process, rules, and practice. Those practices kept Black workers out of its swimming pool, barbershop, and dining area— the very facilities supporting the place where Kennedy worked. Kennedy's House of Representatives' support included support for the elimination of the poll tax and advocated for legislation that supported DC residents forming their own government. It was here that Kennedy also began a perceptible bent toward equal rights through the lens of international politics.[11]

Steven Levingston writes, "The Black plight, by his reckoning, was a foreign-affairs issue; the United States could not reasonably promote democracy abroad if it did not ensure freedom for all its citizens at home. How could America, he asked, make the case that its political system was superior to the Soviet Union's when its own citizens were oppressed and their rights trampled?"[12] This position would inform his actions through most of his presidency, until his last year in the office.

It was also during his stint in the House of Representatives that he positioned himself as somewhat cautious of his vigorous liberal colleagues. Concerning critics who questioned his liberal commitments, he would later state: "I'd be happy to tell them I am not liberal at all. I'm a realist."[13]

THE SENATE RACE

In 1952, John Kennedy decided to challenge respected Massachusetts treasurer, Henry Cabot Lodge Jr., for his seat. Kennedy won by 70,000 votes, with heavy voting support in the Black wards. This put him in the position of having to answer to the rising expectations of the Black community. Black voters lived mostly in the Roxbury and Dorchester areas of Boston and made up less than one percent of his constituency. The Kennedy campaign flooded them with mailings that described Kennedy's long-standing support for civil rights; Kennedy's 1952 speech on the House floor, where Kennedy asked Truman to launch an immediate federal investigation into the Christmas Eve murder of NAACP official Harry T. Moore and his wife, Harriet, who had been killed by a bomb thrown by a segregationist; and that when running for the House he had carried one of the six predominantly Black wards.[14]

A handwritten speech survives from early in his Senate campaign that shows Kennedy beginning to seriously consider civil rights issues. "There is nothing worse in life than racial bigotry," he wrote. He then replaced "bigotry" with "prejudice," to facilitate the next sentence: "There is nothing lower than bigotry." Later in the speech he connected the fight for civil rights with the battle against communism, arguing that a commitment to equal rights was necessary for the strength of the nation.[15]

Philosophically, "civil rights" was on his mind as early as his first Senate run, but he did not really grapple with the issue until late in his presidency. Kennedy would eventually make his bid for the White House. "I have realized . . . that the real source of power is the Executive Branch. . . . Congress retains a restraining influence, but the White House is the real source of power. I work on the labor bill for two years, and nothing happens, but the president makes a fifteen-minute speech and the bill is passed."[16] He clearly understood both the process and the power of the bully pulpit.

On January 2, 1960, he announced from the Senate Caucus room his run for the presidency. In laying out the task before him, Kennedy cited crucial decisions facing American leadership for the next four years: the arms race, the Soviet threat, the diminished stature of American science and education, setbacks in the farm economy, and the decay of American cities.[17]

Although Kennedy understood the power of the bully pulpit, he saw it as reserved for foreign policies and image—his announcement does not show that the six-year-old *Brown* decision was anywhere on his radar. His secretary of 12 years, Evelyn Lincoln, commented, "During the entire campaign the President had stressed the need to start rebuilding the prestige of the United States abroad and he was eager to participate personally in this effort."[18]

At the Democratic convention, though, it was clear that no issue mattered more, both in spirit and in politics, than civil rights. The convention delegates had adopted a civil rights plan that envisioned the elimination of all forms of discrimination based on race, religion, or national origin.

The platform pledged the next administration to demand basic plans for compliance from every school district in the country affected by the *Brown v. Board of Education* decision,[19] and in response delegates from nine states in the Deep South (Alabama, Florida, Georgia, Mississippi, Louisiana, Arkansas, South Carolina, North Carolina, and Virginia) signed a statement of repudiation. The Kennedy campaign found itself on the horns of a dilemma: How could it appeal to Southern states and at the same time impress upon Black voters the presidential nominee had their back?

Immediately after the convention, Kennedy began private meetings to allay fears that he would be an aggressive civil rights president. The governor of Virginia endorsed Kennedy after such a meeting. Kennedy also is reported to have met with Georgia governor Vandiver and to have promised him he would never use federal troops to force Georgia to desegregate its schools.[20]

Were there to be harmful political consequences from the Black constituency as Roy Wilkins, NAACP executive director, warned Kennedy:

> You have disturbed them because, while they know that logic and tradition would seem to dictate that you could not be in the Dixiecrat camp, you are hailed by the Dixiecrat leaders of South Carolina, Georgia and Mississippi, which, with Alabama are the 'worst' states on the Negro question. . . . They feel uneasy over this apparent entente cordiale.[21]

Simeon Booker, *Washington Post* journalist and chief of the Washington Bureau for the Johnson Publishing Company, publisher of *Jet* and *Ebony*, commented on Blacks' initial disappointment and distrust of JFK:

> I think the Kennedys had doped out the Negro position thusly, as one of the Kennedys told me later: "A man has first got to become president before he can help Negroes, and Negroes can't help a man become president, unless it is voting for him at an election." And so their whole strategy was geared to keeping a certain image among the Negro, making statements here and there. . . . And

by taking too strong a view early, they could lose the entire South, the Midwest, the far West. I think intentionally he just stayed away from making any overall approach toward Negroes.[22]

While campaigning vigorously in West Virginia, Kennedy experienced his first look at stark poverty. This marked the beginning of his emotional engagement with the issue—poverty was no longer an abstract concept devoid of a human face.[23]

The poverty issue became part of his bully pulpit, and in 1963, the last year of his presidency, it would find its way into policy initiatives designed to deal with the one-fifth of the nation below the poverty line. These proposed initiatives would later serve as the basis for President Johnson's War on Poverty.

In his runup to the 1960 presidential nomination, the implementation of *Brown* was not anchored in Kennedy's bully pulpit. Civil rights activity was gearing up, and he did not want this potentially nationwide movement to interfere with his economic and foreign affairs agendas. He named his brother, Robert Kennedy, attorney general to help shift those issues from himself and onto someone he trusted to the core.

After Kennedy was elected president, it became clear that his agenda would not give any attention to a full-fledged legislative program for civil rights. He had no interest in meeting face-to-face with civil rights leaders; he directed aides to have meetings and then brief him on the grievances that had been presented. Roy Wilkins felt that Kennedy was turning away from campaign promises. "My illusions faded very quickly."[24]

Kennedy's determination to focus on an extensive economic program (taxes, unemployment, Social Security, and housing) did not leave room for a confrontation with the powerful Southern Democratic block. If he proposed, at this same time, programs or actions on Black inequality, there was a danger of splitting the party and putting his agenda in peril.

Shortly before Inauguration Day, Wilkins publicly criticized the incoming administration for what he saw as an overabundance of caution. "We don't see why we should be Mickey Mouse or Minnie Mouse when it comes to civil rights."[25] The criticism, along with the details of a report titled "The Time Is Now" issued by the National Urban League, was reported in the *New York Times*.

The *Times* article described the report, explaining that it stated that progress on racial equality rested "on the power, the will, and the talent of the President,"[26] and called into question the extent to which Kennedy would use his bully pulpit for civil rights, inclusive of desegregation, and within that, school desegregation. The report argued that Kennedy's pledge to move "in the right direction" with "all deliberate speed" was not good enough—immediate action was called for.[27]

As president-elect, Kennedy had not elevated his bully pulpit to that level.[28]

PLATFORM ON DESEGREGATION

Desegregation, and, specifically, school desegregation, were not among the national issues that drove Kennedy's use of the bully pulpit available to him in the first two years of his presidency. Kennedy's coming of age in the 1940s was very much like that of most of White America, *distant*. His access to the portal of wealth marked a further degree of separation from the Black lives of his fellow countrymen.

Levingston argues that Kennedy had no concept of the lives of Black Americans. He had no sense of the Black church, a formidable force during the first half of the 20th century. He had minimum interaction with Black professionals.[29] Other than the household staff at the Palm Beach and Hyannis residences, his personal interactions with any Blacks were extremely limited.

Blacks were absent from his storied episodes on his PT boat. The Kennedys did not know Blacks until they hit the campaign trail, and even then only engaging celebrities and the press. "What are Negroes like?" Kennedy is reported to have once asked. "I've never spent any time with them."[30]

Robert Kennedy would explain that there was simply a lack of intellectual engagement with the injustice and violence facing Blacks, particularly in the South. Regarding White rioters, the president simply said, "Aren't they bastards?"

In his first 90 days, Kennedy was able to get few of his legislative items through the Legislative Branch: "When I was in Congress, I thought all the power was down at the other end of Pennsylvania (Avenue) at the White House. Now I'm down here and am amazed at all the power those bastards have!"[31] In response to musings in the press that the administration was more talk than action, Kennedy told Arthur Schlesinger that he felt there was no point in riling the public against Congress if the issue was destined to fail, quoting Jefferson: "Great innovations should not be forced on slender majorities."[32]

As the whole Kennedy family had been taught by their father, the goal was to win.

Victor Navasky explains that "Kennedy, who saw himself as a realist, balanced the support of southern racists against a personal and civic obligation to fight for racial justice."[33]

Certainly this Kennedy style helped mute his bully pulpit voice on civil rights. As a result, his actions on civil rights (in the first two years of his term) were pursued through a minimalist-voice of moral persuasion and executive actions emanating from the White House. The Kennedy moral-persuasion stance and its executive leadership moves did set the stage for the pillars of litigation and finally legislation.

By the end of 1960 and into year two, the Kennedy administration's Justice Department had documented a robust record in its attempt to enforce existing court orders and legislation. Parmet writes, "The civil rights division brought over 42 suits in four states to secure voting rights for Blacks. Through the Voter Education project promoted by the administration, 688,800 Blacks were qualified to vote between April 1, 1962, and November 1, 1964. Kennedy also supported the anti-poll tax amendment, which cleared the Congress in September of 1962 and was ratified in two years as the Twenty-fourth Amendment."

The Kennedy administration placed 40 Blacks in important posts during its first two months. Later that year, Thurgood Marshall, who had argued the school segregation case of Topeka, Kansas, before the Supreme Court, was placed on the Second Circuit of Appeals in New York.[34] Additionally, the Kennedy Justice Department intervened in 12 school-desegregation cases. On the other hand, the Kennedy administration, during that time, stuck to its *"no civil rights legislation"* policy without qualification.

On February 28th, 1963, President Kennedy sent a special message to Congress in which he stated, "This message is intended to examine how far we have come in achieving first-class citizenship for all citizens regardless of color; how far we have yet to go and what further tasks remain to be carried out by the Executive and Legislative Branches of the Federal Government, as well as by state and local governments and private citizens and organizations." This was the first time since his inauguration that John Kennedy had appealed directly to Congress on civil rights legislation.

He enunciated the current need: "The cruel disease of discrimination knows no sectional or state boundaries. The continuing attack on this problem must be equally broad. It must be both private and public—it must be conducted at national, state and local levels—and it must include both legislative and executive action."

He reminded Congress of the progress that had been made through "executive action, litigation, persuasion and private initiative—in achieving and protecting equality of opportunity in education, voting, transportation, employment, housing, government and the enjoyment of public accommodations. But pride in our progress must not give way to relaxation of our effort."

He then spoke directly to the Congress: "Nor does progress in the Executive Branch enable the Legislative Branch to escape its own obligations. On the contrary, it is in the light of this nationwide progress and the belief that Congress will wish once again to meet its responsibilities in this matter that I stress in the following agenda of existing and prospective action important legislative as well as administrative measures."

He then turned to *Brown*:

> Nearly nine years have elapsed since the Supreme Court ruled that State laws requiring or permitting segregated schools violate the Constitution. That decision represented both good law and good judgment—it was both legally and morally right. Since that time it has become increasingly clear that neither violence nor legalistic evasions will be tolerated as a means of thwarting court-ordered desegregation, that closed schools are not an answer, and that responsible communities are able to handle the desegregation process in a calm and sensible manner.[35]

This message to Congress began the road to Kennedy's later submission of a civil rights bill and, though delayed, a bully pulpit voice on civil rights and school desegregation.

On February 12, 1963, Kennedy commissioned the Civil Rights Commission to prepare a report on the civil rights record for the past 100 years. Upon receiving the Civil Rights Commission Report, "Freedom to the Free," he said:

> I know it will be useful long after this centennial year is behind us. I am certain that it was no easy task to compress into a single volume the American Negro's century-long struggle to win the full promise of our Constitution and Bill of Rights.[36]

When that report was released, the Kennedy administration was less than pleased. Responding to a question at a President's News Conference on April 24, 1963, Kennedy stated:

> Well, in every case that the Civil Rights Commission described, the United States Government has instituted legal action in order to provide a remedy. The Civil Rights Commission gave a number of cases, the dogs, of a denial of equal rights at the airline terminal, and all of the rest. We are attempting through the established procedures set out by the United States Constitution to give protection, through lawsuits, through decisions by the courts, and a good deal of action has been taken in all of these cases.
>
> Now, it is very difficult. We had outrageous crime, from all accounts, in the State of Alabama, in the shooting of the postman who was attempting in a very traditional way to dramatize the plight of some of our citizens, being assassinated on the road. We have offered to the State of Alabama the services of the FBI in the solution of the crime. We do not have direct jurisdiction, but we are working with every legislative, legal tool at our command to insure protection for the rights of our citizens, and we shall continue to do so. . . . But I can just say to you that the Federal Government has been extremely active in the State of Mississippi, from before Oxford and since, in an attempt to provide for

constitutional guarantees. We hope the State of Mississippi will do it, we hope the local police will do it, we hope the mayors will do it. Where they don't do it, the Federal Government will do it within the limits of our authority.[37]

May 1963 propelled the Kennedy desegregation efforts to move forward. A series of events occurred that impacted a turning point in Kennedy's resolve to move beyond executive programs and select court efforts by his Justice Department. On May 3rd, 13 *"freedom riders"* set out to test a December 1960 Supreme Court ruling that restaurants in interstate bus stations must serve Blacks.

In Anniston, Alabama, mayhem occurred as riders were seriously beaten (*with baseball bats and tire irons*). A second bus arrived in Birmingham, and it is reported that "local authorities were rumored to have assured the Ku Klux Klan that it would have 15 minutes to do as it wished before the police intervened. When the police arrived the Klansmen had withdrawn and the bus station was filled with beaten, bloodied people including some journalists."[38]

Martin Luther King and his associates had launched the first week in April a rolling and massive campaign of protest. O'Reilly reports that the White House or Robert Kennedy's Justice Department gave this effort little attention in the beginning. King and his chief associates, including eight others, were arrested and found guilty of contempt. The demonstrations ramped up that first week in May, and children began to join the protests on the front line.

Much of history of this time concentrates on police commissioner Bull Connor, whose men attacked with nightsticks, electric cattle prods, police dogs, high-pressure fire hoses, and mass arrests, including 1,000 children. But the "pragmatic" president's tone changed. Civil rights was now completely and passionately on his radar. Before Birmingham, he had told Joseph Rauh, civil rights and civil liberties lawyer, "not to push him on civil rights because his criticism was wrong."

Martin writes, Rauh remembers how Kennedy first pushed back at him. However, after Birmingham, Kennedy told Rauh that "the civil rights struggle was going to be a long, tough fight but we have to do it."[39]

On June 11th, after he had federalized the National Guard to push Governor Wallace away from the entrance to the University of Alabama at Tuscaloosa, President Kennedy told the nation on television that:

America faced a moral issue that was not confined to the South and that it was time for bold action. If an American, because his skin is dark cannot eat lunch in a restaurant open to the public, if he cannot send his children to the best public school available, if he cannot vote for the public officials who represent him, if in short, he cannot enjoy the full and free life which all of us want, then who among us would be content to stand in his place? Who among us would be content with counsels of patience and delay?[40]

Edward Kennedy, his brother and a senator from Massachusetts, shared the speech that "laid the groundwork for the Civil Rights Act of 1964."[41] The nation learned later that evening that Medgar Evers, state director of the National Association for the Advancement of Colored People, was killed as he stepped out of his car in his driveway.

On June 19th, John Fitzgerald Kennedy sent an omnibus civil rights bill to Congress. That bill contained language that provided a federal role for a path to sustained school desegregation, had he not been assassinated. How do we weigh his shortened time, and how would he have used his bully pulpit during his second term?

Perhaps Roy Wilkins's words characterize JFK's astuteness:

I don't want this commentary to be principally a comment or an estimate of the Kennedy Administration. I would say what I have said that John Fitzgerald Kennedy had a complete comprehension and an identity with the goals of the Civil Rights Movement. Intellectually he was for it. He understood all the motivations of the Negro community and he felt for the humanity that he wanted to see exhibited by the government of the United States for this segment of the population.

But I think the qualities that Lyndon Johnson later exhibited, and which only Lyndon Johnson could have, by reason of his experience and his study and the use of materials of the government—precisely that lacked in Senator Kennedy forced him to hesitate and weigh and consider what he should do in the civil-rights field I don't think it was from an inner non-conviction. I think he knew this ought to be done. He just didn't know how to manipulate the government to bring it about. Events did push him true, but they didn't push him toward a conviction. They pushed him toward action. He was convinced already, when he was elected—of that I am firmly convinced.[42]

LEGISLATIVE PROFILE AS PRESIDENT

The essence of the massive Civil Rights Act of 1964 was framed during the third year of President Kennedy's first term. He was unable to see it through, as he was assassinated in November 1963, on the one thousand and seventh day of his presidency, in the very month that his Civil Rights Bill, H.R.1731, was referred to the House Rules Committee. The chairman, Howard W. Smith, Democrat from Virginia and a fervent segregationist, refused to grant a rule for the bill's floor debate, just a few days before he boarded Air Force One to fly first to Fort Worth, then on to Dallas.

A report from the *Congressional Quarterly* cites an 83% passage rate of Kennedy's program once it reached the floor of both houses. However, only 43% of the program got to the floor. It should be noted that in spite of Kennedy's deliberate decision not to put forth civil rights legislation for two years, his Housing Act of 1961 was one of the most significant bills in his three years in office.

Subsequently, on becoming president, Kennedy sent 16 separate messages to Congress putting forth his legislative agenda, but none of them mentioned race or civil rights. Conventional wisdom suggests he wanted to end racial discrimination but lacked the momentum to mount a legislative campaign and decided to wait.

JFK AND EISENHOWER'S 1957 CIVIL RIGHTS LEGISLATION

As a senator, Jack was caught in the quandary of seriously addressing the issues of Black America and maneuvering within the Senate in a way that would not undercut his desire to run for president. He had won his Senate seat with the help of a large majority of Black wards in his district. He had to contend with the 22 powerful members of the Senate Southern Caucus. This cohort of senators was determined to *stop* any legislative or political action that would change their sense of a pristine way of life.

Though Richard Russel of Georgia used his powerful tools as leader of the conservative coalition to stop any reform, it was James Eastland, chairman of the Judiciary Committee who best expressed the Southern historic view of Blacks and their rights. He helped and championed the formation of the cabals of White citizens' councils springing up across the South to derail any efforts of Blacks or their recognized allies to gain their constitutional rights. He declared "generations of Southerners, yet unborn, will cherish our memory because they will realize that the fight we now wage will have preserved for them their untainted racial heritage, their culture, and the institutions of the Anglo-Saxon race."[43]

Kennedy positioned himself cautiously; he supported majority leader Lyndon Johnson's maneuvers on the jury-trial amendment of Eisenhower's Civil Rights Bill of 1957. Johnson deemed that in order to ensure passage of the bill, he had to safely guard the jury-trial amendment through. That amendment provided jury trials in voting-rights cases that at the time customarily meant that it would be all-White juries who would hear the cases and therefore would invariably not rule in favor of Blacks.

Roy Wilkins perceived Senator Kennedy in a strained relationship with the NAACP as a result of his 1957 vote, although as a freshman he had voted in favor of a bill outlawing the poll tax and had voted regularly on Rule 22 to get rid of the poll tax. He felt Kennedy substantiated the view that Kennedy "knew little or understood the issues germane to Blacks . . . inclusive of those rights of Negro children in Jackson, Birmingham, and Prince Edward County, Virginia who were still waiting for their government to enforce the school orders of its own Supreme Court."[44]

It is reported by Kenneth O'Reilly that JFK met Roy Wilkins in the Senate restaurant and spent over an hour trying to explain to the NAACP executive director why his vote was "in the movement's best interest."[45] Wilkins went on during the Massachusetts campaign to speak against Kennedy. Kennedy responded to Wilkins, "You came to Pittsfield to say that my record . . . did not deserve the support of the negro voters." Wilkins reportedly responded, "These voters more than quibbling support from a politician intent on an apparent entente cordial with Eastland et al., of Dixie."[46]

This Kennedy legislative vote proved to be the beginning of tensions with the Black civil rights leadership. It could not serve as a basis for a bully pulpit championing desegregation rights for the nation's Black schoolchildren and in the immediate future for Black schoolchildren behind *"the Cotton Curtain."*[47]

Lee C. White, former legislative assistant to Kennedy as senator and assistant special counsel to President Kennedy from 1961–1963, shares in an interview, "One of the campaign themes that the president had played pretty hard was that existing statutory authority gave the president leverage and tremendous opportunity to correct things without going the difficult travail of securing legislation."[48] He completely misread the rising tide of extreme angst among all factions of the civil rights leadership as well as a strong misunderstanding of the role Congress plays in the success of any administration's program.

Within the first three months (March 1961) of his inauguration, Kennedy made a decision not to ask for civil rights legislation in the first session of the 87th Congress. White, in the interview, confirms information that the White House informed the Press that there would be no civil rights legislation, but the emphasis would be on executive action.[49]

In his book, Wilkins lays out his and other leaders' disappointment, within days of Kennedy's election, when they learned that the new president "had no intention of beginning his new administration with a full-scale legislative program for civil rights." Wilkins shares that "Kennedy argued that the issue would divide the Democratic Party and cost him his chance of passing legislation in other fields."[50]

Civil rights leaders were aware of his executive gestures, inclusive of: placing Negroes in top government jobs; appointing Bob Weaver chairman of the Housing and Home Finance Agency, a subcabinet position; appointing Thurgood Marshall to the United States Court of Appeals for the Second Circuit; and raising the number of Black foreign service appointments. "All these gestures could not make up for defaulting on a legislative program. It looked like a holding action," stated Wilkins.[51]

The urgency that civil rights leaders felt might be best illustrated in a letter to Harris Wofford on April 5th, 1961:

Dear Harris,

I have read with much interest your speech before the National Civil-Liberties Clearing House on March 23rd. Since it is a very smooth (but unmistakable) elaboration of the inept message of Ande Hatcher to our District of Columbia branch earlier, I would be more or less correct, I assume, in labeling the sentiments the "official line.

It may be that the Kennedy Administration proceeded in other fields as it is in civil rights, but I would be inclined to doubt it. I will believe until shown otherwise that in any important field, labor, agriculture, industry, finance, housing, health, the leading figures were called in and told, in one way or another, what the Administration had in mind. Whether they cooperated on all phases or on only part of them, they at least knew were they stood.

In civil rights, the information on what the Administration had in mind (I do not count too much the campaign utterances) came through columnists. "Dope" stories by favorably inclined writers, hints by "those close" etc.

For as long as I can remember, the NAACP (commonly thought of as the opposers, the protesters) has been seeking something far beyond mere opposition. It was a pioneer in trying to be "in better gear with the Government." Its trademark, almost has, been "the use of the law and of government to fulfill the promise of the Constitution."

The Kennedy Administration has done with Negro citizens what it has done with a vast member of Americans: it has charmed them. It has intrigued them. Every 72 hours it has delighted them. On the Negro question it on it has smoothed Unguentine on a stinging burn even though for a moment (or for perhaps a year) it cannot do anything about a broken pelvis. It has patted a need even though it could not bind up & joint.

All this is good, not only because people like to have their immediate hurts noticed and attended to, but because the attention to them helps to create a useful moral and political climate.

Experienced observers know that snags have developed, that changes have had to be ordered, that some obeisance to pressures has had to be made. This is politics. The point is not so much whether we have come out thus far with all we were due (we have not), but whether the lines have been set in such a way that we cannot later recover our proper share.

It is plain why the civil-rights legislative line was abandoned, but nothing was accomplished by the maneuver. It did not save the minimum-wage bill from gutting and it will not save other legislation, The Southerners and their Northern satellites, Halleck, Mundt, Bennett, Saltonstall and Company, function whether a civil rights bill is proposed or withheld.

An administration gets as much by whacking them as by wooing them. JFK might as well have had a civil rights bill in the hopper; he might as well have won the Senate rules right (he could have) so he would have a procedure open when he does decide to get behind a civil-rights bill.

I don't suppose we have a quarrel. We do have a difference with the Kennedy Administration and perhaps that difference is rooted in the purpose of the NAACP as contrasted with the purpose of the government of all the people in a time of world crisis. We are concerned (as much as our financial and personnel resources will permit) with Big Integration, but we must, because of the very nature of the domestic scene and of our raison d'etre, be concerned with Little Integration.

The Negro engineers now employed by IMB and Eastman Kodak and General Electric are a part of Big Integration, but the sore thumb fact of 2,500,000 Negro youngsters still in segregated schools seven years after 1954 is Little Integration. So are Police dog attacks in Mississippi. We do not separate the world stage, but we cannot omit East Texas, the Citrus belt Florida, Alabama or the state of John Bell Williams,

As I have indicated, JFK has started well and appears to be going in the right direction, I hope we can be inculged if we stick to our knitting. We may drop a stitch now and then and not match up the border here and there and, while we must keep in mind a relationship between us and the country as a whole, we concentrate in one area. Of course, we risk astigmatism, but wide-angle vision has its drawbacks as well.

S i n c e r e l y ,

Roy Wilkins
Executive Secretary[52]

A month later, Pierre Salinger, press secretary, responded, "The president has made it clear that he does not think it is necessary at this time to enact civil rights legislation."[53]

Bobby Kennedy commented that it "shocked him and made him want to do something about it. But the president didn't believe in sending up civil rights legislation when he felt the Congress and the country weren't ready for it. He didn't believe in just going through the motions on things, said his younger brother."[54] Kennedy was not making any effort to use his bully pulpit to push legislation to address desegregation of America's public schools.

On June 11, 1963, John Fitzgerald Kennedy stepped to the microphones in the Oval Office and delivered *The Report to the American People on Civil Rights*. The events of 1962 and 1963 of the Kennedy presidency had been fraught with a series of actions inclusive of jailing of civil rights leaders: the bombing of Black churches, residences, and businesses; the murder of four Black girls at church on a Sunday morning; police dogs; looting in select cities; defiance of court orders by Governor George Wallace in admitting Blacks to university campuses; and the dispatch of federal troops to the campus of the University of Alabama to quell potential riots.

As the defiant George Wallace saga played out on national television, President Kennedy had been following it with advisor Ted Sorenson. Wallace, after calling the president's actions *"military dictatorship,"* left the campus around 5:00 p.m.

Levingston chronicles Kennedy's reaction as Wallace left the doorway.[55]

Sorenson shares, "The president turned around and said to me, 'I think we'd better give that speech tonight.'" Sorensen was taken aback. "What speech?" he wondered. White House aides had discussed civil rights strategy and the outlines of legislation for a couple weeks, and there was talk about the president addressing the nation. "But no decision had been made," Sorensen recalled, "and no draft had been prepared." Bobby also remembered that the president made a snap decision. Some threshold had been crossed; some epiphany had been reached. "I think he just decided that day," Bobby recalled. "I think he called me up on the phone and said that he was going to do it that night."

The president wanted to go on air at 8 p.m., and he wanted to deliver a major civil rights speech; he was determined to speak on Black rights in a manner he had never done before—in language no president had uttered. Prepared text or no prepared text, he was going to announce civil rights.

The president's political advisors opposed his speaking out publicly, while Robert Kennedy argued in its favor. But the president's aides were no match for the president's brother; no one could defeat Robert Kennedy once his mind was set. He was adamant: the president had to introduce legislation, and he had to do it in a television address. "He felt it, he understood it, and he prevailed."[56]

Kennedy made the decision to ignore Southern politics and move rapidly to mount a legislative program as a resolution to the boiling, explosive mood of the country and to respond to the pleasure of both Martin Luther King and the civil rights leadership who were still not as radicalized as some spinoff leaders were. Though he had moved in vacillating strides, Kennedy was now ready to commit and identify with the movement. President Kennedy directed

Pierre Salinger to alert the television and radio networks to provide him with air time at 8:00 p.m.

In response to those who felt the president was acting with unaccustomed impulsivity, he explained later to his commerce secretary, Luther Hodges, "but there comes a time when a man has to take a stand and history will record that he has to meet these tough situations and ultimately make a decision."[57]

Kennedy's speech was a dramatic moment as he called America's racial tensions a "moral crisis." He said:

> Difficulties over segregation and discrimination exist in every city, in every state of the union, producing in many cities a rising tide of discontent that threatens the public safety, nor is this a partisan issue. In a time of domestic crisis, men of good will and generosity should be able to unite regardless of party or politics. This is not even a legal or legislative issue alone. It is better to settle these matters in the courts than on the streets and new laws are needed at every level. But law alone cannot make men see right.
>
> We are confronted primarily with a moral issue. It is as old as the Scriptures and is as clear as the American Constitution.[58]

There was a resounding roar of hope and relief from the civil rights leadership. Six months earlier in a meeting with Martin Luther King, it is reported that Kennedy had told him he had no plans to propose civil rights legislation in 1963. Dr. King was watching the television with Walter Fauntleroy, and he is reported to have jumped out of his seat and exclaimed, "Walter, can you believe that White man not only stepped up to the plate, he hit it over the fence."

Levingston shares that King immediately sent a telegram to the White House signaling the address as "one of the most eloquent, profound and unequivocal pleas for justice and freedom for all men ever made by any president." He further asserted, "you spoke passionately to the moral issues involved in the integration struggle. I am sure that your encouraging words will bring a sense of hope to the millions of disinherited people of our country. Your message will become a hallmark in the annals of American history."[59]

LEGISLATIVE PROFILE

On June 19, 1963, Kennedy submitted a civil rights bill to Congress. His message to Congress included the following language:

> I am proposing that Congress stay in session until it has enacted an omnibus bill—the most responsible, reasonable and urgently needed solutions. It will go far toward providing reasonable men with the reasonable means of meeting

these problems (civil rights) and it will thus help end the kind of racial strife which our nation can hardly afford.[60]

His accompanying message cited some progress. Nonetheless, he also told Congress, "but persisting inequalities and tensions made it clear that federal action must lead the way, providing both the nation's standard and nationwide solution." In short, he said, "the time has come for the Congress of the United States to join with the Executive and Judicial Branches in making it clear to all that, race has no place in American life or law. The venerable code of equity law commands 'for every wrong a remedy' but in too many communities, in too many parts of the country, wrongs are inflicted on Negro citizens for which no effective remedy at law is clearly and readily available."

In that special message, he addressed the minimal progress toward primary and secondary school desegregation: "Many Negro children entering segregated grade schools at the time of the Supreme Court decision in 1954 will enter segregated high schools this year, having suffered a loss which can never be regained. Indeed, discrimination in education is one basic cause of other inequities and hardships inflicted upon our Negro citizens."

He went on to characterize the delay of enactment of the Supreme Court's decision of 1954 as having placed an undue litigious burden on those who initiated desegregation cases on behalf of their children. He reminded Congress that too often those who brought suits lacked the economic means for maintaining and sustaining the cases and often suffered personal, physical, and economic harassment.

Kennedy stated:

Last week, I addressed to the American people an appeal to conscience—a request for their cooperation in meeting the growing moral crisis in American race-relations. I warned of "a rising tide of discontent that threatens the public safety" in many parts of the country. I emphasized that "the events in Birmingham and elsewhere have so increased the cries for equality that no city or State or legislative body can prudently choose to ignore them." "It is a time to act," I said, "in the Congress, in State and local legislative bodies and, above all, in all of our daily lives.

In the days that have followed, the predictions of increased violence have been tragically borne out. The "fires of frustration and discord" have burned hotter than ever.

On February 28, I sent to the Congress a message urging the enactment this year of three important pieces of civil-rights legislation.[61]

Although these recommendations were transmitted to the Congress some time ago, neither House has yet had an opportunity to vote on any of these essential measures. The Negro's drive for justice, however, has not stood still—nor will it, it is now clear, until full equality is achieved. The growing and understandable dissatisfaction of Negro citizens with the present pace of desegregation, and their increased determination to secure for themselves the equality of opportunity and treatment to which they are rightfully entitled, have underscored what should already have been clear: the necessity of the Congress enacting this year—not only the measures already proposed—but also additional legislation providing legal remedies for the denial of certain individual rights. . . . For these reasons, I am proposing that the Congress stay in session this year until it has enacted—preferably as a single omnibus bill—the most responsible, reasonable, and urgently needed solutions to this problem, solutions which should be acceptable to all fair-minded men. This bill would be known as the "Civil Rights Act of 1963."

In my message of February 28, while commending the progress already made in achieving desegregation of education at all levels as required by the Constitution, I was compelled to point out the slowness of progress toward primary and secondary school desegregation. The Supreme Court has recently voiced the same opinion. Many Negro children entering segregated grade schools at the time of the Supreme Court decision in 1954 will enter segregated high schools this year, having suffered a loss which can never be regained. Indeed, discrimination in education is one basic cause of the other inequities and hardships inflicted upon our Negro citizens. The lack of equal educational opportunity deprives the individual of equal economic opportunity, restricts his contribution as a citizen and community leader, encourages him to drop out of school and imposes a heavy burden on the effort to eliminate discriminatory practices and prejudices from our national life.

These difficulties are among the principal reasons for the delay in carrying out the 1954 decision; and this delay cannot be justified to those who have been hurt as a result. Rights such as these, as the Supreme Court recently said, are "present rights. They are not merely hopes to some future enjoyment of some formalistic constitutional promise. The basic guarantees of our Constitution are warrants for the here and now. . . . "[62]

Kennedy had found the voice to leverage his bully pulpit with Congress.

NOTES

1. Kenneth O'Reilly (1996), *Nixon's Piano: Presidents and Racial Politics from Washington to Clinton* (Free Press), 184.

2. Robert Dallek (2003), *Kennedy an Unfinished Life: John F Kennedy 1917–1963* (Back Bay Books, Little Brown and Company), 28–31.

3. Frederick Logevall (2020), *JFK Coming of Age in the American Century* (Random House), 17.

4. Logevall (2020), *JFK Coming of Age in the American Century*, 56.

5. Ralph G. Martin (1984), *A Hero for Our Time. An Intimate Story of the Kennedy Kears* (Fawcett Crest), 23.

6. Logevall (2020), *JFK Coming of Age in the American Century*, 76.

7. Victor Navasky (2000), *Kennedy Justice* (iUniverse), 443.

8. Barbara Leaming (2006), *Jack Kennedy, the Education of a Statesman* (W.W. Norton and Company), 15.

9. Logevall (2020), *JFK Coming of Age in the American Century*, 74.

10. Steven Levingston (2017), *Kennedy and King: The President, the Pastor and the Battle over Civil Rights* (Hachette Book Group Inc, 2017), 11.

11. Levingston (2017), *Kennedy and King*, 12.

12. Levingston (2017), *Kennedy and King*, 12.

13. Levingston (2017), *Kennedy and King*, 17.

14. Logevall (2020), *JFK Coming of Age in the American Century*, 511.

15. Logevall (2020), *JFK Coming of Age in the American Century*, 512.

16. Martin (1984), *A Hero for Our Time*, 138.

17. Leaming (2006), *Jack Kennedy*, 236.

18. Evelyn Lincoln, *My Twelve Years with John F. Kennedy* (David McKay Company Inc, 1965), 259.

19. Thomas Oliphant and Curtis Wilkie, *The Road to Camelot* (Simon and Schuster Paperbacks, New York, 2017), 250.

20. Levingston (2017), *Kennedy and King*, 81.

21. Oliphant and Wilkie, *The Road to Camelot*, 1430.

22. Simeon Booker, recorded interview by John Stewart, April 24, 1967, John F, Kennedy Library Oral History Program,

23. Martin (1984), *A Hero for Our Time*, 154.

24. Levingston (2017), *Kennedy and King*, 116.

25. Levingston (2017), *Kennedy and King*, 116.

26. Levingston (2017), *Kennedy and King*, 117.

27. Levingston (2017), *Kennedy and King*, 117.

28. Levingston (2017), *Kennedy and King*, 11.

29. Levingston (2017), *Kennedy and King*, 8.

30. Martin (1984), *A Hero for Our Time*, 415.

31. Martin (1984), *A Hero for Our Time*, 366.

32. Martin (1984), *A Hero for Our Time*, 367.

33. Victor Navasky (1971), *Kennedy Justice* (Atheneum), 97–98.

34. Herbert Parmet (1983), *JFK: The Presidency of John F. Kennedy* (Dial press), 256.

35. John F. Kennedy, The President's News Conference Online by Gerhard Peters and John T. Woolley, The American Presidency Project, https//www.presidency.ucsb..edu/node/236989.

36. John F. Kennedy, Remarks Upon Receiving Civil Rights Commission Report "Freedom to the Free." Online by Gerhard Peters and John T. Woolley, The American Presidency Project, https://www.presidency.ucsb.edu/node/236940.

37. John F. Kennedy, The President's News Conference Online by Gerhard Peters and John T, Woolley, The American Presidency Project, https://www.presidency.ucsb.edu/node/2358460.

38. Leaming (2006), *Jack Kennedy*, 297.

39. O'Reilly (1996), *Nixon's Piano, 220.*
40. Edwin O. Guthman and Allen C. Richard (2018), *RFK His Words for Our Times* (William Morrow), 107.
41. Edward M. Kennedy (2009), *True Compass* (Hachette Book Group) 197.
42. Interview with T. H. Baker (April 1969), Oral History transcript, LBJ presidential Library, http:www.discover lbj.org/item/oh-wilkinsr-19690401-1-73-27.
43. Levingston (2017), *Kennedy and King,* 15.
44. Roy Wilkins (1994), *Standing Fast: The Autobiography of Roy Wilkins* (Da Cappo Press).
45. O'Reilly (1996), *Nixon's Piano,* 190.
46. O'Reilly (1996), *Nixon's Piano,* 192.
47. The term *cotton curtain* is a term historically used for the political divide between the South and the rest of the country.
48. Lee C. White (1964, May 26), recorded interview by Milton Gwirtzman, John F. Kennedy Oral History Program.
49. White (1964, May 26), recorded interview by Milton Gwirtzman.
50. Wilkins (1994), *Standing Fast,* 279–82.
51. Wilkins (1994), *Standing Fast,* 281.
52. Papers of John F. Kennedy (1962, March 15), Presidential Papers, White House, Staff Files of Harris Wofford, Alphabetical Files 1956–1962, Roy Wilkins, December 1960, https//www.jFK library.org.assoc.
53. Roy Wilkins (1994), *Standing Fast,* 282.
54. Martin (1984), *A Hero for Our Time,* 417.
55. Levingston (2017), *Kennedy and King,* 400.
56. Levingston (2017), *Kennedy and King,* 400.
57. Levingston (2017), *Kennedy and King,* 401.
58. John F. Kennedy (1963, June 11), speech, radio, and television report to the American people on civil rights, https://www.jfklibrary.org/archives/other-resources/john-f-kennedy-speeches/civil-rights-radio-and-television-report-19630611.
59. Levingston (2017), *Kennedy and King,* 406–7.
60. John F. Kennedy, President John F. Kennedy's message to Congress, https://www.archives.gov/legislative/features/march-on-washington/kennedy.html.
61. These recommendations included school desegregation legislation to provide federal technical and financial assistance to aid school districts in the process of desegregation in compliance with the Constitution.
62. John F. Kennedy, Special message to Congress on civil rights and job opportunities, online by Gerhard Peters and John T. Woolley, The American Presidency Project, https:www.presideny.ucsb.edu/node/23671.

Chapter 3

Lyndon Baines Johnson

Lyndon Baines Johnson—LBJ—leveraged his bully pulpit on education, and within that, school desegregation, with a strong personal theory that had gripped his thinking from the early days of his childhood: "You have got to believe in what you are selling." According to his brother, Sam Houston Johnson, LBJ had heard a salesman say it one day, and it impressed him so much, it became a kind of lifelong mantra: "He was always repeating that."[1]

Lyndon Johnson would expand on this in a discussion with biographer Doris Kearns Goodwin, explaining that "What convinces is conviction. You simply *have* to believe in the argument you are advancing; if you don't, you're as good as dead. The other person will sense that something isn't there, and no chain of reasoning, no matter how logical or elegant or brilliant, will win your case for you."[2]

Johnson was a complex man, a man presented to us by polarizing biographers; but Lyndon Johnson's skillful leadership and conviction made his use of the bully pulpit to impact civil rights in education incredibly effective—the most effective use in the 20th century.

FORMATIVE YEARS

Johnson's social DNA does not suggest naked racism or targeted bigotry as part of his environment in his early years. Johnson was born into a family with a legacy of political experience.

His grandfather, Sam Ealy Johnson Sr., had been elected to political office in the 1920s; his father had been elected to the Texas congress at the age of 27 and stayed there for six terms. His grandfather was an organizer for the biracial People's Party and a staunch campaigner for the 1928 presidential nominee, General James B. Weaver.

LBJ's ancestry, both paternal and maternal great-grandparents, hailed from the South rather than southwest states: Kentucky, Georgia, Louisiana,

Tennessee, and North Carolina. Some, as slave owners, were pioneering planters and farmers. Grandfather Sam Ealy Johnson Sr. and his brother were orphaned at the age of 18 and made their way as successful cattle raisers and drivers, pasturing their herds in Fredericksburg, Texas, before driving them to Kansas City. Johnson Sr. served in the Confederate army through the Civil War.[3]

LBJ's maternal grandfather, Joseph Wilson Baines, was also a Confederate veteran of the Civil War. Educated at Baylor University, he taught school, then studied law and started a law practice, finally serving as secretary of state to Governor John Ireland of Texas.[4]

LBJ grew up in Johnson City (population 323), in the Texas Hill Country. The small town was known for its hospitality and ready welcome to visitors. His siblings included a brother and three sisters.[5] Biographers cite an environment in which Johnson's mother, Rebekah, with a larger-than-life persona, cultivated a climate of overflowing love, high expectations, and joyful pride. A private tutor in "elocution," she taught Johnson to read, memorize, and recite before he was five.[6]

However, it was Johnson's dad, Sam Ealy Johnson Jr., who had the greatest influence on Johnson's political trajectory and the honing of the skills he would eventually use to leverage his bully pulpit. Johnson's early years taught him that his father was an effective, ethical, and skilled legislator.[7]

Johnson's father taught school for three years and had dreamed of becoming a lawyer. In a special election in 1918, he became a representative to the Texas House from the 87th district.[8] He remained a Texas legislator for 12 years.

Sam Johnson had a passion for unpopular causes that was tempered by a pragmatic streak. During the First World War, he opposed a bill that would allow the arrest of and imprisonment of anyone speaking out against the war or the United States' involvement in it. The bill passed in spite of his opposition. While he failed to stop the bill, he gained a whole new constituency of Germans, who were traditionally Republican.[9]

Robert Dallek notes that the height of Johnson's principled pragmatism is exemplified by his support for a state constitutional amendment giving women the right to vote, followed by his opposition the 19th Amendment to the Constitution in accordance with his district's voting.[10]

Sam played a leadership role in ushering Wright Patman's anti–Ku Klux Klan statute through the Texas legislature, which would have made it a crime to parade and to otherwise operate in masks. The measure ultimately failed.

In 1923, Sam walked off the floor of the Texas House rather than support a bill that excluded Blacks in the Democratic Party election.[11] It was Lyndon's father who helped elect Sam Rayburn as speaker of the House. This was fortuitous for Johnson when, as majority leader, he was able to add Sam Rayburn's voice to his bully pulpit.

Sam Johnson's legislative life was mirrored in his son LBJ's genuine interest in leadership, *contra* what many have seen as LBJ's "quest for power."

LBJ loved being Sam Johnson's boy. He harbored the same passion for politics. At a young age, he would hide under tables or stand behind doors to strain and hear every word of his father's evening sessions with political friends. His father would take him on the campaign trail.[12] "Lyndon watched it all at a close range; he imbibed his father's liberal philosophy and imitated Sam's persuasive style of getting really close to someone, nose-to-nose, when he wanted to convince them of something."[13]

After his legislative career, Sam Johnson Jr. began a successful real estate career. This only increased his respect in Johnson City—he was already well-known as being willing and able to help elderly ranchers, veterans, and widows get pensions they often didn't even know they were owed.[14]

A few years after his legislative stint, both the drought and falling cotton prices prompted Sam Ealy to sell the ranch, the proceeds of which were not even able to cover his debts. Sam suffered ridicule and embarrassment.[15]

Several biographers have suggested that this episode in Johnson's formative years inspired his personal quest never to suffer the fate of his father and to avoid failure at any costs, while also attributing his victories to his empathy and sense of hard work.

There were few Blacks or Mexicans in the Texas Hill Country, who traditionally were employed in menial agricultural jobs elsewhere, so White people were called on to pick cotton. As early as nine years old, a young LBJ was one of these.

Later, as a teenager, LBJ worked a road gang for the Texas State Highway Department, gravelling the road to Austin. The work paid almost nothing, and the labor was incredibly hard. Most road gangs were made up of Mexicans and Blacks; the one Johnson was on was all White, but the job was still seen as "nigger work."[16]

Harry McPherson recalled that LBJ "did not pretend, as many southerners did, that Negroes 'really enjoyed' the Southern way of life. He did not romanticize the . . . menial jobs, the political powerlessness."[17]

Contextualizing this characterization of LBJ, Robert A. Caro asks, "How could Lyndon Johnson have romanticized that work? He had done it."[18]

In his early adult years, Johnson craved attention, dressing far more formally than his small-town classmates, wearing a shirt and tie to high school. He was competitive and defiant, qualities that drove him to seek leadership in everything from sports to debates to campus journalism.[19] "Lyndon's defiance—his reluctance to submit to authority—went hand-in-hand with a need to be top dog, to dominate, control, or bend others to his will."[20]

Lyndon's college years were also marked by stories of Lyndon's commanding presence. After LBJ talked himself into a job as the assistant to Southwest Texas State Teachers College president Cecil Evans, he facilitated the notion that in order to approach Evans, one first had to approach Johnson—an undergraduate assistant to an assistant. Evans would even say, "Lyndon, I declare you hadn't been in my office a month before I could hardly tell who was president of the school—you or me."[21]

JOURNEY TO THE PRESIDENCY

"It was there (at Cotulla), in that school, at an early age, that my dream began of an America . . . where race, religion, language, and color didn't count against you."[22]

Johnson's dream began when he was 21 years old, after he took a job as teacher/principal of a segregated school serving Mexican American children in Cotulla, Texas.

While not the only factor shaping his political vision, it undergirded the modus operandi he was to employ and animated LBJ's unyielding bully pulpit during his three years as House staff, two years as a governmental administrator, 11 years as a congressman, 12 years as a senator (six as Senate majority leader), three years as vice president, and ultimately six years as president. It was during his time as director of the Texas National Youth Administration, a New Deal agency that worked toward education and employment for young people, that Johnson began to hone his political skills, developing his capacity to stave off the Southern colleagues who were consumed by intolerance, bigotry, and hate. LBJ, by contrast, started working for the interests of minorities, specifically "the Negro."

Robert Dallek reports that Johnson would pass NYA savings, garnered from White colleges that did not need all their funds, on to Blacks. "The bursar at the Sam Houston College for Negroes in Austin remembers how he would call up and ask: 'You have any boys and girls out there that could use some money? I've got a little extra change here. Can you find a place to put it?'"[23]

Under LBJ, the agency enrolled nearly 25% of eligible Blacks in the Texas College Aid Program while White enrollment languished at 14%; the agency also arranged schooling and training for more than 20,000 young Texans and found work for close to 10,000 others. Bruce Schulman notes that "Johnson carefully steered away from offending the racist sensibilities of most White Texans but did more than any other official in the South to bring New Deal benefits to African Americans."[24]

Almost every biographer notes the seemingly contradictory nature of Johnson's attitudes: While his roots were in the South and his perspective was not dissimilar to that of his neighbors, which in practice meant that he spoke of Blacks as "niggers" in private and referred to them as "Negroes" in formal communications, he yet differed from the majority of Southern Whites in that he was very much interested in providing Blacks with opportunities both economic and political, as exemplified by his work at the Texas NYA.

In 1937, LBJ was elected to Congress, defeating seven more-recognized opponents and all anti–New Deal candidates.

Johnson fared well in the House of Representatives; he was politically astute enough to side with Roosevelt's White House, though it meant elevating tensions with one of his senior mentees, House Speaker Sam Rayburn. He worked hard, and almost all his biographers suggest that his penchant for overworking his staff started during this time and continued through his presidency—yielding results for his Hill Country constituents was paramount. Among them were dollars to renovate schools and build low-cost apartments in the state capital. He was acknowledged by Tom Corcoran "as the best Congressman for a district that *ever was*."[25]

Johnson could see that the House was not going to take him where his ambitious plan was to lead. He told Doris Kearns Goodwin that within three years, he felt "terribly restless and unhappy."[26] Johnson was not interested in the slow climb to power that is characteristic of a career in the House. He set his sights on the Senate, and traded in Sam Rayburn's patronage for FDR's support.[27]

He lost his first attempt for the Senate in 1941. His opponent successfully rode the wave of rising conservatism in Texas as Roosevelt's New Deal program faltered. Governor W. Lee O'Daniel berated the New Deal as a "gang of back-slapping, pie-eating, pussy-footing professional politicians who couldn't run a peanut stand."[28]

During his years in the House, Lyndon Johnson forged a link with the new world of Texas power, the gas and oil brokers. Gas and oil replaced King Cotton in Texas. This was fortuitous for his later moves, including assistance to the party when he chaired a stagnant Democratic Congressional Campaign Committee.

He moved with calculated precision to the right of his Democratic president, Harry Truman. Though he did not, for example, join the segregationist cabal, he openly railed against Truman's civil rights program. Through his voting patterns he carefully prepared his second Senate run; he had to win it, because unlike in his first run, he could not return to his House seat.

At age 40, he secured that Senate seat in a closely contested election, winning by only 87 votes. Joining Johnson in that freshman class of 1948 were colleagues who would go on to work with him as he made his way to the ultimate Senate prize: Majority Leader. The class included Hubert Horatio Humphrey of Minnesota, future vice president of the United States; Paul Douglas of Illinois, a professor at the University of Chicago and a renowned advocate of liberal economic policies; Russel Long, son of Huey Long; and Estes Kefauver, who would lead a Senate committee investigating organized crime.[29]

Only three years later, at age 42, with mild approval from the Senate kingmaker of the time, Richard Russell of Georgia, Johnson entered the ranks of Senate Democratic leadership as a Senate Majority Whip.[30] Johnson is characterized by most biographers as a tireless, indefatigable leader. Schulman credits him as becoming "the most successful and most powerful floor leader the Senate or the nation had ever seen." "Central to Johnson's leadership," says Schulman, "was his personal style that Evans and Novak called 'The treatment.'"[31]

A year later, Johnson ably moved to the position of Minority Leader in 1953, the most junior senator to ever do so. He also successfully won his state's Democratic primary, thus assuring his tenure as a senator for the next six years. During these years he found working with the Democratic liberals different.

Evans and Novak write, "The liberals were emotional, idealistic and firm believers, in their own rhetoric, a manifestation of unrealism Johnson never comprehended."[32] Johnson was aware of his liberal colleagues' suspicions of his Southern roots. His votes, his language, his lack of commitment on civil rights solidified their skepticism. What bothered the liberals the most was his voting record, which began with his arrival in Congress in 1937.

Johnson had a 100% record of voting against every civil rights bill that was sent to the floor during his first 20 in Congress. He had voted *no* on an anti-lynching bill; *no* on a democratic leadership amendment in 1940, eliminating segregation in the armed services; *no* on anti-poll-tax bills in 1942, 1943, and 1945; *no* in 1946 on an anti-discrimination amendment to the federal school lunch program; and *yes* in 1949 on a proposed anti-Negro amendment to a District of Columbia home-rule bill.[33, 34]

Years later, in interviews with Doris Kearns Goodwin, Johnson would justify his vote against the poll-tax bill with a states' rights argument, noting that he actually worked against the poll tax in Texas in the 1950s, and explain his vote against the anti-lynching bill by pointing out that there already were laws against murder and that he believed the point of the bill was really to besmirch the South.[35]

In his own presidential memoir, however, Johnson is more pragmatic: "As a Representative and a Senator, before I became Majority Leader, I did not have the power (to do otherwise). That is a plain and simple fact."[36] And though Johnson despised Democratic liberals, he was astute enough to work with them on issues he could afford to use as leverage without antagonizing any of his Southern base.

He worked with liberals on housing, minimum wages, Social Security, rural electrification, and other bread-and-butter issues, but above all, on civil rights Johnson remained with his Southern base.

The strategy for achieving his goals and the use of his bully pulpit was termed the Johnson System. It was a system that, more often than not, understood when and how to use measures of control.

It utilized his masterful negotiating skills, taking a stance of flexibility when he deemed it to his advantage and moderately working through issues with Southern conservatives and Northern and Midwestern liberals (e.g., some of the very people who came to Congress with him, like Hubert Humphrey).

It relied on relentless, powerfully persuasive conversations; his physical dominance; his ability to read character; the art of skillful head-counting; corralling votes; the deliberate avoidance of a personal vote on any issue that would later interfere with the journey he had decided to travel; and a political and philosophical framework of effectiveness and unbridled will.

Johnson himself described what was necessary to be persuasive: "When you're dealing with all those Senators—the good ones and the crazies, the hard workers and the lazies, the smart ones and the mediocres—you've got to know two things right away. You've got to understand the beliefs and values common to all of them as politicians, the desire for fame and the thirst for honor, and then you've got to understand *the* emotion most controlling that particular senator."[37]

Bruce Schulman argues that, during his first term, if Johnson went all-in with the national liberals, especially on the matter of segregation, he would ruin any chance he had at the presidency. At the same time, if he walked in step with his Southern Democratic colleagues, the taint of insular regionalism would keep him from any position of real leadership. So he walked a moderate middle road, supporting populist causes like education, wages, housing, and farm subsidies, only deviating from national liberal policies on oil and gas and civil rights.[38]

In 1956, two years after the *Brown* decision, Southern congressmen, led by Strom Thurmond, vowed to resist that decision. One hundred and one congressmen and senators signed the "Declaration of Constitutional Principles," better known as the "Southern Manifesto," pledging to resist the *Brown* decision on school integration. Johnson was one of only three Southern senators who refused to sign it. Senator Richard Neuberger, Democrat from Oregon, described LBJ's declining to sign the Manifesto as "one of the most courageous acts of political valor I have ever seen . . . in my adult life."[39]

That same year, when President Eisenhower sent an overarching civil rights bill with real teeth, though it was less ambitious than the Truman doctrine of 1948, Johnson cooperated with the bigoted James O. Eastland, chairman of the powerful Senate Judiciary Committee. The civil rights bill sat in the committee "on hold." Johnson then cooperated with Richard Brevard Russel of Georgia in making sure the bill was not discharged.

With these actions, Johnson, utilizing timing and other elements of the Johnson System and the Treatment, began his influential foray onto the trail that was to become the Civil Rights Act of 1964. An examination of his path to 1964 is more carefully defined in the Legislative Profile Section.

Given Johnson's history of voting against civil rights measures and his actions regarding Eisenhower's 1956 bill, lawmakers and journalists expected nothing different from him when Eisenhower returned the civil rights bill to Congress the next year. Johnson did nothing to discourage such views, allowing himself as much room to maneuver as possible.[40]

Johnson realized that if he could break the Southern logjam by getting the 1957 act limited to a single right, though it would weaken the bill seriously, the South might not filibuster and let the bill come to the floor for the first time in 82 years. Putting his stamp on the bill would "emancipate himself from the Confederate yoke. . . . It would move him into the mainstream of the Democratic Party for the first time since his early days. . . . Unless he plunged into that mainstream, Johnson could not even hope for the presidential nomination."[41]

Caro explains that Johnson believed that "Of all the rights that Black Americans had so long been denied, the right to vote was the one which, if he could get it for them, would be most valuable, for the granting of that right would, he knew, lead—perhaps slowly, but inevitably—to all the others. . . . Give Negroes the vote—give them power—and they could start doing the rest for themselves."[42]

Caro then summarizes Johnson's immediate strategy: "The most important thing wasn't what was in the bill. The most important thing was there was a bill."[43]

Roy Wilkins writes:

The most important figure in the struggle for the 1957 Civil Rights Bill was Lyndon Baines Johnson. . . . The historical, irreversible impact of the Supreme Court's ruling in *Brown v. Board* was not lost on him. . . . He dreamed of becoming President himself and knew that so long as he had Jim Crow wrapped around him, the rest of the country would see him only as a Southerner, a corn-pone Southerner at that, rather than a man of national stature.[44]

Johnson was determined that as majority leader, he was going to pass a civil rights bill using all the tools of his system and advancing his bully pulpit, even if the bill was imperfect.

The wrath Johnson received from the Northern liberals at the watered-down bill was expected. Johnson had developed a compromise that the Southerners would accept by eliminating all provisions that would enforce school desegregation. The Pennsylvania chapter of the NAACP called the bill "weasel worded."

Johnson's press secretary argued that, to the contrary, "It opened a major branch of American government to a tenth of the population for which all legislative doors had been slammed shut."[45] Johnson's shepherding of the 1957 Civil Rights Bill liberated him from the Southern stranglehold. Caro observes that "it was the full flowering of the Johnson system at a level of proficiency not achieved before."[46]

As he moved from senate prominence to the vice presidency, Johnson still felt he was discriminated against as a Southerner: "I don't think anybody from the South will be nominated in my lifetime," Johnson reflected in 1958, "if so, I don't think he will be elected."[47]

Having accepted the role of John F. Kennedy's vice president, Johnson worked effectively and tirelessly on behalf of the ticket. The Democratic Convention of 1960 carried a strong civil rights plank in its platform, and Johnson had a clear role to "hold" the South—to help win eleven of the states of the old Confederacy, as Eisenhower had carried only five in 1956.

Johnson was also expected to help Southern voters tolerate the need to address the Negro issues. On more than one occasion he told audiences that the Negro had waited for more than one hundred years for his freedom: "I think that's long enough, don't you?"[48]

Johnson's relationship with JFK was another issue. After all, as a senator, Kennedy had been at the mercy of the powerful majority leader for eight years. "How much had Jack Kennedy resented having to beg?"[49]

Regardless of the truth of the nature of their relationship, as vice president, Johnson went from being the "second most powerful man in government" to taking a back seat to JFK. Johnson's "decline was swift and merciless."[50]

Though Kennedy intellectually engaged in a civil rights agenda, during his first year in office, Kennedy did not send expanded civil rights legislation to Congress. He did not sense any real interest in Congress, nor was there clear public interest outside the growing demands of civil rights leaders. He turned to the Justice Department and other federal agencies as a response to these demands, demands marked by sit-ins, boycotts, and freedom schools.

The Birmingham riots had gotten the attention of the Kennedy administration, and the young president felt compelled to craft a new civil rights bill. The administration began to draw up civil rights legislation, excluding the involvement of the vice president. After hearing rumors about the bill, LBJ asked to meet with the president. As Johnson entered the meeting, a discussion of the bill was under way with various aides. The president asked if Johnson had anything to add, and Johnson provided advice to the president on two levels, one regarding tactics, and the other regarding the bully pulpit.

Tactically, sending a civil rights bill to Congress at that time would be a mistake, Johnson argued. The Kennedy administration had not yet accomplished their other legislative goals, and it was an old Southern tactic to delay other important bills in the period leading up to a civil rights bill. If any important outstanding legislation was still waiting when the civil rights bill was being considered (and filibustered), the pressure to abandon the civil rights bill would be immense. He also urged Kennedy to put the Johnson System in place, to get all his ducks in a row in order to maximize their chances of success.[51]

The other level of advice he gave regarded the sentiment of Blacks at the time and a call for Kennedy to utilize his bully pulpit. "I think that I know one thing: that the Negroes are tired of this patient stuff and tired of this piecemeal stuff and what they want more than anything else is not an executive order or legislation, they want a moral commitment.... What Negroes are really seeking is moral force and to be sure that we're on their side.... We got a little popgun, and I want to pull out the cannon. The President is the cannon."[52]

PLATFORM ON DESEGREGATION

There are thousands of pages documenting administration and congressional efforts in 1947, 1948, and 1951 to stem the tide of blatant segregation impacting Negroes in American public life. Each of these Congresses had defeated anti-lynching and anti-poll-tax legislation. In spite of their service to the country, Black servicemen, for example, returned to their country only to find themselves unable to access a quality education, let alone the right to vote. Congress remained silent through every administration until Eisenhower in 1956.

Just as Johnson understood how important it was "to count the votes," he also understood the importance of timing as he "worked" Congress. Most historical accounts carefully lay out Johnson's role as majority leader in the passage of Eisenhower's 1957 Civil Rights Bill. We will not discuss details in depth here, but it is important to put it in context.

During the 1940s and the very early 1950s, six different civil rights bills were defeated on the floors of both houses. A lack of public interest, Southern Democratic conservatives, and the Republican bloc almost assured no legislative action in the foreseeable future.

However, in 1956, as political pressures mounted across the country due to *Brown*, defiant refusal by Southern school districts to comply with *Brown* generated some support for compliance in the North and laid the seeds for the desertion of the Democratic Party by Blacks; civil rights appeared on the agenda of Congress again.

Eisenhower's attorney general persuaded him to submit a civil rights bill to Congress. There were three provisions: the creation of a civil rights division within the Justice Department, authority for the Justice Department to intervene on behalf of individuals whose civil rights were being violated, including the right to education, and the appointment of a civil rights commission to recommend further legislation.

In 1956, the House passed a reasonably strong civil rights bill that included the above provisions. When the civil rights bill arrived in the Senate, it was hijacked through a nontraditional route that Johnson had maneuvered, and so it ended up directly in James Eastland's Judiciary Committee. Thus Johnson had steered the direction of the bill so that it would remain in the deep freezer for the remainder of the 85th congressional session.

As noted earlier, Johnson, the "master senator," through his "actions," enabled the Congress during Eisenhower's administration to pass a gutted civil rights bill. Johnson understood it was not a question of the strength of the bill, but that there must be a bill. It was a civil rights bill that passed 72 to 18 after a debate of 121 hours and 31 minutes, with no filibuster.[53] Johnson had begun his foray onto the trail of the civil rights bill that would become law in 1964; however, by tactically maneuvering the elimination of the sections with teeth, it meant that at this time there was no legislative redress for Black children who were still forced to attend segregated schools.

Wells of ink have been spilled to detail the impressive provisions of the Johnson Civil Rights Bills of 1964 and 1965 and most significantly the Voting Rights Act of 1968. However, the public polity spends little ink on Johnson's bully pulpit on the desegregation of schools and the education of Black children.

The Johnson bully pulpit ushered in a vast network of legal frameworks, federal policies, and programs designed to embolden the civil rights in the education of Black schoolchildren. Most, if not all, of these also benefited large numbers of White children, specifically White children in rural communities and in working poor communities.

Johnson unleashed his bully pulpit with a resounding roar to move the implementation of the *Brown* decision through the use of federal tools and policies from the courts (*Green v. County School Board of New Kent County*), from the executive office, and from significant congressional legislation. Discrimination was determined to be illegal in all schools, teeth were put in *Brown*, and as Charles Ogletree observed, "the real changes envisioned by

Brown were now possible." Under President Johnson, the federal government vigorously enforced desegregation, and rapid and dramatic changes were realized in the South. The federal rules implementing the legislation became effective in 1965, and the Justice Department's civil rights lawyers began filing suits. The sanctions imposed by the law and the cut-offs to federal aid were effective tools to regulate school districts that refused to desegregate.[54] Gary Orfield pointed out that, "Just a few years of intensive enforcement was enough to transfer southern schools and create much stricter and desegregation standards."[55]

In discussing Johnson's performance in the passage of the 1964 Civil Rights Bill, Robert Caro writes, "The Presidency of Lyndon Johnson marked the legislative realization of many of the liberal aspirations of the 20th century. . . . He used the power of the presidency for purposes as noble as any in American history."[56]

After President Kennedy's assassination, there were questions about whether Johnson would return to the compromising politician who finessed the Civil Rights Act of 1957. "Civil-rights advocates feared and Southerners hoped that he somehow would perform the same miracle of consensus with the bill that had been submitted by Kennedy."[57]

Johnson was aware of this and assured any and all that he would use all his powers to ensure passage of the bill: "I made my position unmistakably clear: We were not prepared to compromise in any way. . . . I knew that the slightest wavering on my part would give hope to the opposition's strategy of amending the bill to death."[58]

He was no longer Senate majority leader; he was president of the country, and "Power would reveal."

Johnson assured legislative leaders there would be "no compromise on civil rights; I am not going to bend an inch. In the Senate [as Leader] I did as much as I could. But I had to be careful. . . . But I always vowed that if I ever had the power, I'd make sure that every Negro had the same chance as every White man. Now I have it. And I'm going to use it."[59]

At Johnson's ranch, when asked by a group of Southern politicians not to set firm guidelines for implementing the legislation, he retorted, "Nigger, Nigger, Nigger—that's all I hear. You might as well stop, because we're going ahead."[60]

James (Scotty) Reston of the *New York Times* wrote: "More than any other politician since the Civil War, he has, on the race problem, been the most effective mediator between the North and the South. He is the man who induced the Senate to accept the civil-rights legislation which strikes at the disfranchisement of Southern Negroes."[61]

LEGISLATIVE PROFILE AS PRESIDENT

A president's ability to powerfully use the bully pulpit to advance his national platform is most effective when he is able to drive that agenda by successfully engaging the Congress of the United States. Ultimately, it is Congress's support and embrace that advance his political goals and transform those goals into sustainable national legislative programs. Equality for Blacks had been advanced by Eisenhower through the courts and had been advanced by Kennedy through the Executive Branch. Throughout his first four years, Johnson used the legislative path to drive toward equality for Blacks and quality-of-life resolutions for other underserved communities.

Johnson described the bully pulpit and his first weeks as president:

> Teddy Roosevelt used to call the Presidency a "bully pulpit." During my first 30 days in office I preached many sermons from that pulpit. I knew I had to secure the cooperation of the people who were the natural leaders of the nation. I talked with those leaders, from every walk of life. . . . I spoke with Black groups and with individual leaders of the Black community and told them that John Kennedy's dream of equality had not died with him. I assured them that I was going to press for the civil-rights bill with every ounce of energy I possessed. . . . I tried to convince the governors that the nation could not live with racial tensions much longer. I talked to them about the mood of the country, about all the hatred and bitterness and uncertainty that we were experiencing in the wake of President Kennedy's assassination. . . . We have to do something about hate and you have to get to the root of hate. The roots of hate are poverty and disease and illiteracy, and they are broad in the land.[62]

Kearns Goodwin suggests that Johnson's legislative programs were crafted to respond to his sense of the urgency of the current needs of the country, not projecting future needs. She writes, "Every technique reflects the importance being given to movement and speed. . . . While a typical schedule of presidential messages to the Congress consists of one or two a month, in 1965, Johnson transmitted 63 separate documents requesting action on a bewildering variety of legislation."[63]

With his mastery of legislative prowess and techniques, Johnson moved at breakneck speed to get Congress to do a great deal more for civil rights—and specifically the civil rights of Blacks—than had historically ever happened. Richard Kluger, the expert on *Brown* and the Supreme Court, posits that Johnson brokered a deal far beyond what "John Kennedy could probably ever have accomplished."[64] The 1964 Civil Rights Act was passed by the Senate a year to the day after Kennedy had submitted it to Congress. Kennedy's bill died in the House three days before he was assassinated.[65]

Over the next 10 years, due to the Johnson Civil Rights Act, the Justice Department would pursue legal action against more than 500 school districts. The Department of Health, Education, and Welfare would file more than 600 actions aimed at suspending federal aid to school districts that discriminated racially.[66]

Biographers cite many vignettes and examples of Johnson's tactical maneuvering to reach his goals, but one of his most consistent tactics was not to put forth a measure until he could reasonably determine the outcome of the vote.

Clarence Mitchell, of the NAACP, observed that Johnson's legislative moves were "an arithmetic type of consideration." Mitchell remembers, "He said to me when he was in the Senate, 'Clarence, you can get anything that you have the votes to get. How many votes do you have?'"[67]

Another example of his tactical maneuvering comes from his attempt as majority leader to deliver the passage of Eisenhower's 1957 Civil Rights Bill. Johnson needed 33 votes from the Mountain States (Idaho, Montana, Wyoming, Colorado, Utah, New Mexico, and Nevada, coupled with the far western states of Washington and Oregon). Johnson was not going to get votes from his Southern colleagues, so he was unrestrained in using his energy, his political capital, and those storied personal powers of persuasion to figure out what they wanted in exchange for their votes.

Johnson's strategy was to resolve the Hells Canyon controversy. The conflict revolved around who should control the hydroelectric-generating potential of the country's rivers: private corporations or the public.[68] Johnson told Kearns Goodwin, "I began with the assumption that most of the Senators from the Mountain States had never seen a Negro and simply couldn't care all that much about the whole civil rights issue. I knew what they did care about and that was the Hells Canyon issue. So I went to key Southerners and persuaded them to back the westerners on Hells Canyon."[69]

Johnson's civil rights bill gave teeth to the federal government's role in school desegregation. Johnson's commentary in his autobiography, *The Vantage Point*, provides clarity as to his intent, his belief, and his assessment. Johnson closed his own memoirs noting he had given everything that was in him. Johnson says, "John Nance Garner, a great legislative tactician, as well as a good poker player, once told me that there comes a time in every leader's career when he has to put in all his stack, I decided to shove in all my stack on this vital measure."[70]

Johnson recalled an evening at an Urban League dinner. He then mused, seemingly prophetically:

> I looked around the room once more. Most of those present were men and women of my generation. We had given everything we had to the struggle, and

we had seen many of our towering dreams come through. We could look back at landmarks we had established on the trail. But we were not yet in sight of the plateau we had to gain before our country could rest. Turbulence was still in the air; restlessness was rampant. The reigns of leadership were passing from one generation to another and the American struggle for justice was just beginning.[71]

NOTES

1. Robert A. Caro (2003), *Master of the Senate: The Years of Lyndon Johnson* (Random House), 120.
2. Caro (2003), *Master of the Senate*, 120.
3. Clarke Newlon (1964), *L.B.J.: The Man from Johnson City* (Dodd, Mead & Co.), 226.
4. Newlon (1964), *L.B.J.*, 227.
5. Newlon (1964), *L.B.J.*, 226–27.
6. Robert A. Caro (1983), *The Path to Power: The Years of Lyndon Johnson* (Vintage Books), 67.
7. Caro (1983), *The Path to Power*, 50–65.
8. Robert Dallek (1991), *Lone Star Rising: Lyndon Johnson and His Times 1908–1960* (Oxford University Press), 48.
9. Dallek (1991), *Lone Star Rising*, 48.
10. Dallek (1991), *Lone Star Rising*, 148–49.
11. Mark Stern (1992), *Calculating Visions Kennedy, Johnson, and Civil Rights* (Rutgers University Press), 116.
12. Doris Kearns Goodwin (1976), *Lyndon Johnson and the American Dream* (Signet), 36.
13. Bruce J. Schulman (1994), *Lyndon B. Johnson and American Liberalism* (Bedford), 2.
14. Dallek (1991), *Lone Star Rising*, 146.
15. Caro (2003), *Master of the Senate*, 19.
16. Caro (2003), *Master of the Senate*, 718–19.
17. Henry McPherson (1995), *A Political Education: A Washington Memoir* (University of Texas Press), 138.
18. Caro (2003), *Master of the Senate*, 722.
19. Dallek (1991); King (Texas monthly).
20. Dallek (1991), *Lone Star Rising*.
21. Dallek (1991); King (Texas monthly).
22. Johnson presidential remarks, public domain.
23. Dallek (1991), *Lone Star Rising*, 139.
24. Schulman (1994), *Lyndon B. Johnson and American Liberalism*, 16.
25. Caro (1983), *The Path to Power*, 531.
26. Doris Kearns Goodwin (1976), *Lyndon Johnson and the American Dream* (St. Martin's Press), 93.

27. Roland Evans and Robert Novak (1966), *Lyndon B. Johnson: The Exercise of Power* (New American Library), 13.

28. Evans and Novak (1966), *Lyndon B. Johnson*, 14.

29. Evans and Novak (1966), *Lyndon B. Johnson*, 26.

30. Evans and Novak (1966), *Lyndon B. Johnson*, 43

31. Schulman (1994), *Lyndon B. Johnson and American Liberalism*, 42–43.

32. Evans and Novak (1966), *Lyndon B. Johnson*.

33. Evans and Novak (1966), *Lyndon B. Johnson*, 121.

34. Complete House voting Record of Congressman Lyndon Johnson by subject, from May 1937 to December 31, 1948, Box 75, LBJA SF.

35. Goodwin (1976), *Lyndon Johnson and the American Dream*, 232.

36. Lyndon Baines Johnson (1971), *The Vantage Point: Perspectives of the Presidency 1963–1969* (Holt, Rinehart and Winston Inc.), 155.

37. Doris Kearns Goodwin (2018), *Leadership in Turbulent Times* (Simon and Schuster), 197.

38. Schulman (1994), *Lyndon B. Johnson and American Liberalism*, 40.

39. Dallek (1991), *Lone Star Rising*, 496.

40. Evans and Novak (1966), *Lyndon B. Johnson*, 124.

41. Evans and Novak (1966), *Lyndon B. Johnson*, 125.

42. Caro (2003), *Master of the Senate*, 892.

43. Caro (2003), *Master of the Senate*, 893.

44. Tom Mathes and Roy Wilkins (1982), *Standing Fast: The Autobiography of Roy Wilkins* (The Viking Press), 243.

45. Caro (1983), *The Path to Power*, 10.

46. Caro (2003), *Master of the Senate*, 140.

47. Tom Wicker (1991), *JFK and LBJ: The Influence of Personality upon Politics* (Ivan R. Dee), 152.

48. Newlon (1964), *L.B.J.*, 135.

49. Robert A. Caro (2012), *The Passage to Power: The years of Lyndon Johnson* (Vintage Books, 2012), 190.

50. Jeff Shesol (1998), *Mutual Contempt: Lyndon Johnson, Robert Kennedy, and the Feud That Defined a Decade* (W.W. Norton), 75.

51. Caro (2012), *The Passage to Power*, 258.

52. Caro (2012), *The Passage to Power*, 260.

53. Evans and Novak (1966), *Lyndon B. Johnson*, 139.

54. Charles J. Ogletree, Jr. (2005), *All Deliberate Speed: Reflections on the First Half-century of* Brown v. Board of Education (Norton and Company), 132.

55. Gary Orfield and Susan E. Eaton (1996), *Dismantling Desegregation: The Quiet Reversal of* Brown v. Board of Education (The New Press), 8.

56. Robert A. Caro (1990), *Means of Ascent: The Years of Lyndon Johnson* (Knopf), 22.

57. Evans and Novak (1966), *Lyndon B. Johnson*, 376.

58. Johnson (1971), *The Vantage Point*, 157.

59. Caro (2012), *The Passage of Power*, 562.

60. Kenneth O'Reilly (1996), *Nixon's Piano: Presidents and Racial Politics from Washington to Clinton* (Free Press), 243.
61. Newlon (1964), *L B.J.*, 129–30.
62. Johnson (1971), *The Vantage Point*, 29–30.
63. Goodwin (1976), *Lyndon Johnson and the American Dream*, 217.
64. Richard Kluger (1975), *Simple Justice* (Alfred A. Knopf), 759.
65. Kluger (1975), *Simple Justice*, 759.
66. Kluger (1975), *Simple Justice*, 759.
67. O'Reilly (1996), *Nixon's Piano*, 239.
68. Caro (2012), *The Passage to Power*, 59.
69. Goodwin (2018), *Leadership*.
70. Johnson (1971), *The Vantage Point*, 37.
71. Johnson (1971), *The Vantage Point*, 179.

Chapter 4

Richard Milhous Nixon

Much of the Nixon legacy has been chronicled through the lens of Watergate and America's role in Vietnam, with some positive attention given to the opening of relations with China. Discussion of his domestic policy focuses on his proposals for a national Family Assistance Plan, creation of the Environmental Protection Agency, expansion of affirmative action, promotion of Black entrepreneurship, establishment of a wage and price policy, and support for the Voting Rights Act.

There has been a relative lack of attention, however, paid to Nixon's efforts regarding the implementation of *Brown*—the use of his bully pulpit to oppose busing and to pump the brakes on school desegregation generally, a reversal of the momentum built by the previous two administrations.

FORMATIVE YEARS

From a young age, Richard Milhous Nixon's ambition was to elevate his status in life by hard work. At 11 years old, he wrote a letter to the *Los Angeles Times* asking to be considered for the office-boy position they had advertised, noting that he was "willing to come to your office at any time and (would) accept any pay offered."[1]

Many historians have observed that at the core of Nixon's actions was a belief system shaped by the Quaker roots of his mother; his family's station in life was the other primary influence.

> Richard Perlstein argues that Nixon's ambition and his tenacity in seeking the presidency were developed throughout his lifetime of hardship, beginning with working for his abusive father as a child and young man, to his inability to attend Harvard (where he had been accepted) because of financial difficulties, to being snubbed by the only social club at Whittier College, where he'd been

forced to attend, to being passed over for jobs after graduating third in his class at Duke Law.²

Others describe him as a loner and an outsider. Mary Guptill, who worked for the Nixons, recalled Richard as quiet and inwardly focused. In high school, Nixon became a skilled debater; even in high school, he was crafty and deceptive—his coach looked disapprovingly at "his ability to kind of slide around an argument instead of meeting it head-on."³

It was at Whittier College where Nixon began to utilize his outsider status in the development of his leadership skill set. In lieu of fraternities and sororities, Whittier's social life was centered on "literary societies." The Franklins was the only such society for men and was populated by Whittier's economic and cultural elite; Nixon was not asked to join.

Instead, Nixon became a charter member and founding president of a new society, the Orthogonians. Largely made up of football players who were neither culturally nor academically elite, the Orthogonians helped Nixon leverage the average Whittier student's distaste for the overt classism and elitism of the Franklins to run against a Franklin for student-body president and win.⁴

Nixon understood there was a way out for persons who felt undercut by the elite. Throughout his time at Whittier and Duke Law, Nixon would continue to achieve through hard work: "I won . . . not because I was smarter but because I worked longer and harder than some of my gifted colleagues."⁵

Nixon's distrust of privilege was only reinforced when he first encountered systemic racial discrimination while at Duke Law School. Shocked at the racist ideas espoused by many of his classmates, "Nixon became something of a liberal on racial issues."⁶

Nixon's need to win, though, would impact this seemingly liberal view, if, in fact, it was a view he ever held strongly. "Race had always been the best-oiled hinge in the strange contraption that was Nixon's ideology, swinging from one position to the next." He both supported JFK's 1963 civil rights legislation and then attacked it ruthlessly when it went to the House. Expediency was his true ideology.⁷

JOURNEY TO THE PRESIDENCY

Tom Wicker tells us:

> Nixon ran a campaign that was richly financed, measured in pace and tone, and largely issueless. Stressing the advantages of his experience in the presidency rather than the substantive issues of debate, he appealed in broad terms to the "forgotten Americans" citizens who paid their taxes and did not riot. To Nixon

this included middle class Negroes with a stake in society, and it was consistent with his rather generalized campaign pledged to foster Black capitalism. Nixon said, "All we can do is not say anything to do anything which will cause the Negroes to lose confidence in me, because I am going to be President of the United States, and no President can do anything without having the confidence of the Black community.... If I am President... I am not going to owe anything to the Black community."[8]

Nixon's words from the campaign trails from 1960 up to the presidency in 1968 illustrate how Nixon would shape his bully pulpit. At age 32, Nixon was recruited to run against a five-term Democrat for a seat in the House. That Democrat, Jerry Voorhis, a graduate of Hotchkiss and Yale, was clearly a "Franklin" to Nixon, the Orthogonian; Nixon manipulated the public's distrust of Ivy-League elites in any way he could when debating Voorhis. "Nixon adopted, in his first campaign, his signature tactic: making false claims and then taking umbrage when his opponent impugned his integrity."[9]

Early on, Nixon had an admirable civil rights record both as vice president and United States senator. In particular, as vice president he argued that each new Senate (some members change every two years) should be able to adopt new rules for itself by simple majority; for example, the Senate should be able to amend the number of votes needed to end a filibuster, the tool consistently used against civil rights legislation. Ironically, it was LBJ who managed to table such a vote in a bid to hang on to the support of Southern Democrats. Nixon also served as chair of the President's Committee on Government Contracts, working toward ending federal support of businesses engaged in racial discrimination.[10]

But Nixon seems to have held some inner prejudice himself. John Ehrlichman, White House counsel and member of Nixon's inner circle, recalled that the president explained to him, on more than one occasion, that federal programs to address economic, educational, and social disparities were a waste of resources, because "Blacks were *genetically inferior* to Whites. All the federal money and programs we could devise could not change that fact."[11]

During his first presidential campaign, against Kennedy, Nixon's team considered domestic and foreign policy the two key topics to target in order to outpace Kennedy. Nixon reported that he chose to tackle head-on the civil rights issue and the political considerations of how to handle this issue.[12]

On October 19, 1960, Martin Luther King Jr., along with dozens of other protestors, was arrested during a sit-in Atlanta, Georgia. When King was given a four-month sentence based on an old traffic violation, Nixon's apparent silence was deafening.

His press secretary, Herbert Klein, had asked for a comment for the press; Nixon's response was, "I think Dr. King is getting a bum rap. But . . . it would be completely improper for me . . . to call the judge. And Robert Kennedy should have known better than to do so."[13] Nixon seems to have misunderstood that it was JFK, not Robert Kennedy, who reached out, and it was to Coretta Scott King, MLK's wife, not the judge in his trial.

Klein was forced to report that Nixon had no comment, which Nixon said led to Black leaders believing "that I did not care about justice in the King case." In fact, Nixon relates, he tried to get the White House to order an inquiry into King's treatment, though his efforts failed. Years later, Klein painted a different picture, remembering that Nixon's campaign staff saw opportunity in King's difficulties and wanted concrete action from Nixon. Their plan was ignored, though—Nixon thought "it would look like he was pandering."

In 1966, public distastes had diverged in the North and South—while Northerners feared a Southern takeover, Southerners' anxieties over riots dominated regional politics. Nixon, while having supported *Brown v. Board of Education*, the Civil Rights Act of 1964, and the Voting Rights Act of 1965, drew the line at "mob rule," a perfectly ambiguous term—while Northerners believed this was a reference to Southern vigilantes, Southerners saw it as a declaration against Black protests.

In his second attempt at the presidency, Nixon was opposed by Governor Ronald Reagan of California. By now, Nixon was agile on the campaign trail; he was always ambiguous regarding his intentions concerning the desegregation of public schools. He did, however, consistently give out signals that he was sympathetic to the concerns of anti-integrationists in the South.

In May 1968, Nixon traveled to the South in order to secure the support of several shaky allies, ending with a meeting of the region's Republican chairs on May 31. His reception was chilly.

Nixon asked Strom Thurmond to come to Atlanta and put his people in line. Thurmond, supposedly one of Nixon's allies, had been speaking of Reagan with unparalleled deference and admiration. He arrived the next day.

Thurmond and the other Republicans were concerned about the implications of a recent Supreme Court ruling in *Green v. New Kent County*, which had made clear that delays in school integration were no longer acceptable. With this as the fulcrum for the talks, Thurmond suggested that he could guarantee Nixon the nomination if he had assurances from the would-be president regarding *Green*.

Nixon made it clear that even though *Brown* was done and settled, in his view there was little the Constitution allowed the federal government to do in enforcing it, regardless of what had been ruled in *Green*. He also promised that only jurists with similar views would be appointed to the bench and that he would, of course, consult with Thurmond on the matter of a running mate.[14]

Nixon and Thurmond left the meeting arm in arm. Three weeks later, having put his people in line, Thurmond announced that Nixon was the best candidate and that South Carolina was pulling all support for Ronald Reagan.

Later, at the Republican National Convention in Miami, Reagan's shocking popularity forced Nixon to meet and take questions personally from the Southern delegates to shore up their support. When asked by a delegate from North Carolina if he supported "forced busing," Nixon replied:

> I think that busing the child—a child that is two or three grades behind another child and into a strange community—I think that you destroy that child.... I don't think there is any court in this country, any judge in this country, either local or on the Supreme Court ... that is as qualified to ... make the decision as your local school board.[15]

PLATFORM ON DESEGREGATION

It is impossible to describe the bully pulpit of Nixon without a reference to the Southern Strategy, a plan to sway White, mostly Southern voters to vote Republican by appealing to their racial anxieties. A secondary effect was to draw the attention of Whites away from George Wallace. As previously Republican African Americans moved toward the Democratic Party, particularly in the South, Nixon needed to pursue a new group of voters. He chose Southern Whites and waged a campaign that supported traditional, "Dixie" racial attitudes.

Nixon's Southern strategy involved his continued appeasing of Southern Whites by making it clear he would not press forward on integration if he could count on a conservative, Republican South.[16] His promises included a lessened sense of urgency surrounding racial desegregation and the reallocation of power on similar issues in favor of individual states rather than federal control.

Essentially, the Southern strategy offered civil rights opponents a candidate behind whom to rally. He played on the South's downtrodden morale in the wake of sweeping federal reforms under Johnson, even going as far as to state that, on issues of racial relations, "I don't believe you should use the South as a whipping boy."[17] This strategy of divisive rhetoric and catering to White desires led Nixon to the presidency.

Panetta and Gall stated:

Senator Strom Thurmond of South Carolina had urged Nixon to withdraw the work of the government from its efforts of desegregation. Leon Panetta, former director of HEW's Office of Civil Rights during the early days of the Nixon administration, recognized the difficulty Nixon had in attempting to reconcile his campaign promises to Thurmond and the South with the need to obey the court decisions on school desegregation, but saw Nixon giving in to the political pressures from Thurmond, political pressures that HEW was seeking to overcome.[18]

The State, a South Carolina newspaper, in an article quotes Thurmond as saying, "ignore HEW and wait for a better deal."[19] Nixon's liaison to the South, Harry Dent, wrote a January 23, 1969, memo to the president in which he stated, "So far as Southern politics is concerned the Nixon administration will be judged from the beginning on the manner in which the school desegregation guidelines problem is handled. Other issues are important in the South but are dwarfed somewhat by comparison."[20]

As Gulliver and Murphy observed, the Southern Strategy represented:

> A deal between Nixon and the Southern segregationists. . . .[21] The terrible cruelty of the Nixon Administration's indecision on school desegregation was that it gave direct encouragement to those White southerners least reconciled to the ending of an Era. . . . [Moreover], there was a much larger group of troubled White southerners, men and women who were frustrated and uneasy with the rapid pace of social change over the past decade. They had come to believe that such change was inevitable. . . . But Richard Nixon, 37th president of the United States, gave them a reason to hope. . . . That at the very least the direction of change could be somewhat altered . . . that quite possible, for instance, some form of token integration might satisfy the laws and the courts. Had not Nixon said that the Federal Government should get out of the business of trying to run local school districts?[22]

The incongruous pursuit of Nixon's strategy is that Nixon, as vice president of the United States under Eisenhower, had been a civil rights supporter. In 1964, under Eisenhower he had remarked that the pending civil rights bill was "a step forward if it is administered effectively."[23]

Throughout his campaign and presidency, he muffled his message in a very general way and with general language of the law. *His ambiguity enabled him to lead many White Southerners to believe, at heart, he was on their side.*

When he took office on January 21, 1969, he and his secretary of Health Education and Welfare (HEW) found six days after his inauguration that the previous administration had ruled that federal funds for select Southern school districts would be cut off unless the district had submitted desegregation meeting HEW's guidelines.[24] These districts had not done so. Bob

Finch, Nixon's new HEW secretary, granted delays to three of the five Southern school districts. Two of those school districts were in Senator Strom Thurman's districts. This was problematic for Nixon because he had declared "to use the power of the federal treasury to withhold funds in order to carry out federally ordered desegregation schemes was 'going too far.' That kind of action should be very scrupulously examined and in many cases should be rescinded."[25]

Leon Panetta observes that as he and his friends had watched the close election of 1969, they felt hopeful. Nixon proclaimed that the theme of his administration was "Bring Us Together." Nixon had taken this quote from a 13-year-old-girl's sign on the campaign trail in Deshler, Ohio. Panetta hoped he meant it. He had voted for Nixon in 1960 and states:

> In the intervening six years, we learned a great deal about politics and politicians. We had learned more about America's wounds. We had developed a sense of crisis about society, especially about the worsening race relations. Panetta goes on to say, by election-day 1968 we could not buy the product Nixon sold in his campaign. It seemed harsh and reactionary, long on partisan rhetoric, short on humanity; it was not my brand of republicanism.[26]

Nevertheless, after that Nixon tagline, Panetta thought it might be a good sign going forward. Nixon, after all, had shown positive leadership on civil rights when he was both vice president and in the United States Senate.

As Nixon entered the White House, he and his administration were immediately confronted with two political dilemmas prompted by Johnson's legacy on school desegregation:

1. What to do about funding that had been cut off to Mississippi school districts that had ignored the law as determined by Title VI of the Civil Rights Act of 1964.
2. What to do about continuous enforcement of the HEW guidelines whose enforcement protocols had been set up during the Johnson administration.

The first dilemma involved 33 Mississippi school districts who had felt the burn of the HEW Guidelines. HEW had ordered that plans for desegregation be delivered to the court by August 11. At the time of Nixon's election, districts had not submitted any evidence of hewing to the court-ordered desegregation plans.

The first set of HEW desegregation guidelines had said, "To be eligible to receive or to continue to receive (financial) assistance, school officials must eliminate all practices and characteristics of . . . dual or segregated school systems." Those guidelines set up the least-restrictive standards, only requiring that school-district officials submit *assurances* that they would comply. The guidelines did not address faculty desegregation or accepted freedom-of-choice plans.

Thus, in 1966, new, stronger guidelines were issued. These guidelines cemented tough criteria for integrating schools beyond even federal court decrees, calling for districts with less than 10% of Black students attending predominantly White schools to double that number by the next year, for all faculties to be integrated, and while freedom-of-choice plans were permissible, the criterion used to determine whether they were working was the percentage of Black students moving out of segregated schools. As the guidelines became more rigorous, the resistance became more toxic. Nixon coded his anti-busing and anti-integrationist stance in language that appealed to "the people," who valued less federal intrusion and control; this was a clear reflection on the second *Brown* decision, which uses the language *with all deliberate speed*:

> The Administration's policy has not been, is not now, and should not be immediate and total integration. . . . I think it would be an exaggeration to say that the school-integration program is proceeding at a pace entirely consistent with the 1954 Supreme Court decision. Inevitably this decision has had an effect in some areas of the South of building up massive resistance. We should not be surprised by this. However, there has been notable progress. . . . As far as the future is concerned, I believe that the current program of the Administration is the proper one.[27]

Nixon had always provided the South a comfort zone, which explicitly said that:

> we will obey the law but we will delay implementation as long as we can and where we can. . . . After hearing of complaints in the South about enforcement of civil-rights laws, Nixon wrote to Ehrlichman, I want you personally to jump Richardson—Justice—tell them to "knock off this crap." I hold them personally accountable to keep their left-wingers in step with my express policy—do what the law requires and not *one bit* more.[28]

Jim Crow laws were not acceptable, but they do nothing at the federal level to actually repair anything. Nixon's domestic policy in the formative months of his presidency lacked force and direction. In his first speech to Congress, he sent no message on civil rights. However, by June of his first year as president, Nixon had launched a civil rights initiative in three parts: job discrimination, voting rights, and school desegregation. It was in the policy direction of school desegregation that the Nixon administration made its first move. HEW would shift its focus from cutting funds to introducing laws in the federal courts.

Nixon's Justice Department asked the Fifth Circuit to delay the enforcement of integration on the recalcitrant Mississippi school districts. As a result, NAACP lawyers challenged the request for delay. The Fifth Circuit ordered 27 of the school districts to put existing plans into effect by December 31, 1969. President Nixon responded to the Fifth-Circuit decision by ordering HEW and the Justice Department to go to court to appeal the desegregation order. Thus, for the first time since 1954, the federal government, under Nixon's leadership, would argue against desegregation.[29]

Steven Ambrose, Nixon's official biographer, observes that Nixon's bully pulpit needs were contradictory. On the one hand, he wanted voluntary compliance with court orders, and on the other, he wanted the confrontation over by 1970. His judgment was that this would improve his chances during his reelection campaign in 1972. Expediency was the name of the game.

That contradiction played out in concrete terms: Nixon had John Mitchell at the Justice Department working to slow things down and do nothing beyond the bare requirements of the law, but at the same time he had Robert Finch, the secretary of health, education, and welfare, busily trying to work for the implementation of desegregation policies.[30]

All the same, on July 3, 1969, Mitchell and Finch released a statement easing requirements on desegregation. "The administration justified the removal of deadlines and consistent policy by arguing: A policy requiring all school districts, regardless of the difficulties they face, to complete desegregation by the same terminal date is too rigid to be either workable or equitable."[31]

Inclusive in the strategy would be the targeting of judges, not the Nixon administration. On July 3, 1969, with John Mitchel at the helm, a memo to the stringent guidelines angered the strategy of delay. The changes were as follows: No general yearlong delay even though, "there may be sound reasons for limited delay—specifically, bona fide educational and administrative problems in some districts. These districts might therefore be able to talk themselves into reprieve; but an effort but the Mitchel-Dent team to specify 'community resistance' as a good enough reason for delay was not included; there was 'community resistance' to desegregation practically everywhere in the south."[32]

Civil rights leaders recognized this as part of Nixon's push to satisfy White Southerners. Roy Wilkins, executive director of the NAACP, said of this move, "It's almost enough to make you vomit."[33] The next day, headlines included: "President Eases School Deadline on Desegregation" (the *New York Times*), and "President Keeps Promise of His Southern Strategy" (the *Washington Post*). It was clear that the Nixon administration's intention was not to use funding as an effective enforcement mechanism, but rather to incentivize compliance.

Civil rights advocates felt the Nixon administration appeared to be growing hostile toward civil rights legislation. Bishop Stephen Spottswood, NAACP board president, declared that Nixon's message was, "If you're Black, stay back."

In spite of Nixon's seeming lack of interest in or hostility to the maintenance and expansion of civil rights, even among White Southerners who had responded positively to the Southern Strategy, there was confusion and anger regarding Nixon's messaging. His use of the bully pulpit, while effective in gaining the White House, was at odds with both his administration's policy and its enforcement.

Van Davis, a school superintendent in Georgia, had resigned his position after relentless criticism from White parents and students, the very people he was largely concerned with:

> Now, in his campaign he had the Southern people to believe that something could be eased up on it . . . now, he says they're going to abide by the law. . . . I feel very strongly that the Nixon administration is one of our real problems. There are two things, the Nixon administration's failure to take a stand and say what they mean, and then the inconsistencies in enforcing the law . . . these two things have had a terrific impact.[34]

The first year of the Nixon administration can best be contextualized by looking at a study released in December 1969 by the Southern Regional Council, an Atlanta-based biracial research organization. The report observed:

> Somehow, beginning under President Eisenhower at Little Rock, Southern civil rights forces had felt that the tremendous power of the federal executive was behind their efforts. In 1969, it is no longer possible to be so charitable. This year there has seemed to be a deliberate effort at work in the federal administrative machinery to reverse such progress in school desegregation as has already been so dearly won. That effort . . . cynically held out the hope to southern segregationists that the law of the land would not really have to be obeyed.[35]

The Southern Strategy, an appeal to Whites' worst sentiments, was articulated via Nixon's bully pulpit; as a result, his use of the bully pulpit was "anti-Black, not with passion but with a cool, clear-eyed political cynicism."[36]

Fourteen months after his inauguration, Nixon announced during a White House meeting, "I accept Leon Panetta's resignation."[37] Nixon told Ehrlichman that firing Panetta, whose desegregation efforts had not only made him a liability with Southern Whites, but had also been a sign of disloyalty to the president, was "worth dozens of speeches and statements about integrating the schools."[38]

The Panetta resignation prompted a diverse Office of Civil Rights staff to send a very strong letter to the president: "We earnestly hope that you may be prevailed upon to exercise the strong moral leadership that we feel is now essential to avoid a reversal of the Nation's long-standing commitment to equal opportunity."[39]

Shortly after, almost 2,000 employees of HEW signed an open petition asking Robert Finch to explain the administration's civil rights policies in a meeting. Finch, however, was relieved of his duties at HEW and returned to the White House as counselor to the president.

Nixon recognized he needed to change his tactics. The president needed to have more direct control, but he stated to Haldeman and Ehrlichman that there were only three areas where he wished to take "personal responsibility." The first was economic policy, the second was crime, and the third was school integration. "I must resume the responsibility here," he observed, "because it will be the major issue of controversy for the foreseeable future."[40]

In a memo to his advisors Haldeman, Ehrlichman, and Kissinger, Nixon said, "What really matters in campaigns, wars, or in government is to concentrate on the big battles and win them." He further stated that he disagreed with the perspective that one also had to "fight all the little battles" in order to "lay the groundwork for winning the big ones."[41] Nixon recognized that Southern desegregation was a big one.

In order to cement control over this issue, he established the Cabinet Committee on Education. He saw the committee as a way of keeping the "eager beavers" in line.[42] His Orthogonian persona had reappeared. Wicker points out, "The president was determined to make *his* policy that of the administration, in fact as well as form."[43] The courts had ruled against his delaying tactics. He now had to work to counter the rising problem in the South.

Haldeman's diary entries for February of 1970 depict a president who was trying to gain control over an increasingly chaotic situation. From the dismissal of Leon Panetta in an attempt to bring HEW back in line, all the way to floating the idea of getting a "right wing demagogue," running on anti-integration, into a tight race somewhere as a foil to make the Nixon administration look moderate and forward-thinking, school desegregation was an issue about which Nixon felt increasingly desperate.

Nixon and his advisors were convinced that court-ordered integration would do more harm than good; the anger and violence of Southern (and to a lesser extent, Northern) Whites was seen as a symptom rather than the disease.

In his entry for February 17, Haldeman recorded Nixon's support for a congressional move to oppose busing as a message to the judiciary: "P made a *very* strong statement of his position . . . that we may be headed for total chaos unless the courts let up. . . . This has become the major cause of the moment."[44] On March 24, 1970, the Nixon White House released an 8,000-word White paper titled, "Statement about Desegregation of Elementary and Secondary Schools." The document reaffirmed Nixon's personal belief that *Brown v. The Board of Education of Topeka, Kansas* had been correctly decided.

However, the document also cemented Nixon's conviction that the *how* of desegregation should be left to local authorities. Thus, Nixon tried to have his cake and eat it, too; he would stand on the moral side of history in condemning segregation while hiding behind the cloak of federalism when it came to dismantling it. After all, the history of state-sanctioned dual systems in the South was one of local and state control.

The Nixon document also addressed the de-facto segregation in housing patterns, which was relevant in regard to school district boundaries, and claimed that this segregation arose "genuinely" (i.e., by choice on the parts of all concerned), and so no federal remedy was required.

That summer, Nixon met with several members of his administration, including Elliot Richardson, the new HEW secretary. Nixon explained his perspective on Southern-school desegregation: there were no votes in it, so it was a nonpriority, but he wanted to get any confrontations out of the way as soon as possible so as to preclude it being an issue in his campaign for reelection. Reelection was the important thing. "Our enemies will attack us for not doing more. They want to hurt us—get us to hurt ourselves—by making more out of it. Remember: jobs are more important to Negros then everything else."[45]

What worried Nixon the most was the possibility that if desegregation was still a hot issue in 1972, George Wallace would run against him and likely do very well in the South.[46]

Nixon closed the meeting with a series of directives, the most important of which was: "Do only what the law requires, not one thing more."[47]

As Nixon worked though his strategies for the 1972 election, he continued to feed his constituency the picture of a man who was for the civil rights of the Negro, but he used fears of lawlessness as a way of engaging the electorate. He knew his constituencies were more receptive to that than talking about education.

Wallace *did* run, and he *did* do well in the South, but an assassination attempt paralyzed him from the waist down, and he was forced to withdraw from the race. Nixon won reelection in a landslide, winning 60% of the popular vote.

By the time the Watergate scandal broke, on June 17, 1972, school districts had begun the process of responding to court-ordered desegregation strategies, and some historic gains had been made in Southern school desegregation.

The office of the president is not only symbolic, it carries great weight and it affords its occupant a huge bully pulpit. That bully pulpit is enabled by all the president's men. In fact, each of his cabinet positions impact every aspect of the American citizen's public life, inclusive of: what we eat, where we sleep, how we take care of our bodies, how we are protected at our borders, where we live, how our workplace is regulated, how our taxes are impacted, how we spend, how we move across our country, how we are educated, how our rights are protected, and how we access public spaces. Nixon used his cabinet effectively to push his bully pulpit.

As a leader, Nixon did not use his bully pulpit to appeal on the basis of moral judgment, but rather for political expediency—an attitude that was reflected in the advisors he surrounded himself with: John Ehrlichman, H. R. Haldeman, Chuck Colson, and John Dean, among others. People for whom morality outweighed expediency, like Leon Panetta, did not last long in Nixon's circle.

Accordingly, Nixon's rhetoric never positioned desegregation in the context of the value of school integration, but rather as an issue of obedience to the law and a need to save the public schools in the South.

LEGISLATIVE PROFILE

Prior to Nixon's tenure in the White House he had continuously shown support for civil rights and certainly for Eisenhower's Civil Rights Bill of 1957. Martin Luther King, after a meeting he and Ralph Abernathy had with the then–vice president, said, "Let me say how deeply grateful we are to you for your assiduous labor and dauntless courage in seeking to make the Civil Rights Bill a reality. This has impressed people all across the country, both Negro and White. This is certainly an expression of your devotion to the highest mandates of moral law. It is also an expression of your political wisdom. More and more the Negro vote is becoming a decisive favor in National politics."[48]

Nixon, the grandson of an abolitionist whose farm was a way-station on the Underground Railroad,[49] received much praise for supporting just legislative initiatives, including laws banning the poll tax and anti-lynching laws.

He seemed to turn on a dime when he was elected president. His administration was slow in mounting White House legislative functions, particularly since he entered the office without a proposed domestic program intact and certainly no legislative program addressing civil rights, including addressing the nagging school-desegregation issues.

Kennedy and Johnson entered the White House well-prepared to put forth legislative programs. Kennedy had introduced 76% and Johnson 94% of their programs within the first three months in office. During the same period, Nixon had sent to Congress only 12% of his program—mostly minor proposals.[50]

In March 1969, grumbling Republican congresspersons were concerned that President Nixon and his administration had put forth no legislative agenda at all. Nixon asked Ehrlichman to try to "feed into our own executive organization a little more imagination and ingenuity because we seem to be pretty short on ideas."[51]

The postponement of attention to HEW guidelines for school desegregation and an attempt to weaken the Voting Rights Act—this was Nixon's attempt to intervene legislatively. His presidency did not engage Congress in any legislation designed to implement a continuing structural framework for school desegregation.

NOTES

1. Richard Perlstein (2009), *Nixonland: The Rise of a President and the Fracturing of America* (Simon & Schuster), 22.

2. Perlstein (2009), *Nixonland*, 23.

3. Perlstein (2009), *Nixonland*, 22, 221.

4. Perlstein (2009), *Nixonland*, 22.

5. Richard Nixon (1962), *Six Crisis* (Doubleday), 295.

6. Melvin Small (1999), *The Presidency of Richard Nixon* (University Press of Kansas), 51.

7. Perlstein (2009), *Nixonland*, 126.

8. Tom Wicker (1991), *One of Us: Richard Nixon and the American Dream* (Random House), 649.

9. Jill Lepore (2018), *These Truths: A History of the United States* (Norton & Company), 536.

10. Michael Genovese (2001), *The Power of the American Presidency: 1789–2000* (Oxford University Press), 68.

11. John Ehrlichman (1982), *Witness to Power: The Nixon Years* (Simon & Schuster), 223.

12. Nixon (1962), *Six Crisis*, 295.

13. Wicker (1991), *One of Us*, 239.

14. Perlstein (2009), *Nixonland*, 285.

15. Perlstein (2009), *Nixonland*, 300.

16. James W. Ely Jr., and Bradley G. Bond (2014), "Southern Strategy," in *The New Encyclopedia of Southern Culture,* Revised ed., vol. 10. (University of North Carolina Press), 237–56.

17. Gareth Davies (2007), "Richard Nixon and the Desegregation of Southern Schools," *Journal of Policy History, 19*(4), 367–94. *Project MUSE.*

18. Leon Panetta and Peter Gall (1971), *Bring Us Together: The Nixon Team and the Civil Rights Retreat* (Lippincott), 21.

19. Thurmond Strom, December 1968.

20. Panetta and Gall (1971), *Bring Us Together*, 21.

21. Reg Murphy and Hal Gulliver (1971), *The Southern Strategy* (Charles Scribner's Sons).

22. Murphy and Gulliver, *The Southern Strategy.*

23. Perlstein (2009), *Nixonland*, 302.

24. Wicker (1991), *One of Us*, 489

25. Wicker (1991), *One of Us*, 489.

26. Panetta and Gall (1971), *Bring Us Together*, 5–6.

27. Richard Nixon (1967), *The Challenges We Face: Edited and Compiled from the Speeches and Papers of Richard M. Nixon* (Popular books), 185.

28. Stephen C. Halpern (1995), *On the Limits of the Law: The Ironic Legacy of Title VI of the 1964 Civil Rights Act1 90* (Baltimore: John Hopkins University Press).

29. Panetta and Gall (1971), *Bring Us Together*, 254.

30. Ehrlichman (1982), *Witness to Power.*

31. Perlstein (2009), *Nixonland*, 89.

32. Wicker (1991), *One of Us*, 491

33. Davies (2007), *Nixon and the Desegregation of Southern Schools*, 371.

34. Atlanta Constitution, 11 October 1969.

35. Murphy and Gulliver (1971), *The Southern Strategy*, 62–63.

36. Murphy and Gulliver (1971), *The Southern Strategy*, 249.

37. Wicker (1991), *One of Us*, 501.

38. Wicker (1991), *One of Us*, 501.

39. Panetta and Gall (1971), *Bringing Us Together*, 368.

40. Nixon to Haldeman, Ehrlichman (1982), Kissinger, memo, 2 March 1970, in Haldeman office files, box 138, Nixon Project.

41. Nixon to Haldernan, Ehrlichman, Kissinger, memo, 2 March 1970.

42. Originally, it was called the Cabinet Committee on School Desegregation, but this was felt to be too inflammatory.

43. Wicker (1991), *One of Us*, 501.

44. Haldeman Diaries, entry for 17 February 1970. Events in Lamar were covered in Nixon's news summary for 4 March 1970, in POF; box 31, Nixon Project.

45. Ehrlichman (1982), *Witness to Power*, 230–40.

46. See Ehrlichman's notes on the meeting, 4 August 1970, in Ehrlichman office files, box 4. See also Garment's summary in memo to Nixon, 5 August 1970, POF; box 7, Nixon Project.

47. Ehrlichman (1982), *Witness to Power*, 230.

48. Stephen E. Ambrose (1987), *Nixon: The Education of a Politician 1913–1962* (Simon and Schuster), 434.
49. Ambrose (1987), *Nixon*, 9.
50. Melvin Small (1999), *The Presidency of Richard Nixon*, 155–56.
51. Perlstein (2009), *Nixonland*, 89.

Chapter 5

Gerald Rudolph Ford

Just as the Nixon presidency walked into Lyndon Johnson's great society programs, Ford walked into Nixon's busing controversy in Boston. Ford's bully pulpit commitment to the country's desegregation efforts is best illuminated by his voice on the busing. Ford's tenure was impacted by three desegregation cases: *Keyes, Milliken*, and *Hennigan* (Boston).

FORMATIVE YEARS

"Jerry" Ford was born Leslie L. King Jr. His mother divorced his father when he was two years old, and he was later adopted by Gerald Ford Sr., who, by age forty had developed a successful paint business. However, where the Nixon family environment was one of scrappiness, the Ford family environment appeared "*orderly, serene, and happy.*"[1]

Gerald Ford did not resent the status of fellow classmates in school or college. He characterized his school days as follows: "Everyone . . . had more good qualities than bad. If I understood and tried to accentuate those good qualities in others, I could get along much better.[2] According to one of his biographers, 'he wore a suit and ties to school most of the time instead of a casual shirt, slacks, and a sweater that were so common'"—which suggests a family determined to maintain the outward signs of middle-class respectability.[3] A former classmate remembered him in 1974 as having not been a rich boy—but a regular guy.[4]

In *A Time to Heal*, Ford recalls how the family would spend quality time in the summer at Lake Michigan and the Pere Marquette River. Ford describes his stepfather (adopted father) as "a marvelous family man. Neither of the parents could be described as secure-economically; but emotionally both were very secure. And if I retain that characteristic today, I owe it to them."[5]

Ford's mother also had a profound effect on "Jerry." Ford writes in *A Time to Heal*, that a friend showed him a quote:

> To laugh often and love much; to win the respect of intelligent persons and the affection of children; to earn the approbation of honest critics and endure the betrayal of false friends; to appreciate beauty; to find the best in others; to give other of one's self; to leave the world a bit better, whether by a healthy child, a garden patch, or a redeem social condition; do you have played and laughed with enthusiasm and son with exaltation; To know even one life has brains easier because you have lived.[6]

He said he thought immediately of his mother, Dorothy Gardner. He indicated this was the credo by which he lived.[7]

The athletically skillful Ford would enter sports early in his middle years, concentrating on football. "Athletics," Ford said of his parents' beliefs, "built a boy's character." They did not exclude academic rigor; in fact, he graduated in the top 5% of his high school class.

It was at the University of Michigan that Ford's sense of racial justice emerged. As a member of the U of M football team, he earned the status of most valuable player. Yet the most noteworthy event of his stellar college sports career was his threat to quit the team in 1934 out of fury when the visiting Georgia Tech team refused to take the field if Ford's African American teammate played:

> I was a University of Michigan senior, preparing with my Wolverine teammates for a football game against visiting Georgia Tech. Among the best players on that year's Michigan squad was Willis Ward, a close friend of mine whom the Southern school reputedly wanted dropped from our roster because he was Black. My classmates were just as adamant that he should take the field. In the end, Willis decided, on his own, not to play.
>
> His sacrifice led me to question how educational administrators could capitulate to raw prejudice. A university, after all, is both a preserver of tradition and a hotbed of innovation.
>
> That game against Georgia Tech was Michigan's only victory that year. The story of Willis Ward's benching is not a great moment in the school's stories football history, but people close to both men say it speaks to Ford's character. The incident was on Ford's mind in 1999 when he took one of the final political stands of his long life by writing an op-ed piece for The New York Times supporting the University of Michigan and its use of affirmative action in its admissions policies.[8]

Twenty-five years after his presidency, Ford publicly defended the University of Michigan's affirmative-action admission policy, in 1999. He stated:

> At its core, affirmative action should try to offset past injustices by fashioning a campus population more truly reflective of modern American and our hopes

for the future. Unfortunately, a pair of lawsuits brought against my alma mater poses a threat to such diversity. Not content to oppose formal quotas, plaintiffs suing the University of Michigan would prohibit that and other universities from even considering race as one of many factors weighed by admissions counselors.[9]

JOURNEY TO THE PRESIDENCY

After attending Yale Law School, Ford joined the navy as part of the Pacific Operation. After serving four years in the U.S. Navy, Ford opened a successful law practice with a friend. He continued a steady interest in politics and joined a Republican reform group, who opposed the local political establishment.

Ford was able to win a seat in Michigan's Fifth Congressional district, defeating a five-term Republican incumbent, and then his Democratic opponent, in November 1948.

Ford, a Congressional insider, was chosen by his colleagues twice for significant leadership roles, first, as chairman of the Republican Conference and then as a minority leader.[10]

John Robert Greene observes in *Gerald Ford: Life Before the Presidency*:

> During his first few terms in Congress, Ford demonstrated an ability to work with members of both parties, won a reputation among his colleagues for hard work and integrity, and earned the trust of his fellow Republicans on the Hill, including a young California legislator named Richard Nixon.
>
> Ford supported General Dwight D. Eisenhower's bid for the Republican presidential nomination in 1952—largely because he agreed with Eisenhower's foreign policy views—and was pleased that Nixon won the 2nd spot on the ticket. Indeed, Ford emerged as one of Nixon's greatest defenders when, after both the nomination and the election, Nixon found himself embroiled in controversy.[11,12]

In the House, Ford aligned with a coalition of progressive, moderate Republicans and liberal Democrats. At one point during his House of Representatives stint, his voting with the conservative coalition (Republicans and Conservative democrats) fell to 64%, which made him the fourth most liberal member of the 11-man delegation from Michigan.[13]

While in Congress, Ford built a reservoir of friendly relationships among other Congressional leaders. He was thus in a position of quality leadership on major domestic policy issues.

In the House, Ford developed a *"floating coalition strategy"*: a strategy designed to adhere to "never voting against the southern democrats unless it was absolutely necessary," so they would be available to support him the next time around. According to Reichley, Ford believed that a close alliance with the Southern Democrats would hobble the Republicans.[14]

Ford, as a House leader, played an active role in deterring court-ordered busing as Nixon expanded his Southern Strategy. His state of Michigan had strong anti-busing supporters including liberal Democrats. His closest confidant, Hartment, is to have said:

> He believed that many Blacks agreed with him. He felt that what he was doing was needed to preserve the neighborhood school.
>
> Ford's position against busing further antagonized the civil rights community, which had not forgotten his efforts to dilute the open housing bill in 1968. At the House Judiciary Committee hearings in Nixon's nomination of Ford to be vice-president in 1973, Clarence Mitchell, director of the Washington office of the NAACP, testified that Ford has taken a, "restrictive approach to civil rights."[15]

A tangled web surrounding Ford's bully pulpit developed during the Johnson administration. Ford as the minority leader led the Republicans in staunchly opposing most of Johnson's domestic legislation, including the Great Society's program.

When Agnew was forced to resign in the fall of 1973, Ford was not Nixon's first choice as VP; John Connally, of Texas, had been tapped earlier. Upon hearing from his confidential sources, both Democrat and Republican, that Connally would be hard to confirm, Nixon rejected both Reagan and Rockefeller as he felt either choice would split the party. He then chose Ford. Nixon later wrote, "Ford was qualified to be president . . . his views on both domestic and foreign policy were very close to mine . . . and there was no question he would be the easiest to get confirmed."[16]

PLATFORM ON DESEGREGATION

When Ford entered the presidency, he had not been elected for any office other than representative to the 5th Congressional District of Michigan. He had never aspired to be president from all accounts detailing his trajectory. Nixon's legacy left a tainted suspicion of the political establishment and a very low level of trust in institutions of the government. Ford's personal portrait, one of character, comradery, and conciliation, was closer to the norms of the "*upper echelon*" of the American political community and in direct contrast to Richard Nixon.[17]

Kalman points out, after Nixon:

the national mood had not changed so quickly since Franklin Roosevelt relieved Herbert Hoover. From the Democratic side of the aisle, Senator Mansfield declared, "The sun is shining again." The mainstream media agreed. The New Republic compared the nation to a child who had swallowed something nasty and thrown up and feels better. Mr. Ford is everything that Nixon wasn't, with warmth and openness and decency, and he has engendered national affection.[18]

Just as Nixon had crafted a Southern motif to embolden and enable his success in becoming president, Ford's strategies, positions, and voice on busing became one of the anchors of his presidential actions.

Ford had opposed the 1971 *Swann v. Charlotte-Mecklenburg* school district decision. The Supreme Court sustained the busing of inner-city Black students and White suburban students served to reverse the effects of pre-*Brown de jure segregation* within a school district. *Swann* proclaimed busing as a necessary tool to end desegregation. The decision provided the opportunity for federal courts to take over desegregation decisions after a school district's *de jure* violation.

This decision was echoed by a federal judge who ordered busing across district lines in the Richmond, Virginia, case (*Bradley v. School Board of the City of Richmond*). The Richmond case further addressed segregated teacher assignments.

In the mid-1970s, a significant number of northern cities were answering to federal courts on segregated schools: Baltimore, Detroit, Indianapolis, Kansas City, multiple districts in Ohio [Akron, Cincinnati, Cleveland, Columbus, Dayton, and Youngstown), Louisville, Milwaukee, Omaha, St. Louis, and Wilmington, Delaware.

The Gallup poll reported that though a large majority of the nation favored integration in voice, only 5% of the nation favored busing to achieve it.

In June 1974, Judge Arthur Wendell Garrity Jr. found that racial segregation existed in every Boston school at all grade levels. He ruled the Boston schools were unconstitutionally segregated.

J. Harvie Wilkinson III writes:

> The sorriest chapter of the whole northern story was that of Boston, Massachusetts. Boston was not easily dismissed, like Birmingham, as a regional aberration. Indeed, Boston and Massachusetts were the pride of the American liberalism: the political and literary pacesetter for the new nation, the home for one of the world's foremost universities, the only State to have resisted the Nixon landslide of 1972.

Wilkinson suggested:

but busing by court order humbled and embarrassed Boston, a fact that gave some in the South a sick satisfaction. "Because there has been progress in the South," wrote the Dallas Times Herald, "Southerners should not gloat over the violence in Boston. It is sad. It is tragic. Southerners have learned from experience just how much so." As indeed it was. That racial violence should so possess this historic city in the Charles was a national tragedy of the first rank.[19]

Boston's school committee, from the very beginning, took no responsibility to implement the court order directed at Boston's desegregation; rather, it responded to the loud, organized, and highly vocal anti-desegregation section of the Boston community. The school committee appealed all of the judge's rulings. The superintendent took a different stance. He showed a willingness to cooperate with the court. He had a three-year contract; at the end of that contract, he was not reappointed.[20]

During the summer of Ford's new term, Boston roared out of control, from Mayor Kevin White to the anti-busing coalition to the state legislature to the school committee.

Events unfolded as follows:

September 9, 1974: Mayor White appears on educational television in Boston with a lengthy address, which includes the following statements: "We are faced with the unpleasant task of implementing a court order. . . . The city has exhausted all legal avenues of appeal at a cost of in excess of a million dollars. . . . I'm for integration but against forced busing. They are not mutually exclusive. People who would boycott schools are asked to weigh the decision carefully, but it is their decision to make. Parents should attend open houses at schools before making a final decision to not to send students to the school."

The U.S. Commission on Civil Rights, in its report "Desegregating Boston Public Schools," observed: "The mayor's position . . . strongly inferred that it was legitimate to boycott schools. It is not. Boycotting schools runs afoul of a panoply of state laws and can result in criminal prosecution."

September 12, 1974: School opens. The Tactical Police Force is called to quell disturbances at South High. Most other schools show few incidents. Enrollment in the school system is down 10,000 from a possible enrollment of about 82,000. The boycott was participated even in neighborhoods not involved in Phase I but where a citywide plan was expected. The average enrollment during the 1974–1975 school year was about 60,000.

September. 22, 1974: State Senator Bulger, State Representative Flaherty, and Mrs. Hicks issue a Declaration of Clarification: There is resistance in South Boston because "it is against our children's interest to send them to school in crime-infested Roxbury." (The statement was accompanied by charts showing neighborhood crime statistics.) "Routine, everyday violence ravages the Black community (but is hidden from the public by a conspiratorial press."

October 2, 1974: After two weeks of boycott, White attendance has risen. On this day, however, a riot breaks out in the South Boston lunchroom, legitimating the fearful reaction White parents might have had about their children's schools. From this time on, at least 25 police are stationed inside South High and 300 outside.

October 3, 1974: On National Boycott Day, attendance is 41,800, the lowest it will ever be in the course of the conflict.

October 7, 1974: A South Boston mob pulls Andre Yvon Jean-Louis from his car and beats him, as well as beating the police who try to interfere.

October 7, 1974: Mayor White asks Judge Garrity to assign federal marshals to Boston. He declared that he was able to maintain public safety and orderly implementation of the court's order in 90% of the city, but that he could no longer guarantee the safety of the students in South Boston and Hyde Park high schools.

President Ford sent a taped 30-second voice message to Boston radio and television station:

> Boston is a fine, proud City. The cradle of liberty. Where many of the freedoms that we all so cherish today in this Country, were born, 200 years ago. The people of Boston share a tradition for reason, fairness and respect for the rights of others. Now, in a difficult period for all of you, it is a time to reflect on all that your City means to you. To react ill to the finest tradition of your City's people. It is up to you, every one of you, every parent, child, to reject violence of any kind in your City. To reject hatred and the shrill voices of the violent few, who simply don't care about the lives of your children.[21]

Roy Wilkins observed, "I thought he had jumped to the forefront of the mob. . . . He was leading the way against the courts and the 14th Amendment, the *Brown* decision and Black children. He undermined us as a craven retreat and a capitulation to the lawlessness and ignorance of the people who are fanning the race issue."[22]

In the fall, the fury exploded, and two high school students were stabbed, the superintendent closed schools, the school committee defied Judge Garrity's order and refused to submit a plan. The judge threatened the school committee with a receivership. On December 29, Mayor White, in a press release, announced that the city would pay the costs of the Supreme Court appeal and said that "citywide busing should not be imposed as long as [there were] widespread boycotts."[23]

Ford, through his bully pulpit, gave the militant anti-busing, anti-desegregation group his assurances that the federal government would not help the Boston police keep order as Judge Garrity's order was being implemented.

Months after assuming the presidency, his response to Boston's school desegregation plan was as follows:

> At the outset, I wish to make it very, very direct: I deplore the violence that I have read about and seen on television. I think that is most unfortunate. I would like to add this, however: The court decision in that case [*Morgan v. Hennigan*], in my judgment, was not the best solution to quality education in Boston. I have consistently opposed forced busing to achieve racial balance as a solution to quality education, and therefore, I respectfully disagree with the judge's order.
>
> But having said that, I think it is of maximum importance that the citizens of Boston respect the law. And I hope and trust that it is not necessary to call in Federal officials or Federal law enforcement agencies. Now, the marshals, if my information is accurate, are under the jurisdiction of the court, not directly under my jurisdiction. As far as I know, no specific request has come to me for any further Federal involvement, and therefore, I am not in a position to act under those circumstances.[24]

But, in fact, Ford turned down Massachusetts's governor sergeant's appeal for federal troops.[25]

One of Ford's aides said, "It was not based on racism per se, at least not in his own mind. He was a product of neighborhood schools in Grand Rapids, and thought that was a very positive experience that all American children should have."[26]

President Ford was simply clueless about the Black experience in public education.

O'Reilly reports that Ford had the Justice Department look for "a proper record in a case that would justify . . . a proceeding before the Supreme Court to see if the court would review its decision in the *Brown* case and the several thereafter." He later retracted that request, but as O'Reilly points out, he continued to "trace the busing controversy to *Brown*."

He continued to use his bully pulpit not only to speak out against busing but used his office to order studies (for purposes of finding legitimate arguments for the courts) that would document what he saw as the deleterious effects of busing.

LEGISLATIVE PROFILE

His administration submitted legislation to Congress that would restrict the judiciary's "use of 'radical remedies'," when addressing the problem of segregation in the schools. Ford suggested at the time of its submission to

Congress that the purpose of the proposed School Desegregation Standards and Assistance Bill was to protect "community control of schools."[27]

Before Nixon resigned in March 1974, the House of Representatives passed an anti-busing addition to HR 69, the Education Amendments of 1974. Six days after the House HR 69 conference report, the Senate adopted the conference report, sending it to Nixon's desk on August 7th, 1974.[28] Casper Weinberger, secretary of health, education, and welfare, expressed his opinion:

> "While the bill's busing provisions fall short of your desire to retain the House provisions," Secretary of Health, Education, and Welfare Caspar Weinberger wrote Nixon, "the measure does strengthen the existing law against busing and contains many of the provisions you originally sought." Given the obdurate attitude of the Senate and the size of the House vote accepting this compromise. Weinberger recommended that Nixon sign the legislation. But when Nixon resigned due to the Watergate scandal on August 9, the busing controversy fell to President Gerald Ford.[29][30]

Ford's first major Oval Office signing ceremony was to approve HR69 on August 21, 1974. It contained the ESCH Amendment (Education Amendment of 1974):

> The amendment, sponsored by Michigan Republican Marvin Esch, "prohibited federal courts or agencies from ordering busing of students to any but the school closest or next closest to the student's" home and "provided that any school district under a federal court order or desegregation plan in effect on the date of HR 69 could ask that the case be reopened and made to comply with the provisions of Title II." The Esch Amendment to the Education Amendment of 1974 was rejected by the senate 46 to 47.
>
> The conference report on the bill added a Senate amendment as "prohibited busing beyond the school next closest to a student's home but allowing courts to mandate additional busing if it were required to guarantee the students civil rights." The conferees also replaced the House reopener provision with language permitting parents or the school district to reopen a case only if the time or distance traveled was so great as to endanger the health of the student or impinge on the educational process. Whereas the House bill had required the termination of a busing order of a federal court determined that desegregation had been achieved, the conference report merely permitted such termination.[31]

The amendment offered other segregation techniques, including free transfers, revised attendance zones, magnet schools, and school closings. However, the statute provided a qualification, which said if it was necessary to bus a youngster out of his neighborhood to satisfy constitutional guarantee of equal rights, it was acceptable.

President Ford's counsel suggested to him that though HR 69's busing provisions were not flawless, they were acceptable. "While falling short of the administration's wishes," White House aide Roger Semerad wrote, "the bill includes several favorable new measures to limit forced busing and holding that remedy as a last resort."[32]

Ford indicated that he was pleased to sign the bill as the first major piece of legislation at the outset of his new administration. He promised to "spend whatever money necessary to implement the ESCH administration," yet he vetoed the appropriations, naming it "inflationary." In signing the bill he said,

> As enacted, H.R. 69 contains an ordered and reasoned approach to dealing with the remaining problems of segregation in our schools, but I regret that it lacks an effective provision for automatically re-evaluating existing court orders. This omission means that a different standard will be applied to those districts which are already being compelled to carry out extensive busing plans and those districts which will now work out desegregation plans under the more rational standards set forth in this bill. Double standards are unfair, and this one is no exception.
>
> I believe that all school districts, North and South, East and West, should be able to adopt reasonable and just plans for desegregation which will not result in children being bused from their neighborhoods. Another troublesome feature of this bill would inject the Congress into the process of administering education laws. For instance, some administrative and regulatory decisions of the Department of Health, Education, and Welfare would be subjected to various forms of Congressional review and possible veto.
>
> As a veteran of the Congress, I fully appreciate the frustrations that can result in dealing with the executive branch, but I am equally convinced that attempting to stretch the constitutional role of the Congress is not the best remedy. The Congress can and should hold the executive branch to account for its performance, but for the Congress to attempt to administer Federal programs is questionable on practical as well as constitutional grounds. I have asked the Attorney General for advice on these provisions.[33]

The Ford administration, unchallenged, continued to pivot to *"the language of quality education"* to avoid the action of federal courts in the desegregation of schools. The reader must be reminded that the federal court had ordered busing to achieve desegregation, not "quality education." It is the view of the author that at this same time, deficit-based thinking about all Black children began to shadow policy discussions. Rarely or hardly ever in all of his remarks on segregation, except within the context of the ESCH amendments to HR 69, did Ford use the term *school desegregation*.[34]

Ford continued to set in motion agitated and volatile racial tensions surrounding federal action and the courts. "The President has promised to uphold court orders, while insisting that the courts have gone too far, he has told those who have fought desegregation bitterly that his legislation will not affect court orders and litigation in progress."[35]

Key members of his administration began to privately question these emphases. Attorney General Edward Levi argued that the ESCH alternative to busing was unrealistic and expensive. Secretary of Transportation William Coleman, the only African American in the cabinet, attached Ford's implication that busing had been less than a last resort: "History will show . . . that the Federal judges acted with great restraint, judgement, and wisdom in assisting the court-ordered busing."[36]

Richard Parsons, an African American member of the president's Domestic Council, addressed "the conceptual and political inadequacies" of Ford's positions:

> As a conceptual matter, if one opposes busing, for whatever reason, one must either indicate the alternative means by which the constitutional objective (indeed requirement) of desegregation of public school systems can be achieved or simultaneously indicate his opposition to the very objective which busing seeks to facilitate. The alternatives which we have focused on—i.e., improving teacher-pupil ratios, physical plants and curriculum—address the broader question of quality education, not the question of school desegregation.
>
> That is to say, since busing is the law of the land, like it or not, he ought to be actively encouraging people to comply with the law and not fueling frustrations with the law by criticizing it.[37]

On October 10, 1975, Mitch Kehetia of the *Macomb Daily* interviewed President Ford on his position:

> Well, we have a Constitution, and the courts have the obligation to interpret the Constitution. And the Court, back in 1954, made the basic decision which, in effect, has precipitated the numerous court decisions that result in court-ordered forced busing to achieve racial balance in public school systems.
>
> They allege that this is the way that the courts ought to achieve quality education. I strongly, vehemently disagree with the Court's decision, based on the Constitution, as the best way to achieve quality education. I have had that view for 10 years or more.
>
> I think it is deplorable, I think it is the wrong answer, and I just hope that the judges will use in their wisdom a way to find a better answer to what is going on at the present time.[38]

Ford suddenly began to blame the *Brown* decision in many of his public responses. On March 12, 1976, in a Remarks and a Question-and-Answer Session with members of the Northern Illinois Newspaper Association in Chicago, President Ford was asked about foreseeable changes to the stance of HEW or the courts.

Ford responded:

> Of course, the problem is forced on the country under a judgment or a decision of the United States Supreme Court that came about in the mid-1950s on the basis that it was a constitutional violation of the rights of individuals to perpetuate segregation in public school systems. Now, the courts make that judgment. Nobody in the executive branch can change that judgment.
>
> I strongly disagree with the radical remedies of forced busing to achieve racial balance. I don't think that accomplishes what we all want, which is quality education. I think it is harmful to quality education, and I think there are some recent studies that prove that. So, if the courts will be more moderate, and we can help in any other way, I think that is the real answer.[39]

When questioned by civil rights leadership as to the use of *quality education* as a code word to avoid discussing desegregation, Ford continued to let his audiences know that he disagreed with the civil rights leaders and that he would address desegregation in forthcoming legislation. His intent was to limit the role of the courts.[40] Ford said, "The Justice Department . . . is in the process of preparing legislation . . . which would seek to limit the courts . . . to . . . the areas where the local school board has violated the constitutional rights of individuals—in this case, students." He then disavowed such 'rights': "Busing itself is not a constitutional right, nor is it a lack of constitutional right. It is only a remedy."[41]

The legislation that the Ford administration proposed required that courts "determine the extent to which acts of unlawful discrimination have caused a greater degree of racial concentration in schools or school systems than would have existed otherwise, and to confine the relief provided to correcting the racial imbalance caused by these unlawful acts." The bill generally would have limited court-ordered busing to no more than five years, and would have established a bipartisan National Community and Education Committee to help communities prepare for desegregation and preclude violence.[42,43]

Four and a half months later, Ford's solicitor general, Robert Bork, challenged a busing decision. He argued that a Federal Court "went too far" in ordering the consolidation of the city and ten suburban Wilmington, Delaware, school districts.[44,45]

In transmitting proposed school busing legislation, Ford documents elements of his bully pulpit:

> To the Congress of the United States:
> - In its fullest sense, the issue is how we protect the civil rights of all Americans without unduly restricting the Individual freedom of any American. It concerns the responsibility of government to provide quality education, and equality of education, to every American.

- It concerns our obligation to eliminate, as swiftly as humanly possible, the occasions of controversy and division from the fulfillment of this responsibility.
- I am totally dedicated to quality education in America—and to the principle that public education is predominantly the concern of the community in which people live. Throughout the history of our Nation, the education of our children, especially at the elementary and secondary levels, has been a community endeavor. The concept of public education is now written into our history as deeply as any tenet of American belief.
- In recent years, we have seen many communities in the country lose control of their public schools to the Federal Courts because they failed to voluntarily correct the effects of willful and official denial of the rights of some children in their schools.
- It is my belief that in their earnest desire to carry out the decisions of the Supreme Court, some judges of lower Federal Courts have gone too far. They have: resorted too quickly to the remedy of massive busing of public school children; extended busing too broadly; and maintained control of schools for too long.
- It is this overextension of court control that has transformed a simple judicial tool, busing, into a cause of widespread controversy and slowed our progress toward the total elimination of segregation.
- Whether busing helps school children get a better education is not a settled question. The record is mixed. Certainly, busing has assisted in bringing about the desegregation of our schools. But it is a tragic reality that, in some areas, busing under court order has brought fear to both Black students and White students—and to their parents.

My bill recognizes that the busing remedy is transitional by its very nature and that when a community makes good-faith efforts to comply, busing ought to be limited in duration. Therefore, the bill provides that three years after the busing remedy has been imposed a court shall be required to determine whether to continue the remedy.

Should the court determine that a continuation is necessary, it could do so only for an additional two years. Thereafter, the court could continue busing only in the most extraordinary circumstances, where there has been a failure or delay of other remedial efforts or where the residual effects of unlawful discrimination are unusually severe.

Great concern has been expressed that submission of this bill at this time would encourage those who are resisting court-ordered desegregation—sometimes to the point of violence. Let me here state, simply and directly, that this Administration will not tolerate unlawful segregation. We will act swiftly and effectively against anyone who engages in violence.[46]

The bill would have limited court-ordered busing to no more than five years and was not passed into law. Within a week of the submission, Ford lost the presidency to the election of Jimmy Carter.

Ford attempted to continue this tentative cordial relationship by energetically presenting his view on domestic policy issues inclusive of civil rights and urban affairs to African American organizations and audiences. In his language, "Blacks in our society have too often been mentally segregated by some thinkers and planners who acted as if Blacks did not have the same expectations and problems as other Americans, I promised as the very beginning of my administration to be president of all people, and I am keeping that pledge."

On the other hand, he did direct federal agencies to increase opportunities in federal services for African Americans. Ford also named a Black cabinet secretary, William Coleman Jr, and the first Black Air Force Star General, Daniel "Chappie" James.

As Freedman and James point out in their chapter on Ford: "no civil rights issue drew more attention and generated more national divisiveness during his presidency than the controversy over court requiring busing to desegregate public schools what Ford and other critics labeled 'forced busing.'"[47]

NOTES

1. James A. Reichley (1981), *Conservatives in an Age of Change: The Nixon and Ford Administrations* (The Brookings Institution).

2. Gerald R. Ford (1987), *A Time to Heal: The Autobiography of Gerald R. Ford* (Norwalk, CT: Easton Press), 46.

3. Bud Vestal (1974), *Jerry Ford Up Close: An Investigative Biography* (Berkley), 58.

4. Ford (1987), *A Time to Heal*, 29.

5. Ford (1987), *A Time to Heal*, 45.

6. Ford (1987), *A Time to Heal*, 142.

7. Ford (1987), *A Time to Heal*, 4.

8. Ford (1987), *A Time to Heal*, 45.

9. Archived records NPR. July 4, 2013.

10. Betty Ford with Chris Chase (1979), *The Times of My Life* (Ballantine Books), 61, 132.

11. John Robert Greene (2017, July 17), "Gerald Ford: Life Before the Presidency," Miller Center, https://millercenter.org/president/ford/life-before-the-presidency.

12. Greene (2017, July 17), "Gerald Ford."

13. Congressional Quarterly Almanac; Volume VI, 81st Congress, 2nd Session—1960 (Congressional Quarterly News Features, 1951, p. 847), *American Political Science Review* 6 (1950): 60–61. https://doi.org/10.1017/s0003055400301769.

14. Reichley (1981), *Conservatives in an Age of Change*, 86.
15. Reichley (1981), *Conservatives in an Age of Change*, 279.
16. Richard M. Nixon (1978), *RN: The Memoirs of Richard Nixon* (Grosset & Dunlap), 926.
17. Laura Kalman (n.d.), "Right Star Rising: A New Politics, 1974–1980," *The SHAFR Guide Online*, 5, https://doi.org/10.1163/2468-1733_shafr_sim180220004.
18. "The Sun Is Shining Again" (1974, August 26), *Newsweek* (quoting Mansfield; TRB: Postmortem New Republic).
19. Harvie J. Wilkinson III (1979), *From* Brown *to* Bakke*: The Supreme Court and School Integration: 1954–1978 (*Oxford University Press).
20. Walter G. Stephan (1980), *School Desegregation Past Present, and Future* (Plenum Press), 63.
21. *Boston Globe*, October 11, 1974.
22. Roy Wilkins and Tom Mathews (1982), *Standing Fast: The Autobiography of Roy Wilkins* (Viking Press).
23. Arthur L. Stinchcombe and D. Garth Taylor (1980), "On Democracy and School Integration," *School Desegregation*, 157–86, https://doi.org/10.1007/978-1-4615-9155-9_8.
24. Gerald R. Ford, The President's News Conference Online by Gerhard Peters and John T. Woolley, The American Presidency Project, https://www.presidency.ucsb.edu/node/255942.
25. "Federal troops ask for Boston" (1974, October 16), *New York Times*, A1.
26. Kenneth O'Reilly (1996), *Nixon's Piano: Presidents and Racial Politics from Washington to Clinton* (New York: Free Press), 334.
27. Public Papers of the President of the United States: Gerald Ford (1976–1977), Washington, D.C. Government Printing Office, 1979.
28. Gary Orfield, "Congress, the President, and Anti-busing Legislation, 1966–1974," in Douglas, *School Busing*, 31, 36–37. *Milliken v. Bradley*, 418 U.S. 717 (1974), "Anti-busing Amendments Added to Education Bill," 16.
29. Memorandum from Caspar Weinberger to the president, August 5, 1974, David Lissy Files, Box 4, GRFPL, p. 2.
30. Lawrence J. McAndrews (1997), "Missing the Bus: Gerald Ford and School Desegregation," *Presidential Studies Quarterly, 27*(4), 791–804, http://www.jstor.org/stable/27551801.
31. McAndrews (1997), "Missing the Bus."
32. McAndrews (1997), "Missing the Bus," 793.
33. Gerald R. Ford, Statement on the Education Amendments of 1974. Online by Gerhard Peters and John T. Woolley, The American Presidency Project, https://www.presidency.ucsb.edu/node/255924.
34. "Survey Finds Law Cited by Ford Is Unused in Most Busing Cases" (1975, September 21), *New York Times*, A41.
35. McAndrews (1997), "Missing the Bus."
36. Minutes of the cabinet meeting (1975, September 17), James E. Connor File, Box 5, GRFPL, pp. 3–4.

37. Memorandum from Dick Parsons to Jim Cannon and Phil Buchen, October 23, 1975, James Cannon Files, Box 5, GRFPL, pp. 4–6.

38. Gerald R. Ford, The President's News Conference Online by Gerhard Peters and John T. Woolley, The American Presidency Project https://www.presidency.ucsb.edu/node/257743.

39. Gerald R. Ford, Remarks and a Question-and-Answer Session With Members of the Northern Illinois Newspaper Association in Chicago. Online by Gerhard Peters and John T. Woolley, The American Presidency Project, https://www.presidency.ucsb.edu/node/257657.

40. McAndrews (1997), "Missing the Bus."

41. Interview with the president on "Face the Nation," 2–4.

42. President's television message on busing (1976, June 24), James Cannon Files, Box 6, GRFPL, pp. 1, 3; "Education," in President Ford 1976 Factbook, September 9, 1976, Richard Cheney Files, Box 18, GRFPL, p. 9.

43. McAndrews (1997), "Missing the Bus."

44. Memorandum from Philip Buchen and James Cannon to the President, October 28, 1976, James Cannon Files, Box 6, GRFPL, p. 2.

45. McAndrews (1997), "Missing the Bus."

46. Gerald R. Ford, Special Message to the Congress Transmitting Proposed School Busing Legislation Online by Gerhard Peters and John T. Woolley, The American Presidency Project, https://www.presidency.ucsb.edu/node/257630.

47. Eric Freedman, Stephen Jones, and Jennifer Hoewe (2012), *Gerald Ford, Race, and the Presidency* (Dome), 6.

Chapter 6

James Earl Carter

Jimmy Carter, relatively unknown, came to the White House with a plurality of 0.04% votes. He had two calling cards that powered his bully pulpit on the desegregation of public schools: a Black card, based on his affinity for Blacks; and a paradoxical segregationist card.

Chuck Stone, a prominent Black journalist and retired Tuskegee airman, pointed to the irony that "the descendants of Black slaves united to provide the balance of power for a Georgia redneck's election as the 39th president of the United States."

FORMATIVE YEARS

Carter grew up in Archery, Georgia, an unincorporated, predominantly Black community two and a half miles from Plains, Georgia, on a farm his father purchased in 1928.

There were two White, landowning families in Archery: the Carters and the Watsons. Ernest Watson was a section foreman for the Seaboard Airline Railroad.[2] Later other White families moved into the general area, but the Carters had little contact with them. He lived, worked, and played with Black youth from the age of four until he left to go to college in 1941. "When not working, my Black playmates and I spent as much time as possible in the woods hunting and fishing or just exploring."[3]

In his autobiography *A Full Life*, Carter recalls that as a young child he never considered the socioeconomic or legal differences that existed between the Black families of Archery and his own White family.[4] He avers this in spite of also noting any number of differences that he was obviously aware of: the Black families on the farm paying deference to his father, mother, and other members of the family; the fact that his family owned motor vehicles while Black folks walked or rode mules; and the segregation of the schools.

He also offers the figure of William Decker Johnson, a resident of Archery, who was a bishop in the African Methodist Episcopal Church, as being "the epitome of prestige and success" to Carter and "many others." Apparently, one wealthy Black man was enough to balance out everything else in young Carter's experience.

When he attended school in Plains, Carter was friendly with the other students in the all-White Plains High School, but he states that he "felt more at home . . . with my Black friends. . . . There were never any rankings among us except those derived from who caught the biggest fish, picked the most cotton, had performed better in the last baseball game, or prevailed in a wrestling match or foot race."[5]

Carter suggests that the root of his awakening came as a result of an incident that occurred, at age 14, when he was working in the field with his Black friends. Young adulthood had come upon them, and Carter had begun playing varsity basketball, was engaging in social events in Plains, and had become interested in girls.

As he and his friends approached the pasture gate, his friends hung back to let him go through first; young Carter suspected a prank was about to be played upon him. But nothing happened, and over the years he began to suspect that his friends' parents had warned them it was time to begin treating him with a deference that had apparently been absent when they were children.[6]

Carter attributes his attitude toward his Black playmates and neighbors to his mother. "Even when I was a child, my mother was known within our community for her refusal to accept any restraints on her treatment of Black citizens." Carter's sister would bring up the disapproving comments made by other White women, but this did not bother his mother in the least.[7]

On the other hand, Carter's father was a strict segregationist, believing that the separation of the races was a biblical tenet that was confirmed by the existence of Jim Crow laws. Carter claims that in spite of this, his "father always treated his African-American employees and customers with meticulous fairness and respect."[8]

In his inaugural address as governor of Georgia in 1971, Carter made national news with his use of his Black card: "The time for racial discrimination is over. No poor, rural, weak, or Black person should ever again have to bear the additional burden of being deprived of the opportunity of an education, a job, or simple justice."[9] *Time* magazine ran a drawing of Carter on its cover with the headline "Dixie Whistles a Different Tune." Whether for symbolic or political reasons, Carter placed a portrait of Dr. King in the governor's office.

Carter moved to further establish his civil rights credentials in his campaign autobiography, *Why Not the Best?* It loudly proclaimed his willingness to befriend Blacks and do the right thing during his state's Jim Crow days.[10] He received endorsements from Martin Luther King's father, Coretta Scott King, and Georgia congressman and civil rights activist Andrew Young. He frequented Black churches. His wife, Rosalynn, campaigned regularly in Black neighborhoods, slept in Black hotels, and ate in Black restaurants.[11]

Roy Wilkins, who like other civil rights leaders decided to take a wait-and-see stance, wrote, "There was always something of the prize schoolboy about Jimmy Carter, but it was hard not to like him."[12]

Andrew Young said in support of Carter, "John Kennedy read about racism and poverty in a sociology class at Harvard, but Jimmy Carter lived it." Young further commented, "We grew up alike. I grew up in New Orleans in a White neighborhood, playing with White kids but going to school with only Black kids. Jimmy Carter grew up surrounded by Black playmates but went to school only with White kids."[13]

As Carter forged his way to the White House, his second calling card came into play. Carter's actions and words suggested the purposeful and calculated building of an image that portrayed him (when necessary) as a person of layered poverty and a conservative segregationist.

Carter's mother, however, conveys a different image:

"We—didn't have much money," stated Miss Lillian, "but we had everything we needed. Jimmy's book *Why Not the Best?* makes us sound so poor you want to get out a hat and take up a collection." Jimmy Carter's attitude toward being poor and what should be done to solve "being poor" seems more northern liberal than southern conservative.[14]

O'Reilly observes that was always truth in the two personas Carter had developed and propagated, "that of a Joan Baez red-dirt Georgia farm boy from Plains . . . and that of the Annapolis graduate and card-carrying nuclear engineer."[15]

In an interview in 1976, he told a reporter about his special relationship with the poor of America. "I do have unique experience," he said, "and one of the strongest and best of these is my relationship with poor people. That's where I came from. That's where I live. Those are my people—not only Whites, but particularly Blacks."

JOURNEY TO THE PRESIDENCY

At the end of his naval career, Jimmy and Rosalynn became very active in various civic activities and programs in the local community. Annapolis, for

Jimmy Carter, had been a way out of Plains and had put him into a wider world. His stint as a navy man, though, did not fulfill his larger ambitions.[16]

When the Carters returned to Georgia in 1953, they lived what was in many ways a typical middle-class lifestyle. Jimmy joined community organizations, taught Sunday school, and worked on his late father's seed business. Rosalynn took care of the household, but then eventually managed the financial side of the business, a rather progressive endeavor in the 1950s.[17]

Leslie Wheeler writes that Carter's more-than-a-decade away from Georgia had changed him—his experiences had awakened the humanitarian sensibilities instilled in him by his mother, which is why "he was destined to be more than just another country politician, seeking to care for his own."[18]

Their return to Plains in 1953 placed them on a complicated path. They had to work through the aftermath of the 1954 Supreme Court decision. Positions hardened and community polarization set in. Sumter County became the 70th county in the Third Congressional District to organize a county unit of the States' Rights Council of Georgia.

Before *Brown*, Whites who broke with convention in their relationships with Blacks by treating them with something approaching equality, like Carter's mother, Miss Lillian, may have been looked at askance, but were generally tolerated. After *Brown*, any White who was not vocally opposed to school integration became a pariah, subject to boycott and physical violence.[19]

Carter refused to join the White Citizens' Council in spite of threatened boycotts of his growing business. The Plains Council had been organized by the Plains chief of police and a local Baptist preacher, who was also the railroad depot agent. Out of concern for his financial and physical well-being—he was the only White man in the area to refuse—friends and customers offered to pay his five-dollar dues. Carter responded, "I would as soon flush five dollars down the toilet." He would later write that he had been willing to leave town if it became necessary.[20]

As a result of this decision, there was a brief boycott of their business, filling station attendants refused to serve them, and they were expelled from the Americus Country Club; no doubt there were other small but painful indignities.[21]

In November 1955, the county grand jury, the governing body for the country, appointed Jimmy Carter to the Board of Education. James Earl Carter Sr. had served on the board for more than 10 years. The younger Carter, literally taking his father's seat, remained on the board until January 1963, when he resigned to serve in the Georgia State Senate.

The Sumter County Board of Education focused on the equalization of facilities for Black students and ignored desegregation until the county schools desegregated in 1964. As a school board member, Carter witnessed the inequalities between Black and White schools and the backlash of the

White community in response to the state legislature's clumsy equalization attempts.

After he joined the board, matters pertaining to educational efficiency—consolidation, planning, testing, and surveys—became more prominent on the board's agenda. Equity in 1950s Georgia consisted of equalizing facilities and expanding access to programs. While Carter served on the board, it completed a building program to upgrade the educational facilities for Black students and established a classroom for White children with special needs.

Despite *Brown*, the schools in Sumter County remained segregated. At his second board meeting, Carter made the suggestion that the board inspect all the schools under their supervision. The visits to the schools for White children went very well. Board members were impressed by the students and found the facilities in reasonable shape.

The board members, however, were embarrassed by the state of the schools for Black children. In an interview later, the county superintendent at the time, W. W. Foy, described how there were five barely adequate elementary schools for Black children along with over 30 schools being held in Black churches and even private homes, each staffed by only one or two teachers. Due to the antiquated heating, the schools were "fire traps." Foy's strongest memory was of "large teenage boys trying to sit on chairs designed for children of kindergarten age." The board ended the tour without visiting all of the school sites for Black children.[22]

Before Carter became a member of the board, the state had approved a new program to build four elementary schools and one high school for Black children. After construction began, a small number of White citizens in the town of Leslie objected to the location of one of the elementary schools, claiming that it would force White and Black children to walk along the same streets.

Carter motioned to notify the State about the objections of the White people. The State denied the request to move the location, and Carter rescinded his previous motion.

It is difficult to ascertain what Carter's real concerns were in this situation—political expediency (there were a number of reasons to forecast that the State would deny the request; amplifying the White neighbors' protest would mollify them while changing nothing) or even protecting Black children from the outcome of any friction.[23] But 22 years later, only a month after being elected president, the *New York Times* reported on the American Civil Liberties Union's use of Carter's resolution to delay the building of the school as evidence of a historical pattern of discrimination in Sumter County.[24]

Peter Bourne suggests that a truly integrationist approach at the time was untenable and that Carter, while seeking better treatment for Blacks, was largely conventional in his thinking, accepting the inequities of the time as inevitable. Sumter County Attorney Warren Fortson, who was ostracized by the White community for forming a biracial city council committee in Americus, even compared the issue of integration with contemporary attitudes about child molestation—it was completely taboo.[25]

Carter provides a characteristically mild take on the period:

> Although the school integration decision of the Supreme Court in *Brown v. Board of Education* came the year after we returned home, "separate but equal" was not challenged or changed in our community. Having witnessed President Truman's end of segregation in the military, Rosalynn and I supported in a relatively unobtrusive way the evolutionary process of ending the more oppressive elements of racial distinctions in our community.[26]

Carter became chairman of the school board in 1961. He proceeded to promulgate a plan his father had considered when he was on the school board, the consolidation of the Sumter County and the Americus school districts. Earl Carter believed that such consolidation would enrich offerings for Plains students, in addition to concerns of being swallowed up by a consolidated system. The local communities, on the other hand, were concerned that such a merger might be a harbinger of pressure to integrate the schools.

Carter, fellow board members, and Warren Fortson developed a detailed plan (which still called for separate schools for Blacks and Whites) that had to get voter approval. Carter "naively" assumed that a factual presentation would sway parents, who would do what was best for their children. He traveled the county giving speeches, while his wife and others worked to get the message out through phone calls, letters, and the media.[27]

Lead opposition came from members of his own family—his uncle and his cousin Hugh Carter, a state senator. The anti-consolidation forces prevailed, using fear of integration as their primary tool, even though Carter's tenure as a board member had mirrored that of an anti-integrationist/segregationist. His plan for consolidation maintained separate Black and White schools; he never objected to the fact that White teachers were eligible for sick-pay while Black teachers were not; and he voted to use surplus sick-leave funds to give White teachers a raise, but not Black teachers.[28]

The consolidation effort afforded Carter both his first look at campaigning and his first political defeat. As so many Carter biographers point out, including Carter himself, he did not like to lose; thus, he would work harder.

Carter began to set his sights on another challenge, a bigger one, one he could win. He would run for a Georgia state senate seat. The senate race was an eventful one. Carter lost due to vote rigging on the part of a long-standing Democratic party boss who ruled his fiefdom—Quitman County—through outright, blatant corruption. After learning of the illegal tactics that took place on that Election Day, Carter engaged the help of an *Atlanta Journal* reporter to give the election statewide publicity.

Eventually, the vote was tossed out in Quitman County, and Carter would win in a second round of voting.[29]

Carter would later reflect on the win: "If . . . I have one political attribute as the cause of my success, it would be tenacity. Once I get onto something I am awfully hard to change. That may also be a cause of some of my political failures."[30]

During the first session of his Georgia Senate tenure, the summer of 1963 was bristling with racial turmoil across the South, including Carter's hometown region: from the activities of the Student Nonviolent Coordinating Committee (SNCC) to a student beating on the streets of Americus, Georgia, to young Black youths' attempts to purchase tickets to attend the local movie theater to the jailing of protestors (including twenty young girls aged nine to thirteen) for a month in cells with no beds or mattresses. Americus, Georgia, in Carter's backyard, became the focus of national attention.[31]

The silence of Carter during this time is deafening. There is no record of public comments.[32] Carter was not part of the group of prominent citizens in Americus working to deescalate the anger and polarization that was only growing.[33]

In Atlanta, Carter's environment was one of relative liberality; people were working hard to put segregation behind them. The schools were integrated, the city hospital had integrated its wards, and the downtown restaurants were beginning to serve Blacks.

When Carter went home to Sumter County, though, he faced a different atmosphere. The local leadership was still adamantly opposed to integration. Carter saw that change was coming; desegregation was inevitable. But to "publicly endorse integration was political suicide."[34]

Carter instead adapted a strategy that relied on avoiding direct confrontation in order to allow the inexorable creep of progress to do its work. This strategy would manifest again in President Carter's use of the bully pulpit with regard to the desegregation of schools.

In the summer of 1964, during a special session called to consider the Fair Elections Act, Carter gave his first serious speeches in the Senate. He pressed his colleagues to abolish the racist "30 questions," commonly used in the South to keep Blacks from being able to register to vote. The questions were mocking and often impossible to answer.

Carter would later recall the fear he felt at the likely reaction from his constituency back home; but he was too committed to back down. In fact, the subject matter was not particularly radical for Atlanta, and the speech was not reported in the press there, nor was it covered in Americus; it did not even turn up in the *Senate Journal*.[35]

Carter believed that in order to avoid race issues, it was best to champion other issues that affected rural Georgians, both Black and White, where government might make a positive difference.[36] He concentrated on energy policy, tax reform, health issues, welfare reform, and Social Security financing.[37] He earned a reputation as a moderate.

Carter made two runs for governor. His first attempt, in 1966, saw the manipulation of his "Black" calling card. He painted his main primary rival as too liberal, associating him with LBJ while at the same time arguing that the Democratic nominee had to have the support of "responsible" Black and White voters.[38] He would lose the primary.

His second run, in 1970, was carefully planned in its double appeal. He told Black leaders, "You won't like my campaign, but you'll be proud of my record as governor." Carter would utilize his second calling card, that of the "segregationist," in this election, which would remain controversial throughout his career. He positioned himself to the right of the incumbent governor as a "redneck" and a conservative.

Carter worked hard to convince rural, White, and blue collar voters that he understood them and sympathized with them. He stated repeatedly that Georgians were conservative, as was he, but that conservative did not necessarily mean racist.

But Carter was certainly threading the needle of courting that constituency without saying anything overtly racist. Language is highly coded in the politics of the South, something voters are very aware of. Carter praised Alabama Governor George Wallace and pointed out that he expected to get a lot of votes from people who supported Wallace for president. At the same time, he touted his support among NAACP leadership and the Black church. "The remarkable thing was that probably both statements were true. They were diminishingly true as the campaign neared an end." By the campaign's end, most Black voters were supporting Carter's liberal rivals while White segregationists had moved into Carter's tent.[39]

Carter prevailed. Leslie Wheeler suggests that most Georgians wanted a person in the governor's office who had just a hint of racism, and the Blacks who supported Carter accepted his use of the segregationist calling card.

Leroy Johnson, a Black senator from Atlanta, stated, "I understand why he ran that kind of ultra-conservative campaign . . . you have to do that to win. And that's the main thing. I don't believe you can win in this state without being a racist. Five years from now, perhaps—but not now."[40]

Carter's one-term gubernatorial program concentrated on the state's reorganization: efficiency, cost reduction, and budget reform. He continued his quest to upgrade the state's educational program. He did engage a policy of promoting Blacks and women to his staff, to major policy boards and agencies, and to the court system. However, Governor Carter did not use his office or his leadership acumen to foster the continued desegregation of Georgia's schools.

Carter's tenure as governor, in fact, established his uneasiness with, if not outright hostility to, "forced" busing. He once referred to the busing of students "the most serious threat to education I can remember."[41]

As ever, Carter sought to improve the lives of Black citizens materially and civically while declining to endorse an integrationist position that would cost him much of the White vote. Carter, like his predecessors Ford and Nixon, chose not to use his voice in his leadership to assure the intent or promise of *Brown*. He did not see desegregation moving toward integration as a positive, enriching the quality of education for Black and White children alike.

Carter's presidential campaign saw more of the same; yet on the national level, there were more eyes to notice and voices to criticize that he seemed to be on both sides of the integration issue.

In May 1976, the *New York Times* ran a piece that noted his seeming inconsistencies: he recently had told a reporter that he thought private schools should not be able to refuse Black students; previously in the year he had wondered why the federal government wanted to ensure that "every student" be admitted without regard to race or religion; and at another time he said that with the exception of schools like Jewish yeshivas, private schools should be required to be open to all admissions, regardless of whether they received federal funds or had tax-exempt status.[42]

In April 1976, having won the primaries, Carter said while discussing public housing that he thought community members should be able to preserve the "ethnic purity" of their neighborhoods; while he would not support enforced neighborhood integration, neither would he allow discrimination.

Asked for clarification a few days later, Carter doubled down, apparently unaware of the implications of his words: "I have nothing against a community that is made up of people who are Polish, Czechoslovakians, French Canadians, or Blacks who are trying to maintain the ethnic purity of their neighborhoods."

The press hounded him all day on the issue, and the next day, after ABC correspondent Sam Donaldson brought up the "Hitlerian" connotations of "ethnic purity," Carter finally got angry. "If anyone derived from my statement the connotation that I have an inclination to racism, then I would resent that, because it's certainly not true."[43]

Nevertheless, Black leadership was appalled, and 17 members of the Congressional Black Caucus condemned his statement.

Even if Carter had missed the enormity of his gaffe, Rosalynn had not, and she called him, impressing upon him the need to apologize.

The next day he issued a statement apologizing for the use of the term "ethnic purity." He and his campaign then immediately began organizing a rally in Atlanta aimed predominantly at Black voters. The images of Carter and Martin Luther King Sr. together at the rally helped calm the controversy.[44]

In his campaign platform, Carter remained opposed to busing, stating that the enforced transportation of students outside their neighborhoods in pursuit of desegregation was a tool of last resort.

PLATFORM ON DESEGREGATION

In the election, Carter received 95% of the Black vote and 45% of the White vote. He carried every Southern state except Virginia. He had unapologetically embraced the power of the 1965 Voter Rights Act. John Lewis, the leader of the Voter Education Project, said, "The Voting Rights Act created the climate for someone like Jimmy Carter to become the Democratic nominee and be elected President."[45]

He appointed the first Black division head at the Department of Justice, the first Black female cabinet member, and the first Black ambassador to the United Nations. Carter named more Blacks, Latinos, and women to the federal judiciary than all previous administrations combined.

As president, Carter kept to the path he'd followed on his way to the White House—he affirmed the use of the federal government's resources and power to oppose discrimination but opposed forced integration of any sort.

On April 11, 1978, Bob Haiman of the *St. Petersburg Times* asked President Carter about leadership with regard to the lack of progress for Black Americans since 1968. He quoted a Carnegie Corporation report that examined the Nation's separate and unequal societies: "'It's because there seems to be no leader who is capable of evoking the Nation's latent sense of conscience and mobilizing it to action.' My question, sir, is, could you be that leader, should you be that leader, are you that leader, and if you are, then how do you plan to lead?"

Haiman spoke directly to the bully pulpit Carter now had the opportunity to wield. Carter's response emphasized the economic gains made by minority groups and the financial investment in those groups made by the federal government under his leadership. He noted that minority groups still had a long way to go and that he felt "responsible to make sure that they go that long way toward equality of opportunity." He made no mention of integration.[46]

Later that year, Senators Eagleton (D-Missouri) and Biden (D-Delaware) proposed an amendment to a Labor, Health, Education, and Welfare appropriations bill. The amendment provided that none of the funds appropriated would be used in any way to "bus" students out of their neighborhoods.

It was clear that the Eagleton-Biden amendment would thwart the efforts of HEW's Office of Civil Rights to enforce desegregation of northern schools.[47] In spite of this, Carter signed the bill into law.

The US Commission on Civil Rights produced a status report that expressed concern about the Eagleton-Biden amendment along with other legislative efforts that "undermined the ability of the Executive and Judicial branches to guarantee the Nation's children and young people their constitutional rights. It has thus acted against widely accepted civil-rights goals and contributed to a lessening of the national will with respect to equal rights in the vital area of public education."[48]

In spite of this report from his own administration, Carter never raised his voice to rally against the aggressions of the legislative branch. In essence, he was complicit in their actions.

In a series of town hall meetings in 1980, Carter again reiterated his opposition to busing and his discomfort with federal intrusion in local school matters generally, while also stating his consistent opinion that federal funds could and should be used to provide equal opportunity.

The 35th president of the United States demonstrated a commitment to civil rights at certain select levels, pushing against voter suppression and using his Justice Department to investigate and thwart activities of the Ku Klux Klan. He directed his agencies and cabinet to actively pursue equal opportunity in employment for Blacks and other minorities and women.

Just as he was at the state level, he was very intentional about opening employment opportunities to Blacks in the federal government. Yet Carter failed to use his voice, his office, and his bully pulpit to push forward America's quest to assure that Blacks are equally included in all aspects of the fabric of the country.

Carter's own solicitor general, Drew Days, questioned "whether we can continue to look to the litigious model as the principal method for achieving civil-rights progress given its significant shortcomings and wavering public acceptance."

Nathaniel R. Jones, attorney, judge, law professor, and general counsel of the NAACP, answered Days with a quote from Thurgood Marshall:

> Desegregation is not and was never expected to be an easy task. Racial attitudes ingrained in our Nation's childhood and adolescence are not quickly thrown aside. But just as the inconvenience of some cannot be allowed to stand in the way of the rights of others, so public opposition, no matter how strident, cannot be permitted to direct this court from enforcement of constitutional principles at issue.[49]

When the nation was still wrestling with the desegregation issue, after the setbacks of Nixon and Ford, the country needed a leader to help Americans see the need for change and to assist them through the process of correcting a historic wrong. There is no instrument better equipped for that process than the bully pulpit of the presidency; yet, Carter neglected it.

LEGISLATIVE PROFILE AS PRESIDENT

Carter's successful and robust legislative agenda did not include a priority that promoted school desegregation. He did successfully give full cabinet status to education by establishing the Department of Education.

The Miller Center of Public Affairs at the University of Virginia reports that Carter's legislative passing rate was just under that of LBJ, at 70%. Robert C. Byrd, Senate majority leader, observed that his legislative achievements had been overlooked by too many. With an "extensive and ambitious" legislative agenda, "he won more often than he lost" and "could be justly proud of his legislative accomplishments. History will be more kind to Mr. Carter than were his contemporaries."[50]

NOTES

1. Chuck Stone (1977, Jan–Feb), "Black Political Power in the Carter Era," *The Black Scholar,* 8(4), 6–15.
2. Jimmy Carter (2016), *A Full Life: Reflections at Ninety* (Simon & Schuster), 11.
3. Carter (2016), *A Full Life*, 12.
4. Carter (2016), *A Full Life*, 22.
5. Carter (2016), *A Full Life*, 24.
6. Carter (2016), *A Full Life*, 24.
7. Carter (2016), *A Full Life*, 28.
8. Carter (2016), *A Full Life*, 28.
9. Carter (2016), *A Full Life*, 101.
10. Carter (2016), *A Full Life*, 336.
11. Betty Glad (1980), *In Search of the Great White House* (Norton), 323–25.
12. Roy Wilkins and Tom Mathews (1980), *Standing Fast: The Autobiography of Roy Wilkins* (Viking Press), 339–40.
13. "Andrew Young" (1977, July), *Playboy,* 67.
14. Jeffrey St. John (1976), *Jimmy Carter's Betrayal of the South* (Green Hill Publishers), 25.
15. Kenneth O'Reilly (1996), *Nixon's Piano: Presidents and Racial Politics from Washington to Clinton* (Free Press), 337.
16. St, John (1976), *Jimmy Carter's Betrayal of the South*, 25.

17. Deanna L. Michael (2008), *Jimmy Carter as Educational Policymaker: Equal Opportunity and Efficiency* (SUNY Press), 14.

18. Leslie Wheeler (1976), *Jimmy Who?: An Examination of Presidential Candidate Jimmy Carter, the Man, His Career, His Stands on the Issues* (Barron's Woodbury), 25.

19. Peter G. Bourne (1997), *Jimmy Carter: A comprehensive Biography from Plains to Post-presidency* (Scribner), 96.

20. Bourne (1997), *Jimmy Carter*, 97.

21. John Bourne (1995, February 10), *Interview with Chip Carter*.

22. Michael (2008), *Jimmy Carter as Educational Policymaker*, 16.

23. Michael (2008), *Jimmy Carter as Educational Policymaker*, 17.

24. *New York Times*, "ATLANTA," December 21.

25. Bourne (1997), *Jimmy Carter*, 115.

26. Carter (2016), *A Full Life*, 77–78.

27. Bourne (1997), *Jimmy Carter*, 106.

28. Wheeler (1976), *Jimmy Who?*, 32–33.

29. Bourne (1997), *Jimmy Carter*, 121–28.

30. Bourne (1997) *Jimmy Carter*, 131.

31. Bourne (1997), *Jimmy Carter*, 134–35.

32. Bourne (1997), *Jimmy Carter*, 136.

33. Bourne (1997), *Jimmy Carter*, 137.

34. Bourne (1997), *Jimmy Carter, 143*.

35. Bourne (1997), *Jimmy Carter*, 144.

36. Bourne (1997), *Jimmy Carter*, 150.

37. Richard Neustadt (1990), *Presidential Power and Modern Presidents* (The Free Press), 239.

38. Bourne (1997), *Jimmy Carter*, 158.

39. Reg Murphy and Hal Gulliver (1971), *The Southern Strategy* (Scribner).

40. Bourne (1997), *Jimmy Carter*, 199.

41. Wheeler (1976), *Jimmy Who?*, 80–81.

42. Charles Mohr (1976, May 26), "Carter on Busing," *New York Times*, https://www.nytimes.com/1976/05/26/archives/carter-on-busing.html.

43. Bourne (1997), *Jimmy Carter*, 312–13.

44. Bourne (1997), *Jimmy Carter*, 311–12.

45. Ari Berman (2015, September 3), "Op-Ed: How Jimmy Carter Championed Civil Rights—and Ronald Reagan Didn't," *Los Angeles Times*, https://www.latimes.com/opinion/op-ed/la-oe-0906-berman-carter-civil-rights-20150906-story.html.

46. Jimmy Carter, The President's News Conference Online by Gerhard Peters and John T, Woolley, The American Presidency Project, https://www.presidency.ucsb.edu/node/245096.

47. *Washington Post* (1977, July 5), "The Anti-busing Game," www.washingtonpost.com/politics/1977/07/05/the-anti-busing-game.

48. Arthur Fleming (1977, July 22), Chairman, US Commission on Civil Rights Testimony before Senate Judiciary Committee, 95th Congress, 1st session.

49. Nathaniel R. Jones (1984), "The Desegregation of Urban Schools Thirty Years after *Brown*," *University of Colorado Law Review, 55*, 556.

50. Stuart E. Eizenstat (2018), *President Carter the White House Years* (St. Martin's Press), 11.

Chapter 7

Ronald Wilson Reagan

The public school desegregation imprint on President Reagan can be earmarked as: "His Administration Turned Back the Clock on School Desegregation."

Ronald Reagan's voice on the desegregation of America's schools resonated with language that was intransigent, interminable, and uncompromising in its opposition to busing. While Ford, Nixon, and Carter had opposed busing as a tool to implement the "promise of *Brown*," their bully pulpit voices were less divisive.

A strong characterization of Reagan's bully pulpit is illustrated in commentary by Nathan Glazer. He argues, "A legitimate, moral, and constitutional effort to eliminate the unconstitutional separation of the races has been turned into something else."[1]

Reagan viewed federal responses (especially by the courts) as invasive, as egregious, and as a useless effort to regroup the races in education by elaborate transportation systems.

FORMATIVE YEARS

Reagan was born in a Democratic household in the north-central town of Tampico, Illinois. Before the Depression, Reagan's family moved to Dixon, Illinois, where his father operated a shoe store.

In his early years, he followed the politics of his father, a Roosevelt supporter and a New Dealer. As he prepared to run for governor, he published an autobiography, *Where's the Rest of Me?* His official biographer, Edmund Morris, writes:

> The autobiography was designed to frame his father's importance, as a sense of responsibility. "Reagan describes a charming but weak man who failed to realize the potential of life because of alcoholism. He remembers his father as

a restless man, burning with ambition to succeed." Politically, he saw his father as "sentimental democrat who believed fervently in the rights of the working man." He was also a Roman Catholic at a time when anti-Catholic prejudice flourished in America.[2]

In the autobiography, according to Cannon, Reagan's father would not allow him or his brother to see the film *The Birth of a Nation* because it glorified the Ku Klux Klan. Cannon observes he would remember that because at the time of that movie, he was only four years old.[3]

Reagan's mother, however, was central to his cultivation. Anderson Marvin said, "she had a flair for acting and helped him build his movie career."[4]

In Dixon, Reagan's dad rented near the northside of town enabling *"Dutch"* to qualify to go to school at Dixon High School Northside. This pleased both Reagan and his mother as they both aspired to a middle-class status.[5]

It was at Illinois Eureka College, a college smaller than the average Illinois high school, located 70 miles from his birth home of Tampico, Illinois, that Ronald *"Dutch"* Reagan's trajectory toward the presidency first took root in the construct of both his mother and father's basic values, though he would later veer from his father's morals.

His lifeguard skills, honed in high school in Dixon, afforded him money to go to the college. "Half of my college," he told his biographer with pride, "lifeguard money paid for half of my college education, and dishwashing the other half."[6]

An incident happened at Eureka College that involved faculty and students protesting and striking to oust the president. Reagan became actively involved in student unrest and strikes (reminiscent of his father's sense of justice). Reagan was one of the speakers at the campuswide strike rally, which resulted in a motion by acclamation to force the resignation of the college president, Bert Wilson.

Reagan reflected:

> I discovered that night that an audience has a feel to it and, in the parlance of the theater that audience and I were together. When I came to actually presenting the motion (sic) there was no need for a parliamentary procedure . . . they came to their feet with a roar—even the faculty members voted by acclamation. It was like heady wine.[7]

Commentary by most Reagan chroniclers attest to his speaking ability and speechmaking as a major arsenal during the Reagan administration. Martin Anderson, a White House insider, reports that he had the ability to move large audiences just as he had done as freshman at Eureka College when he was selected to be the spokesman for a successful student strike. Anderson reports further that Reagan never forgot it and honed his skills to continue that pattern.[8] The author attributes the president's success as a two-term president as his "ability to speak, to inspire, and move those who think America watched and listened to him."[9]

Ronald Reagan had found his voice, a voice that would anchor his bully pulpit for many years to come, inclusive of his bully pulpit on school desegregation/integration.

Cannon described him as:

> Widely popular, and people liked to hear him talk. He succeeded at everything he tried. At a time when one-fourth of all Americans were out of work, he convinced a station manager to hire him for a part-time sports announcing job for which better-qualified applicants had already been rejected.[10]

There is considerable ink on Reagan's screen actor years from 1937–1942. Reagan's perception of himself is that he was brought up without bigotry or prejudice . . . and certainly during his screen-actor years, his record does include fighting discrimination in employment opportunities.

In 1947, he was elected president of the Screen Actors Guild (SAG), a labor union representing actors. Schultz says, "He soon learned the art of negotiations and was reelected in 1952 and 1959."[11]

It was also during his tenure as president of the Screen Actors Guild (SAG) that he began the trajectory toward conservative republicanism. The SAG served as a forum for many issues of the day, including the strong communist serge within the ranks of Hollywood personnel. Reagan, reminiscent of the Eureka strike, used his voice to persuade his fellow members to settle a strike policy; thus, SAG remained neutral during that fraught period. His trajectory continued when he was hired to be a spokesperson for General Electric (GE), where the messaging to the GE family bordered on the debate between the liberal sense of a more robust role of the government and the conservative sense of lesser role of the federal government.[12]

In a letter to Nixon, Reagan explains the shift to being a Republican when he heard "it frightening" in the acceptance speech of John Kennedy at the Democratic National Convention. Reagan was bothered by Kennedy's idea of the "challenging new world" being one in which the "the Federal Government will do more and of course spend more." Reagan's aversion to the government's solving problems is echoed in a letter to a citizen:

> Dear Mrs. Willingford,
>   I can't tell you how much your letter meant to me. I'm truly grateful and very proud. I guess we who call ourselves Republicans haven't done a very good job of explaining what it is we really want for the people. Maybe we've been so

busy trying to fight against programs of the government because we don't think they'll solve the problem that we haven't taken the time to explain that we do want the problems solved.

I started out as a Democrat, casting my first vote for Franklin D. Roosevelt in 1932. One of the things that disturbed me over the years was my party's indifference to the situation in the South, where Blacks were denied their constitutional rights for so long. And, of course, the South was a one-party region, solidly Democrat. It seemed that Washington would do nothing to upset that situation. My first Republican vote was for Eisenhower and I didn't get around to becoming a Republican until 1962.[13]

JOURNEY TO THE PRESIDENCY

In 1964, the televised speech, in support of Barry Goldwater, channeled Reagan's now-steady argument against "*big government*," an argument to be later used as his bully pulpit arguments against investment in education and desegregation. The speech, heralded as a hit, encouraged California businesses to recruit him for governor. He easily won.

Cannon points out that Reagan's past had not prepared him for the "*everydayness*" of governor.[14] His early confidant, Nofziger, mused that Reagan had "materialized out of thin air with no political background, no political cronies, and no political machine. He didn't even run his own campaign."[15]

His general attitude toward the role of government is reflected in a line from remarks to the American Society of Newspaper editors on April 9, 1986. He said:

> I have always stated that the nearest thing to eternal life we'll see on this earth is a government program. It is my intention to curb the size and influence of the federal establishment and to demand recognition of the distinction between the powers granted to the Federal Government reserved to the states or to the people. . . . All of us—All of us need to be reminded that the Federal Government did not create the states; the states created the Federal Government.[16]

His governorship would be marked nationally by his response to the unrest on California University's public colleges. It is said that his actions (National Guard presence on campuses complete with shotguns, teargas, and bayonets) were consistent with his now fully formed conservative philosophy.

Cannon observes, "What distinguished Reagan in his long climb to the presidency was perseverance towards his goal. Social conservatism (from the era of civil rights to Vietnam to the federal role in education) had prompted a robust environment for a cultural climate of 'us and them'." Cannon goes on to point out that Reagan "was not immune to the laws of political gravity. For all of his amicability, he could be highly manipulative in pursuing his goals."[17]

Consistent with this understanding, on August 3, 1980, Reagan began his election campaign for president in Neshoba County, Mississippi, where civil rights activists Andrew Goodman and Michael Schwerner had been brutally murdered in 1964. "I believe in State's rights," Reagan told the all-but-a-few-White crowd at the county fair.[18] His opponent, Jimmy Carter, likened Reagan's words to "the stirrings of hate and the rebirth of code, words like State's rights."[19]

Reagan was assuring the mostly White crowd of thousands that he would restore to the States and to local community governments the power that properly belonged to them.

In response to a question at the Carter-Reagan presidential debate, when asked his opinion of a multiracial society in a nation, where "Blacks and other non-Whites are increasing in numbers in our cities. Many of them feel that they are facing a hostility from Whites that prevents them from joining the economic mainstream of our society. There is racial confrontation in the schools, on jobs, and in housing, as non-Whites seek to reap the benefits of a free society. What do you think is the Nation's future as a multiracial society?"[20]

Reagan responded:

I believe in it. I am eternally optimistic, and I happen to believe that we've made great progress from the days when I was young and when this country didn't even know it had a racial problem. I know those things can grow out of despair in an inner city, when there's hopelessness at home, lack of work, and so forth. But I believe that all of us together—and I believe the Presidency is what Teddy Roosevelt said it was; it's a bully pulpit—and I think that something can be done from there, because the goal for all of us should be that one day, things will be done neither because of nor in spite of any of the differences between us—ethnic differences or racial differences, whatever they may be—that we will have total equal opportunity for all people. And I would do everything I could in my power to bring that about."[21]

PLATFORM ON DESEGREGATION

There was a stark contrast in presidential support for school desegregation in the transition from Carter to Reagan and a pronounced divergence in the president's support for civil rights. In spite of his poor performance in using his bully pulpit to advance the path for desegregation, Carter held a supportive constituency within the civil rights community and was supportive of the tenets of the civil rights leadership.

Reagan's message, as characterized by Kenneth O'Reilly of *Nixon's Piano*, was that "racial injustice no longer existed and any past injustices were not an issue. The issue was African American's behavior and self-destructive values (crime, drugs, teenage pregnancy, laziness, etc.)."[22]

Reagan, in fact, did not meet with the civil rights leadership until his second term. On the campaign trail of his successful run for presidency in 1980, he told Lauren Barrett that "the Voting Rights Act had been 'humiliating' to the South."[23]

O'Reilly posits a picture of how Reagan built an economic coalition (known on the streets as the Reagan Democrats) that used language and implemented actions that slid eventually into anti-Black rhetoric. He points out, "while Reagan offered corporate America cash through tax-rate cuts depreciation he offered the rest of White America little more than anti-Black rhetoric."[24] Conversely, the living standard of working- and middle-class White America began to slide. The Reagan bully pulpit and his administration began to focus on mostly White small business. The economic interest of poor people and the working and labor classes, which once held the Roosevelt coalition together, became toxic. Race was the wedge that Reagan's people used to split the coalition. Race became the marker for fracturing the coalition.

O Reilly surmises, "If Reagan's spoken promise was to get the government off the backs of the American people, his unspoken promise was to get '*the niggers*' off the backs of the White middle and working classes who had lost control of their schools and neighborhood while paying taxes to support busing, Medicaid, public housing in the city suburbs." Groups sprang up like SPONGE (the Society for the Prevention Of Niggers Getting Everything).[25]

President Reagan was quite calculating within the construct of advocacy for civil rights. He would assert support for racial justice; yet the voice of his cabinet members (often speaking in consort with his thoughts) would express the opposite. Many times they would hurl toward language that blamed the very people who fought for their rights for their inability to gain their rights.

He called the inner-city homeless "campers." "One problem that we've had . . . is the people who are sleeping on the grates," he remarked on *Good Morning America*. "The homeless, who are homeless, you might say by choice." It should be noted that Black unemployment was at 14% on the day he took office and the Black poverty rate at 36% in eighteen months of his first term.

Marian Wright Edleman, of the Children's Defense Fund, accused the president of using his office "to repeal or weaken everything, every single federal children's program and every program protecting the poor." President Reagan retorted, "In the war on poverty, poverty won."[26]

Reagan used his bully pulpit to popularize the notion that welfare recipients were on the take. He successfully put a Black face on the welfare issue by constantly advancing the story of Chicago's Linda Taylor as a *"welfare Queen."* He would tell the story to congressional leaders, foreign leaders, and personal contacts, inflating the story each time so that Ms. Taylor had, "eighty names, thirty addresses, twelve Social Security cards." According to the story as it advanced, she collected "veteran's benefits on four non-existing deceased husbands" and other welfare-state funds to produce a tax-free income of over $150,000. (Note: Ms. Taylor had been convicted in 1977 for fraud and perjury involving $8,000 on public-aid checks.)[27]

On affirmative action, Reagan's 1986 budget proposals called affirmative action goals, timetables, and quotas "a tax on the employment of White males."

One of his cabinet members, Edwin Meese, corroborated the Reagan position, stating "counting by race is a form of racism." He suggested that, "even if you engaged in affirmative action practices that did not adhere to quotas as nothing short of a legal, moral, and constitutional tragedy."[28]

Reagan continued to use his bully pulpit to advance his assault on affirmative action in his speeches, including the notion of reverse discrimination. He appropriated and distorted the matter, saying, "If you happen to belong to an ethnic group not recognized by the Federal Government as entitled to special treatment, you are the victim of reverse discrimination."[29]

On voting rights, Reagan had opposed the Voting Rights Act of 1965 citing constitutional grounds for his stance. With his "aw shucks" manner, President Reagan was slow to lend his voice to the Voting Rights Act.

Reagan alleged that he was "in complete sympathy with the goals and purposes of the legislation." He offered, however, that he could see in it "flaws and faults" that were dangerous enough to cause him to oppose renewal altogether.[30]

Drew Days observes, "Few could miss the stark contrast between the posture of this administration, sitting on its hands while the congress struggled, and the vigorous and constructive assistance provided by earlier administrations, particularly the Johnson and Ford administrations, at the time of original passage in 1965 and the 1975 extension of the Voting Rights Act."[31]

Blacks throughout his administration had a testy relationship with Reagan, and it was in particular their response to the way he used his voice. They saw him as constantly speaking "in code."

Kenneth O'Reilly, in *Nixon's Piano*, shares that Reagan, on rare occasions, would contact an African American critic who questioned his commitment to racial equality. He reports, "Roger Wilkins, for one, received a telephone call after writing a critical newspaper column. The president relayed the Jack Reagan and Burky stories, but they failed to change Wilkins's mind, 'any fair reading of that column would reveal that I had called him an ignorant bigot . . . any fair reading of my mind would reveal that this is exactly what I think.'"[32]

Nancy Reagan observed, "A lot of lies are told by people who go into politics. But the only one that ever got Ronnie steamed up was the occasional allegation that he was a bigot."[33]

An Urban League Report of 1987 posited that on the national level, six years of Reagan policies had produced "no gains for Blacks."[34]

In an interview by Tom Wicker with Eddie N. Williams, director of the Joint Center for Political Studies, Williams observed, "the word Black is not part of [Reagan's] lexicon."[35] There were scholars who raised the question by the time Reagan was president, including Drew Days, Carter's assistant attorney general, as to how long advocates could continue to look to the litigation model as the veritable method for achieving civil rights, given wavering public acceptance and measured shortcomings of litigation.

However, Days suggests on matters of race and constitutional rights there is an efficacy in litigation. He reminds us of Thurgood Marshall's argument in Milliken, "desegregation is not and was never expected to be an easy task. Racial attitudes ingrained in our Nation's childhood and adolescence are not quickly thrown aside [but] just as the inconvenience of some cannot be allowed to stand in the way of the rights of others, so public opposition, no matter how strident, cannot be permitted to divert the court from [the] enforcement of constitutional principles at issue."[36]

Drew Days, in *Turning Back the Clock*, concludes:

> Civil rights enforcement at the national level during the period of almost 40 years before the Reagan Administration took office had several salient features. First, successive administrations, irrespective of party, attempted to build upon the previous principles of civil-rights law to achieve increasingly effective enforcement of basic civil rights.
>
> Though there were variations with respect to emphasis and allocation of resources from administration to administration, the momentum of civil-rights enforcement was basically forward. Second, despite differences in ideology, each administration was willing to alter its initial views on civil-rights enforcement in the face of reality: techniques that proved ineffective were abandoned in favor of more potent approaches. Third, no administration openly challenged the authority of Supreme Court rulings, even those it did not wholly embrace.

Days calls out:

> The Reagan Administration has been the exception. It has consistently shown in matters of civil rights to move in precisely the opposite direction from former administrations. It has sought to undermine the achievements of preceding

administrations, Republican and Democratic. Mechanically repeating stock phrases about "busing being bad" and quotas being "unfair" as articles of faith, its officials have demonstrated an extreme ideological rigidity, refusing to yield in the face of even the most compelling facts and reasoning to the contrary.[37]

"One of the things Reagan recognized as being done well from Washington was using the bully pulpit in education," observed Chester E. Finn. Finn, who served as the Education Department's assistant secretary for educational research and improvement, said "he realized that Washington was a good podium from which to steer the National discussion."[38]

Reagan's use of his voice may best be described in a letter from Nixon to Reagan long before he became president. When Reagan lost the nomination to Ford in 1976, Nixon in a letter to Reagan said, "The millions who saw and heard you on TV during the convention had to conclude—even in some cases did not agree with your philosophy—that you were an eloquent and persuasive advocate of your point of view."[39] This was so true of Reagan's bully pulpit voice. He never raised it for school desegregation or school integration.

The manner in which Reagan used his bully pulpit could be most disarming. Donald Regan observed, "The President has a unique talent; he is serious internally. When he has made a decision, he lives with it. He does not fret over it. And most of all, he does not change his mind."[40] Martin Anderson describes another trait. "He is a warmly ruthless man" with "stubborn patience."[41]

The major strategies used by the Reagan administration to overcome a path forward in desegregating the schools included limiting the power of the courts, particularly as related to busing, tapping the Justice Department's office of civil rights to block implementation of court-ordered remedies, assaulting the health of a selected segment of the nation's public schools, drafting opposing federal legislation, and using the budget as a tool for crippling those federal programs that supported school integration.

Reagan, as observed by Wicker, was *"visibly"* reluctant to enforce the work of his own administration's agencies when they tried to implement civil rights policies and court remedies as they were legally bound to do.[42]

Over time the courts weighed inferences and presumptions to fairly allocate the burdens in school desegregation litigation (*Keyes v. School District*, No 1,413 U.S.189 (1973). It rendered that the finding of State-imposed segregation in a substantial portion of the school district creates a rebuttable presumption of an entirely segregated district requiring a systemwide remedy.

Drew Days in *Turning Back* provides a useful explanation as follows:

After almost 20 years of reviewing school desegregation cases, the Supreme Court decided in 1973 that it was very unlikely that Black or Hispanic plaintiffs seeking desegregation would be able to prove that the racial composition of every school, in every section of a district, resulted from intentionally segregative actions by school officials.

Experience has taught the court, however, that where plaintiffs could show that the school board had closed schools, opened schools, or changed boundaries or grade structures in one substantial part of the system to create or maintain segregation, it was likely that the same segregative intent infected the rest of the system as well.

Drawing from rules of evidence and burdens of proof familiar to other areas of law, the court determined that where plaintiffs could present evidence of such segregation, a system wide remedy would be appropriate unless the school board could rebut the presumption that its illegal action pervaded the district. The Supreme Court merely placed the burden on the party possessing any arguable exculpatory evidence to produce it. This is a rule born of both painful experience and logic.[43]

Reagan's response to Keys through his attorney general for civil rights was that the Reagan Justice Department would not rely upon the Keys presumption. "That, in fact, it would only initiate system-wide desegregation litigation, if it uncovered 'direct' evidence of pervasive intentional discrimination. As the courts began to refine their position on the duty of school districts to eradicate '*root and branch*' vestiges of unconstitutional."[44]

Reagan's Justice Department continued to thwart the intentions of the court. *Green* (*Green v. New Kent County)* found that school boards had the affirmative duty to develop desegregation plans that promised "realistically to work and . . . realistically to work now."[45] The Reagan administration disagreed. They were clear that they did not see the role of the school board's affirmative duty to desegregate. Attorney General Reynolds, in speaking for the administration, saw the role of the Justice Department's responsibility in enforcing only school-district desegregation remedies.

Only if it is "to remove remaining state-enforced racial barriers to open student enrollment," there can be no doubt as to the intent of the Reagan vision of court-ordered remedies (including busing) on segregation/desegregation. To make it "*as plain as day*," in response to a question about busing, Reynolds responded in a *New York Times* article on October 16, 1981, "Compulsory busing of students in order to achieve racial balance in the public school is not an acceptable remedy." He went on to say, "as a matter of administrative policy, this theme has been endorsed by the President, the Vice President, the Secretary of Education and me."[46]

The administration continued to attempt to roll back court remedies, by taking sides in school board cases with histories of resistance to compliance with *Brown*. Examples include but are not limited to:

- An amicus brief for the Nashville School Board (a board that had not begun any desegregation effort until 1971, 17 years after *Brown*. In that case, the Supreme Court denied review; not one justice dissented.[47]
- Joined the East Baton Rouge, Louisiana, School Board in a challenge to a desegregation plan ordered into effect three years earlier.[48] The administration sought a stay in order to "afford (it) an opportunity to prepare and present a more effective and less intrusive desegregation program than the plan presently in operation."[49]
- Succeeded in rolling back the court-imposed desegregation plan in Norfolk, Virginia (*Riddick v. School Board of the City of Norfolk, Virginia*), mirroring Reagan's understanding of the use of his bully pulpit. Reynolds testified before the Senate sub committee on the judiciary hearing on separation of powers said, "We all probably can agree that the achievement of this objective, eradication of state-imposed racial segregation, is central to the constitutional promise of equal protection of the law. In recent years, however we have witnessed growing public disillusionment with some of the remedies used to accomplish the constitutional imperative of eliminating racial discrimination in public schooling."[50]

The courts did use "public opinion" as a proxy for achieving justice. But President Reagan knew how to play to the audience. In fact, in *Cooper v. Aaron,* The Supreme Court held that public opposition to desegregation techniques was not a proper legal consideration.[51]

Reagan used his bully pulpit to play to parents who had become very concerned about the direction of the country regarding school desegregation.

Reagan's assaults on the courts were robust and heavy handed in his quest to stop the desegregation path the nation was taking. As that path became more problematic, Reagan's major bully pulpit strategy was to raise the rhetoric of *"forced busing"* to fuel used to propel rockets into space. The yellow school bus had always been as American as apple pie in the 20th century. *The New York Times*, in an article, cited statistics on busing for desegregation that indicated "only a small fraction of children enrolled in public schools are bused solely for purposes of desegregation. In 1980, for example, over 97% of public school busing was for purposes having nothing to do with desegregation."[52]

Within a year of taking office, the Reagan administration portrayed clearly, through his personal and official voice in a series of statements. As Drew Days points out:

> Assistant Attorney General stated in 1981, "In keeping with this overarching philosophy [that the constitution must be color-blind], the Justice Department

will, in school cases as in all other cases handled but the Civil Rights Division, refrain from selling race-conscious remedies, such as court-ordered busing, solely for the purpose of achieving a particular racial balance."[53]

Reynolds told a Senate Subcommittee, "Accordingly, the Department will henceforth, on a finding by a court of de jure racial segregation, seek a desegregation remedy, rather than court-ordered busing. . . ." Assistant Attorney General Reynolds, "states succinctly, we have concluded that involuntary busing has largely failed in two major respects: It had failed to elicit public support, and it has failed to advance the overriding goal of equal educational opportunity."[54]

Reynolds remarked in a *New York Times* article during that same time, "integrated education . . . we are not going to compel children who do not want to choose to have an integrated education to have one."[55]

Reynolds showed his ruthlessness. In a South Carolina case, Reynolds referred to Black parents as "*those bastards*" and vowed to block their participation by making them jump through every hoop.[56]

In 1988, as late as the 3rd year of his second term, in spite of all the Reagan disruptions, he stated, "Busing takes innocent children out of the neighborhood schools and makes them pawns in a social experiment that nobody wants. And we've found out that it failed."[57]

Reagan engaged in other political decisions that established his opposition to court-ordered remedies, legislative remedies, and busing, as tools of desegregation. Significant among those decisions was the use of the power of the purse. Just after he assumed office, he promoted and signed the Omnibus Budget Reconciliation Act of 1981.[58] This act terminated funding for scores of federal programs designed to help districts meet compliance with court orders that needed assistance in meeting those orders. The largest and most significantly effective was the Emergency School Aid Act of 1972 (ESAA).[59]

The ESAA was passed to "(a) meet the special needs incident to the elimination of racial segregation and discrimination among students and faculty in elementary and secondary schools, and (b) to encourage the voluntary elimination, reduction, or prevention of racial isolation in elementary and secondary schools with substantial proportions of minority group students."[60]

These monies provided planning grant monies to school districts across the nation who sought to voluntarily desegregate its school system. (ESAA was a Nixon bill.) He read public opinion on private/public schools and skillfully exploited it from his bully pulpit. The president robustly attempted to help finance segregated academies who had responded to the May 17, 1954, Supreme Court decision by setting up private academies whereby Whites could place their children without concern for integrated classrooms.

President Reagan was unable to sustain this effort as he feigned ignorance. In a visit to a Black high school in Chicago, he said, "I was under the impression that the problem of segregated schools had been settled."[61]

On the campaign trail during his run against Ford, Reagan posted vouchers as an anecdote to busing. Parents would use these vouchers to enroll their children directly in schools of their choice.

Reagan surmised:

> The Federal Government might, through vouchers or tax credits, aid students to enroll in school of their choice. There need be a little, if any connection between federal department and educational institution and thus no possibility of control. Indirect aid would enhance the ability of parents with limited means to enroll their children at a school which they regard as best for their children. While segregation simply has no place in American public schools, neither has forced busing. It has wrought too much damage already. . . . Busing is a social experiment that has failed.[62]

Under the cover of *A Nation at Risk*, Reagan was able to complete the pivot that had begun with Richard Nixon. The policy language of the Nixon administration turned from desegregation to compensatory education and "*inner-city*" schools. Reagan's use of the report repositioned the intent and purpose of *Brown*.

An educational cottage industry was born with conceptual language: disadvantage (a lexicon) for Black and Hispanic students low test scores, low expectations, achievement gap, tool boxes or kits to model "*what works*," school reform, standardized testing and assessment. More significantly, the report was seen as an engine to drive competition into the bedrock of educational teaching and learning. The shift was subtle, and most in the civil rights community and the Black community missed it. Black students for the most part were back to being victims, lacking skill sets.

Susan Eaton commented, "The school desegregation movement did not fail. Rather, the Government failed to actively support desegregation." She goes on to say, "Desegregation was never meant to be a remedy for low test scores. Rather, it was and is one underlying condition with the potential to engender higher-quality schooling, improved race relations, and in the long run, a more democratic, more equal society."[63]

Though *A Nation at Risk* was meant to provide information on how or why our schools were "*failing*," Reagan's Department of Education, headed by Bill Bennett, began to broadcast the "*failing schools narrative*," warning the nation of a "*rising tide of mediocrity*" so severe even our national security was at risk. It was hijacked by the Reagan administration as a boost for choice; as a lever to void the federal government of federal desegregation enforcement including busing as a way to add the lane of cost benefit in education.

Anya Kamentz shares, "the authors of the report admitted that it was flawed from its beginning." She said the authors were convinced that schools were failing; so they went looking for proof. In her article, Kamentz shares the suppression of the Sandia report: "It was not useful to the Administration as it found just the opposite. Most categories of students were showing steady improvement. Conceptually, this did not fit the political needs or the Administration or the bully pulpit of the President."[64]

In 1982, Rev. Jesse Jackson criticized President Ronald Reagan's attacks on busing as an enabler in achieving desegregation for "targeting: not the bus, but us."[65] By 2002, the United States Supreme Court ended the Charlotte, North Carolina, plan, which had launched the era of court-ordered busing.

The bully pulpit of Reagan's legacy may be best captured by Sean Edwards: "What he saw as his mission was clear in his call for abolishing the brand-new federal Department of Education, and it was reflected in his opposition to mandatory busing for school desegregation . . . his antipathy towards teachers' unions and his second-term appointment of a famously combative Secretary of Education who scorned the education establishment."[66]

The legacy of Ronald Reagan within the construct of school desegregation could not be more clear. His charismatic bully pulpit launched a bold, full, and frontal attack on school desegregation.

LEGISLATIVE PROFILE AS PRESIDENT

Continuing its attack on federal courts, the Reagan administration supported legislation that would deprive federal district courts of the ability to order busing remedies and that would allow challenges to existing desegregation orders that required busing. Such legislation would take away the attorney general's power to seek busing remedies. Those federal court remedies had for years—in the 1960s and 1970s—contributed greatly to the increased integration of Black students in the nation's schools.

Drew Days points out:

> Congress had rejected this proposed legislation thus far. If enacted however, the bill could place the Federal Government in a position where, although it could identify a public school district which was operating in violation of the Constitution, it would be powerless to correct the situation. For this reason, justice department officials from the Eisenhower, Nixon, Johnson, and Carter administrations have argued against the legislation's constitutionality.

In fact, "four former attorneys General and three former solicitors general signed a letter in March, 1982 which was sent to members of the senate judiciary committee expressing their unanimous view that congress may not restrict federal court jurisdiction to enforce *Brown* and their opposition to various legislative proposals designed to achieve that result."[67]

The Reagan administration did nothing to put in enforcement mechanisms for Title VI, the guts of the legislative remedy for desegregation. His support of the office of civil rights under Title VI was abysmal. The Reagan administration ushered in a period of assaults on the role of the federal government in school desegregation and an assault on the courts and the law.

NOTES

1. Nathan Glazer (1972, March), *Commentary Magazine, 7*.
2. Edmund Morris (1999), *Dutch: A Memoir of Ronald Reagan* (Random House), 40.
3. Lou Cannon (1991), *President Reagan: The Role of a Lifetime* (Simon & Schuster), 208.
4. Ronald Reagan, Kiron K. Skinner, Annelise Graebner Anderson, and Martin Anderson (2005), *Reagan: A Life in Letters* (Simon & Schuster), 42.
5. Roger Morris (1990), *Richard Milhous Nixon: The Rise of an American Politician* (Henry Holt and Company), 50–51.
6. Morris (1990), *Richard Milhous Nixon*, 69.
7. Morris (1990), *Richard Milhous Nixon*, 74.
8. Martin Anderson (1988), *Revolution* (Harcourt Brace Jovanovich), 54.
9. Anderson (1988), *Revolution*, 55.
10. Cannon (1991), *President Reagan*, 33.
11. Garry Schultz (2004), *Reagan: A Life of Letters* (Free Press), 124.
12. Cannon (1991), *President Reagan*, 88.
13. Reagan, Skinner, Anderson, and Anderson (2005), *Reagan*, 37.
14. Cannon (1991), *President Reagan*, 43.
15. "Ron Flied by the Seat of His Paints?" (1983, December 18), *New York Daily News*.
16. "Public Papers of Ronald Reagan" (1986, April), Ronald Reagan Presidential Library.
17. Cannon (1991), *President Reagan*.
18. Tom Wicker (1991), *One of Us: Richard Nixon and the American Dream* (Random House), 11.
19. Jimmy Carter, Presidential Debate in Cleveland Online by Gerhard Peters and John T. Woolley, The American Presidency Project, https://www.presidency.ucsb.edu/node/217132.
20. Jimmy Carter, Presidential Debate in Cleveland Online.

21. Jimmy Carter, Presidential Debate in Cleveland Online.
22. Kenneth O'Reilly (1996), *Nixon's Piano: Presidents and Racial Politics from Washington to Clinton* (Free Press), 362.
23. Laurence I. Barrett (1984), *Gambling with History: Ronald Reagan in the White House* (Penguin Books), 426.
24. Barrett (1984), *Gambling with History*, 364.
25. O'Reilly (1996), *Nixon's Piano*, 360.
26. Roger Wilkinson (1982), *A Man's Life* (Simon and Schuster), 369–70.
27. O'Reilly (1996), *Nixon's Piano*, 360.
28. *Wall Street Journal*, October 24, 1985.
29. Ronald Reagan (1983), *A Time for Choosing: The Speeches of Ronald Reagan, 1961–1982* (Regnery Gateway in cooperation with Americans for the Reagan Agenda), 169.
30. Randall Kennedy, *Persuasion and Distortion: A Commentary on the Affirmative Action debate*, 1342 fn. 56. *Harvard Law Review*. April, 1986.
31. Drew Days (1984), "Turning Back the Clock: The Reagan Administration and Civil Rights," 339, https://openyls.law.yale.edu/bitstream/handle/20.500.13051/722/Turning_Back_the_Clock_The_Reagan_Administration_and_Civil_Rights.pdf.
32. Days (1984), "Turning Back the Clock," 359.
33. Nancy Reagan, and William Novak (1989), *My Turn: The Memoirs of Nancy Reagan* (Random House), 107.
34. *State of Black America*, 1987, "A Report of the Urban League."
35. Tom Reagan (1987), Interview with Eddie N. Williams.
36. *Milliken v. Bradley*, 418 U.S. 717.814 (1974).
37. Days (1984), "Turning Back the Clock," 346–47.
38. Education Week, https://www.edweek.org/ew/articles/2004/06/16/40/reagan.h23.html.
39. Reagan, Skinner, Anderson, and Anderson (2005), *Reagan*, 708.
40. Ann Reilly Dowd (1986), "What Managers Can Learn from Manager Reagan," *Fortune Magazine*, 41, https://archive.fortune.com/magazines/fortune/fortune_archive/1986/09/15/68052/index.htm.
41. Anderson (1988), *Revolution*, 288.
42. Wicker (1991), *One of Us*, 16.
43. Days (1984), "Turning Back the Clock," 324.
44. *Green v. County School Board*, 391 U.S. 430, 438 (1968).
45. Id. at 439 (Greene).
46. Gary Orfield and Susan Eaton (2015, June 29), "Back to Segregation," *The Nation*, 17, https://www.thenation.com/article/archive/back-segregation/.
47. Brief for the United States as Amicus Curiae in support of Petitioners, *Metropolitan County Bd. of Education v Kelly*, 103 S.Ct, 834 (1983).
48. Motion by the United States to Stay Further Proceedings in the Court of Appeals, *Davis v. East Baton Rouge Parish School Bd.*, No.81–3476 5th Cir. August 16, 1982.
49. Id. at 3. "Greenhouse Issue: New Attacks" (1982, August 12), *New York Times*, A25, col. 1.

50. "School Desegregation: Hearings before the Subcommittee On Civil and Constitutional Rights of the House Comm. on the Judiciary," 97th Cong., 1st session 614 (1981), Statement of William B. Reynolds, Assistant Attorney General, Civil Rights Division.

51. *Cooper v. Aaron*, 358 U.S 1, 16 (1958).

52. *New York Times*, December 4, 1980, A31, col.3.

53. Address, Education Commission of the States, National Project on Desegregation Strategies Workshop at 8 (September 27, 1981), Chicago, IL.

54. Address (September 27, 1981).

55. *New York Times*, November 20, 1981, A14, column 1.

56. O'Reilly (1996), *Nixon's Piano*, 370.

57. Frye Gaillard (1988), *The Dream Long Deferred* (The University of North Carolina Press).

58. L No. 97–15, 95 Stat 357.

59. 20 U.S.C1601 et seq.

60. Emergency School Aid Act.

61. Mark Hertsgaard (1985), *On Bended Knee: The Press and the Reagan Presidency* (*Wall Street Journal*).

62. Box 39, folder "Reagan Issues Busing of the Ron Nessen Papers" at the Gerald R. Ford Presidential Library.

63. Gary Orfield and Susan Eaton (1996), *Harvard Project on School Desegregation* (The New Press).

64. Anya Kamentz (2018), "What a Nation at Risk Got Wrong and Right about U.S. Schools," NPREd.

65. Larry McAndrews (2009, winter-spring), "Not the Bus but Us: George W. Bush and School Desegregation," *Educational Foundations, 23*(1–2), 67, https://eric.ed.gov/?id=EJ869701.

66. Sean Cavanagh (2004, June 16), "Regan's Legacy: A Nation at Risk, Boost for Choice," *Education Week*, https://www.edweek.org/ew/articles/2004/06/16/40reagan.h23.html.

67. Days (1984), "Turning Back the Clock," 1984.

Chapter 8

Conclusion

If one were to characterize the checkered journey of school desegregation over the course of three and a half decades as a musical composition, it would begin on President Dwight David Eisenhower's watch with the peal of a trumpet and end with the muffled sound of a bass on the watch of President Ronald Wilson Reagan.

All seven U.S. presidents from Eisenhower to Reagan were faced with one of the deepest conflicts in the history of the country: school desegregation/integration. Each of them was also equipped with a bully pulpit that was shaped by three factors: the president's belief system, the tone in the public square, and the noise of the political establishment.

The *Brown* court held that *state-imposed* racial segregation in public education was unconstitutional. As Judge Robert Carter, who argued one of the five cases of *Brown*, states, "What makes *Brown* historic is its fall out effect. It radicalized race relations in the country, removing Blacks from the status of supplicants to full citizenship under the law, with entitlement by law to the rights and privileges of all other citizens."[1]

During the implementation of *Brown II*, a series of court decisions on desegregation remedies established another important principle; racial integration in education as part of our democratic fabric is an appropriate societal goal and as a remedy for past discriminations in education.

Sixty-nine years after *Brown*, headlines in newspapers, articles in scholarly journals, and discourse in school districts nationwide still call for processes to address what remains *de facto* segregation in public schools.

"Schools Are Still Segregated and Black Children Are Paying a Price"[2]
"When a School Desegregates Who Gets Left Behind?"[3]
"Reconsidering the Benefits of Desegregation"[4]
The seven presidents' bully pulpit portals include the following

EISENHOWER

Eisenhower stalled on school desegregation by putting his finger in the dike. He was adamant about his respect for the constitution and the rule of law. A national hero, he had goodwill to burn but still did only what he had to do, like sending federal troops to Little Rock to protect schoolchildren from violence when they exercised their constitutional rights. Wasting the opportunity afforded him by his bully pulpit, during his entire tenure as president he failed to make any strong, unambiguous statement in support of *Brown*.

KENNEDY

By 1960, civil rights, including school desegregation/integration, had emerged as an explosive domestic issue. For two and a half years, Kennedy was hesitant to engage with the implications of *Brown*. While he spoke in favor of school desegregation, he was cautious and vacillated. He was reluctant to propose civil rights legislation for fear of losing support of Southern Democrats, whose support he needed to pass his foreign policy proposals.

Upon the events of Birmingham and the defiance of George Wallace, Kennedy's bully pulpit came alive. He was the first president to say that civil rights were a moral issue. He used the bully pulpit to appeal to the American public's sense of honesty, common decency, and notion that change could take place. His eloquent public appeals began to tug at the nation's conscience.

JOHNSON

Even though LBJ was warned that supporting strong civil rights legislation would put him on the path to waning political capital and power, Johnson pushed hard for what he believed was right. As a result of Johnson's courage, the strong Southern Democratic coalition turned Republican almost immediately.

A master negotiator, Johnson finessed the Congress into passing the Civil Rights Act of 1964. Johnson's legislation provided two concrete provisions that provided teeth to the federal government for enforcing compliance among school districts that failed to plan for school desegregation, including lawsuits and the withholding of federal funds.

NIXON

Nixon began the retreat from the federal role in addressing desegregation compliance set forth in the Johnson legislation.

He used "the bus" as a euphemism for law and order, utilizing his bully pulpit to appeal to the Southern base but also to ethnic neighborhoods in the North. Both Southern and Northern Democratic congressional members, along with conservative Republicans, bought into and promoted Nixon's use of "forced busing" as a coded term for antagonism toward the enforcing of *Brown*. He compellingly and consistently used his bully pulpit to oppose the busing of children to achieve racial balance. Nixon's demagoguery on the busing issue was balanced with a calculated push to imply that he was more interested in addressing the quality of education in all schools; desegregation was unnecessary.

Despite Nixon's retreat from a federal role in enforcing *Brown*, two years into his presidency, desegregation was working. Only 8.7% of Black students were attending all-Black schools, and one half of all Black students in the South were in predominantly White schools.

This, however, was not Nixon's doing, and, in fact, it happened in spite of him. Rather, it was the result of the legal and legislative work of his predecessors, Johnson and Kennedy.

FORD

During his 800-plus-day term, in which he was considered moderately conservative, Ford encouraged opposition to busing from his bully pulpit. When he took office, the controversy had moved north, to Boston, Massachusetts. His voice, actions, or lack thereof demonstrated an assertive and negative attitude toward court-ordered enforcement.

While he supported the *Brown* decision, he used his bully pulpit to argue that the courts had gone too far in ordering "forced busing." His message encouraged a violent resistance in Boston.

Ford believed enough in the intent of *Brown* that he was willing to lead the country to find an alternative to court-ordered remedies. By this time he had public support throughout the country in resistance to "forced busing." Ford was most comfortable working with Congress and used his bully pulpit to leverage alternative legislation.

Four months before his loss to Jimmy Carter, Ford unveiled legislation that would have limited court-ordered busing to no more than five years and would have established a process to help communities prepare for desegregation and to find ways to curb violence.

CARTER

Jimmy Carter had a lifetime of experience with the issues surrounding race. Yet more than any other of his predecessors, he was an enigma when it came to school desegregation. He provided strong leadership for many seemingly intractable problems around race. His administration was probably the strongest of the seven in assuring access to job opportunities and higher education regardless of race. He had a supportive constituency in the civil rights community, but his bully pulpit was silent on the dilemma of school segregation; he left matters of school district compliance to his surrogates. He simply dropped the ball.

REAGAN

Reagan's use of the bully pulpit was a disjuncture from that of the other six presidents.

His predecessors had employed their bully pulpits in starts, fits, lapses, steps forward, and steps backward, but nevertheless there was always movement. Reagan never raised his voice for school desegregation.

His bully pulpit used coded language to mischaracterize the intent and practice of school desegregation. Adversity on school desegregation on his watch reached high levels of heated rhetoric among much of the nation's constituencies. Aided by his attorney general, Bradford Reynolds, he brought the progress of school desegregation to a crashing halt.

Approaching seven decades after *Brown*, America's public schools still collectively face the task of eliminating *de facto* school segregation from its purple mountains, from its fruited plains, and from sea to shining sea. None of the presidents succeeding Ronald Reagan, inclusive of George Herbert Bush, William Clinton, George Walker Bush, Barack Hussein Obama, and Donald Trump, has used his bully pulpit to try to resolve this intractable issue of *de facto* public school segregation and to further the promise of *Brown* . . . the racial integration of America's public schools.

NOTES

1. Robert L. Carter (1987–1988), *Michigan Law Review*, 1085.

2. Economic Policy Institute, February 12, 2020.
3. *New York Times*, March 22, 2022.
4. *The Hechinger Report*, August 18, 2022.

Bibliography

Adair, A. V. (1984). *Desegregation: The Illusion of Black Progress*. University Press.
Adams, S. (1961). *First-Hand Report: The Story of the Eisenhower Administration*. Harper and Brothers.
Aistrup, J. A. (1996). *The Southern Strategy Revisited: Republican Top-Down Advancement in the South*. University Press of Kentucky.
Aitken, J. (1993). *Nixon: A Life*. Regnery Publishing INC.
Alba, R. D., Logan, J. R., & Stults, B. J. (2014). "How Segregated Are Middle Class Americans?" *Social Problems. 47*(4), 543–58. https://doi.org/10.2307/3097134.
Alter, J. (2020). *His Very Best: Jimmy Carter, a Life*. Simon & Schuster.
Ambrose, S. (1989). *Nixon, vol. 2: The Triumph of a Politician, 1962–1972*. Simon & Schuster.
Anderson, C. R. (2011). "What Do You See? The Supreme Court Decision in Pics and the Resegregation of Two Southern School Districts." *Teacher College Record, 113*(4), 755–86.
Anderson, J. D. (1988). *The Education of Blacks in the South, 1860–1935*. The University of North Carolina Press.
Anderson, T. J., Lee, E. C. (1967). "The 1966 Election in California." *Western Political Quarterly, 20*, 553.
Apple, M. (2004). "Creating Difference: Neo-Liberalism, Neo-Conservatism and the Politics of Education Reform." *Education Policy, 18*(1), 12–44.
Ashman, C. R. (1972). *The People vs. Angela Davis: The Trial of the Century*. Pinacle.
Back, A. (2003). "Exposing the 'Whole Segregation Myth': The Harlem Nine and New York City's School Desegregation Battles." In J. Theoharis & K. Woodard (Eds.), *Freedom North: Black Freedom Struggles Outside the South, 1940–1980* (pp. 65–91). Palgrave Macmillan.
Baker, T. H. (Interviewer). (1982, October 7). "Homefront USA: Interview of Bayrd Rustin" (Tape #1, Episode 111) [TV series episode]. In R. Ellison (Series Producer),*Vietnam: A Television History*. https//:www.discoverlbj.org/item/oh rust inb-1969061761-74-65.
Ball, S. J. (1990). *Politics and Policy Making in Education*. Routledge.

Baptiste, H. P., & Sanchez, R. (2004). "American Presidents and Their Attitudes, Beliefs, and Actions Surrounding Multicultural Education: A Series of Research Studies in Education Policy (Fourth Installment)." *Multicultural Education, 12*(1), 33–40.

Barone, M. (1990). *Our Country: The Shaping of America from Roosevelt to Reagan*. Free Press.

Bell, D. (1980). *Shades of Brown: New Perspectives on School Desegregation*. Teacher's College.

Bell, T. H. (1986). "Education Policy Development in the Reagan Administration." *The Phi Delta Kappan, 67*(7), 487–493.

Berliner, D. C. & Biddle, B. J. (1995). *The Manufactured Crisis*. Addison-Wesley Publishing.

Berman, A. (2015, September 3). "Op-Ed: How Jimmy Carter Championed Civil Rights—and Ronald Reagan Didn't." *Los Angeles Times*. https://www.latimes.com/opinion/op-ed/la-oe-0906-berman-carter-civil-rights-20150906-story.html

Blight, D. W., & Scharfstein, A. (2012, May 16). "King's Forgotten Manifesto." *The New York Times*.

Blood, T., & Henderson, B. (1996). *State of the Union: A Report on President Clinton's First Four Years in Office*. General Publishing Group.

Blumenthal, S. (2003). *The Clinton Wars*. Plume.

Board of Education of Oklahoma v. Dowell, 498 U.S. 237 (1991)

Bolling v. Sharpe, 347 U.S. 497 (1954)

Booker, C. B. (2000). *African-Americans and the Presidency*. Franklin Watts.

Bourne, P. G. (1997). *Jimmy Carter: A Comprehensive Biography from Plains to Post-Presidency*. Scribner.

Boyarsky, B. (1968). *The Rise of Ronald Reagan*. Random House.

Branch, T. (1989). *Parting of the Waters: American in the King Years*. Simon & Schuster.

Braunstein, P., & Doyle, M. (Eds.). (2001). *Imagine Imagine Nation: The American Counterculture of the 1960s and '70s*. Routledge.

Briggs v. Elliot, 342 U.S. 350, (1952)

Brown v. Board of Education of Topeka, 347 U.S. 483 (1954)

Brown v. Board of Education of Topeka, 349 U.S. 294 (1955)

Brown v. Board: Timeline of School Integration in the U.S. (2012). "Teaching tolerance: A project of the southern poverty law center." http://www.tolerance.org/magazine/number-25- spring-2004/brown-v- board-timeline- school-integration-us.

Brown, C. S. (1973). "Negro Protest and White Power Structure: The Boston School Controversy, 1963–1966." [Doctoral dissertation, Boston University].

Brown, L. (1992). "Group Asks Parents to Pull Students from School Monday. WAAK-UP Calls for Boycott of School District." *Sentinel Voice*.

Brownell, H. (1993). *Advising Ike: The Memoirs of Attorney General Herbert Brownell*. University Press of Kansas.

Brownell, H., & Burke, J. P. (1993). *Advising Ike: The Memoirs of Attorney General Herbert Brownell*. University of Kansas Press

Buchen, P. W. (1976). Memo from Philip W. Buchen to Ford, 4/21/76. Domestic Council, F.L. May, Assoc. Dir. for Housing, Community Affairs, & Communications, Box 8, GRFL.

Burk, R. F. (1985). *The Eisenhower Administration and Black Civil Rights*. University of Tennessee Press.

Campbell, D. (2003). Noam Chomsky on Reagan's Legacy. www.commondreams org /headlines03/0303-09.htm.

Carmine, E. G., & Stimson, J. A. (1990). *Issue Evolution: Race and the Transformation of American Politics*. Princeton University Press

Carnoy, M., & Levin, H. (1985). *Schooling and Work in the Democratic State*. Stanford University Press.

Caro, R. A. (1983). *The Path to Power: The Years of Lyndon Johnson*. Vintage Books.

Caro, R. A. (2003). *Master of the Senate: The Years of Lyndon Johnson*. Random House.

Caro, Robert A. (2012). *The Passage to Power: The Years of Lyndon Johnson*. Vintage Books.

Carroll, P. N. (1990). *It Seemed Like Nothing Happened: America in the 1970s*. Rutgers University Press.

Carter, D. T. (1996). *The Politics of Rage: George Wallace, the Origin of the New Conservatism, and the Transformation of American Politics*. Louisiana State University Press.

Carter, J. (2010) *White House Diary*. Farrar, Stauss and Ginoux.

Carter, J. (2016). *A Full Life: Reflections at Ninety*. Simon & Schuster.

Chester, L., Hodgson, G., and Page, B. (1969). *An American Melodrama: The Presidential Campaign of 1968*. Viking Press, 1969.

Citera. "Bill Clinton's Race Initiative." 105–9.

Clark County School District. (1968). "Status Report on the District's Integration Policy."

Clark County School District. (1983). "A Comparison of Achievement Gains Black Students versus White Students 1980–81 to 1982–83."

Clark County School District. (n.d.) "An Overview of Clark County School District Desegregation."

Clark Hine, D. (2004). "African Americans and the Clinton Presidency: Reckoning with Race, 1992–2000." In T. G. Shields, J. M. Wayne, and D. R. Kelley, *The Clinton Riddle: Perspectives on the Forty-Second President* (pp. 79–91). University of Arkansas Press.

Clinton, W. (2004). *My Life*. Alfred A. Knopf.

Cohen, J. E. (1995). "Presidential Rhetoric and the Public Agenda." *American Journal of Political Science, 39*(1), 87–107.

Congressional Record. (1968). "Ford's Statement on the House Floor Supporting the Fair Housing Act." Congressional Record, H2814.

Crouse, T. (1974). *The Boys on the Bus*. Ballantine Books.

Cummings v. Richmond County Board of Education. 175 U.S. 528, (1899).

Dallek, M. (2000). *The Right Moment: Ronald Reagan's First Victory and the Decisive Turning Point in American Politics*. Free Press.

Dallek, R. (1991). *Lone Star Rising: Lyndon Johnson and His Times, 1908–1960*. Oxford University Press.

Dallek, R. (1999). *Flawed Giant: Lyndon Johnson and His Times, 1961–1973*. Oxford University Press.

Danielson, M. N. (1976). *The Politics of Exclusion*. Columbia University Press.

Davies, G. (2007). "Richard Nixon and the Desegregation of Southern Schools." *Journal of Policy History, 19*(4), 367–94.

Davis v. County School Board in Prince Edward County, 103 F. Supp. 337 (1952).

Days, D. S., III. (1984). "Turning Back the Clock: The Reagan Administration and Civil Rights." *Harvard Civil Rights-Civil Liberties Law Review, 19*(2).

Degregorio, W. A. (1991). *The Complete Book of U.S. Presidents*. Barricade Books. (Original work published 1924)

Dent, H. (1978). *The Prodigal South Returns to Power*. Wiley.

"'Desegregating' St. Louis." (1981, May 22). *Chicago Tribune*; May 22, 1981; ProQuest Historical Newspapers: Chicago Tribune (1849–1988), pg. 19.

Dimond, P. R. (1985). *Beyond Busing*. University of Michigan Press.

Dougherty, J. (2004). *More Than One Struggle: The Evolution of Black School Reform in Milwaukee*. The University of North Carolina Press.

Dreier, P. (2004). *Urban Suffering Grew under Reagan*. www.commondreams.org/views04/061001.htm.

DuBois, W.E.B. (1935). "Does the Negro Need Separate Schools?" *The Journal of Negro Education, 4*(3), 328–35.

Dulles, F. R. (1968). *The Civil Rights Commission, 1957–1965*. University of Michigan Press.

Edsall, T. B., & Edsall, M. (1991). *Chain Reaction: The Impact of Race, Rights, and Taxes on American Politics*. W. W. Norton.

Edwards, G. C., III, & Wood, B. D. (1999). "Who Influences Whom? The President, Congress, and the Media." *American Political Science Review, 93*, 328–44.

Eggen, D. (2005, November 13). "Civil Rights Focus Shift Rolls Staff at Justice." *Washington Post*, A1.

Ehrlichman, J. (1982). *Witness to Power: The Nixon Years*. Simon & Schuster.

Eisenhower, D. (1955, January 6). State of the Union Address.

Eisenhower, D. D. (1963). *Mandate for Change*. DoubleDay.

Eisenhower, D. D. (1981). *At Ease: Stories I Tell to Friends*. Eastern Acorn Press.

Eisenhower, S. (2020). *How Ike Led: The Principles behind Eisenhower's Biggest Decisions*. Thomas Dunne Books.

Epperson, L. (2008). "Undercover Power: Examining the Role of the Executive Branch in Determining the Meaning and Scope of School Integration Jurisprudence." *Berkeley Journal of African-American Law & Policy, 10*(2), 146–80.

Evans, R. & Novak, R. (1966). *Lyndon B. Johnson: The Exercise of Power*. New American Library.

Ewald, W.B. (1981). *Eisenhower the President: Crucial Days, 1951–1960*. Prentice Hall Direct.

Fairclough, A. (1995). *Race and Democracy: The Civil Rights Struggle in Louisiana, 1915–1972*. University of Georgia Press.

Farkas, G., Grobe, R., Sheehan, D., Shuan, Y. (1990). "Cultural Resources and School Success: Gender, Ethnicity, and Poverty Groups Within an Urban District." *American Sociological Review, 55*(1), 127–142.

Feeney, M. (1994). *Nixon at the Movies: A Book about Belief.* University of Chicago Press.

Ferguson, R. F., & Mehta, J. (2004). "An Unfinished Journey: The Legacy of *Brown* and the Narrowing of the Achievement Gap." *Phi Delta Kappan, 85*(9), 656–69.

Fletcher, M. A. (2002, September 16). "Civil Rights Watchdog Once Outspoken Critic: Education Official Softens Controversial Views." *Washington Post*, A17.

Ford, G. R. (1975, January 14). "Remarks on the Anniversary of the Birth of Martin Luther King, Jr." http://www.presidency.ucsb.edu/ws/?pid=4927.

Ford, G. R. (1975, July 1). "Remarks at the Annual Convention of the National Association for the Advancement of Colored People." www.presidency.ucsb.edu/ws/?pid=5037

Ford, G. R. (1976, August 3). "Statement on Signing the Housing Authorization Act of 1976." http://www.presidency.ucsb.edu/ws/?pid=62S8.

Ford, G. R. (1976, February 10). "Message on the Observance of Black History Month." http://fwww.presidency.ucsb.edu/ws/?pid-6288.

Ford, G. R. (1979). *A Time to Heal: The Autobiography of Gerald R. Ford.* Harper and Row.

Ford, G. R. (1987). *A Time to Heal: The Autobiography of Gerald R. Ford.* Easton Press.

Freeman v. Pitts, 503 U.S. 467 (1992)

Gebhart v. Belton, 33 Del. Ch. 144, 87 A. 2d 862 (1952), affirmed 91 A. 2d 137 152 (1952).

Genovese, M. A. (2001). *The Power of the American Presidency: 1789–2000.* Oxford University Press.

Goetz, E. G. (2003). *Clearing the Way: Deconcentrating the Poor in Urban America.* Urban Institute Press

Gonyea, D. (2013, July 4). "The Civil Rights Stand of a Young Gerald Ford." All Things Considered, NPR.

Goodwin, D. K. (2018). *Leadership in Turbulent Times.* Simon & Schuster.

Grant, J. (1968). *Black Protest.* Fawcett World Library.

Green v. County School Board of New Kent County, 391 U.S. 430 (1968).

Greenberg, D. (2004). *Nixon's Shadow: The History of an Image.* W.W. Norton.

Greenhouse, L. (1982, May 7). Busing Bill Backed by Administration. *New York Times*, A1.

Guinier, L. (1998). *Lift Every Voice: Turning a Civil Rights Setback into a New Vision of Social Justice.* Simon & Schuster.

Haldeman, H. R. (1994). *The Haldeman Diaries: Inside the Nixon White House.* G.P. Putnam's Sons.

Hannah-Jane, N. (2015, June 25). "Living Apart: How the Government Betrayed a Landmark Civil Right State." *ProPublica.*

Harvey, G. E. (2014). "Southern Strategy." In J. W. Ely Jr. & B. G. Bond (Eds.), *The New Encyclopedia of Southern Culture: Revised Ed., Volume 10* (pp. 237–256). UNC Press.

Henry, A. J. (2007). *Justice, Presidents and Senators: A History of the U.S. Supreme Court Appointments from Washington to Bush II*. Rowman & Littlefield Publishers.

Hill, K.Q. (1988). "The Policy Agendas of the President and the Mass Public: A Research Validation and Extension." *Journal of Political Science, 42*(4), 1328–1334.

Hill, L. (2004). *The Deacons for Defense: Armed Resistance and the Civil Rights Movement*. University of North Carolina Press.

Hitchcock, W. I. (2018). *The Age of Eisenhower: America and the World in the 1950s*. Simon & Schuster Paperbacks.

Hodgson, G. (1976). *America in Our Time: From World War II to NixonWhat Happened and Why*. Doubleday.

Holmes, S. A. (2001, January 15). "In His Final Week, Clinton Issues Proposals on Race." *New York Times*, A11.

Hughes, E. J. (1972). *The Living Presidency.*. McCann and Geoghegan, Inc.

"(Inviting?) M---- America: J. Frank Dobbs, Texas Bar-----: 1903, 1963." (1963, May 17). Congressional Record in A3138-39.

Jacoby, T. (1998). *Someone Else's House: America's Unfinished Struggle for Integration*. Free Press.

Jamieson, K. H. (1996). *Packaging the President: A History and Criticism of Presidential Campaign Advertising (third edition)*. Oxford University Press.

Johnson, L.B. (1971). *The Vantage Point*. Holt, Rinehart and Winston.

Kalman, L. (2022). *"Right Star Rising: A New Politics, 1974–1980."* The SHAFR Guide Online. https://doi.org/10.1163/2468-1733_shafr_sim180220004.

Kennedy, E. M. (2011). *True Compass: A Memoir*. Grand Central Publishing.

Kent, F. R., Jr. (1953, December 8). "High Court Told It Has Duty to End School Segregation." *Washington Post*.

Kerns, D. (1976). *Lyndon Johnson and the American Dream*. Signet.

Kluger, R. (1971, August 19). Interview with Phillip Elman.

Kluger, R. (1986). *Simple Justice*. Alfred A. Knopf.

Kotlowski, D.J. (2009). *Nixon's Civil Rights: Politics, Principle, and Policy*. Harvard University Press.

Kotz, N. (2005). *Judgement Days: Lyndon Baines Johnson, Martin Luther King, Jr., and the Laws that Changed America*. Houghton Mifflin.

Ladson-Billings, G. (2004) "Landing on the Wrong Note: The Price We Paid for Brown." *Educational Researcher, 33*(7), 3–13.

Ladson-Billings, G. (2006). "From the Achievement Gap to the Education Debt: Understanding Achievement in U.S. Schools." *Educational Researcher 35*(7), 3–12.

Lahman, N. (1998). *The Reagan Presidency and the Politics of Race: In Pursuit of Color-blind Justice and Limited Government*. Prager Publishers.

LaTour, J. (2009). "Battling Reagan, the Union-busting President." DC37 AFSCME ALC-CIO Public Employee Press. 19 July 2012 https://www.dc37.net/wp-content/uploads/about/graphics/pdf/Battling_Reagan.pdf.

Lepore, J. (2018). *These Truths: A History of the United States*. Norton & Company.
Levingston, S. (2017). *Kennedy and King: The President, the Pastor and the Battle over Civil Rights*. Hachette Press.
Levy, P. B. (Ed.). (1998). *America in the Sixties—Left, Right, and Center: A Documentary History*. Praeger.
Lukas, A. (1976). *Nightmare: The Underside of the Nixon Years*. Viking.
Mason, R. (2004). *Richard Nixon and the Quest for a New Majority*. University of North Carolina Press.
Matthews, C. (1997). *Kennedy and Nixon: The Rivalry That Shaped Postwar America*. Free Press.
Matthews, C. (2011). *Jack Kennedy: Elusive Hero*. Simon & Schuster.
McAndrews, L. J. (1997). "Missing the Bus: Gerald Ford and School Desegregation." *Presidential Studies Quarterly, 27*(4), 791–804. http://www.jstor.org/stable/2755180
Minow, M. (2008). "After *Brown*: What Would Martin Luther King Say?" *Lewis & Clark Law Review, 12*(3). ssrn.com/abstract=1276340
Morris, E. (1999). *Dutch: A Memoir of Ronald Reagan*. Random House.
Morrow, F.E. (1963). *Black Man in the White House: A Diary of the Eisenhower Years by the Administrative Officer for Special Projects, the White House, 1955–1961*. Coward-McCann.
Murphy, R, & Gulliver, H. (1971). *The Southern Strategy*. Scribner.
Myrdal, G. (1944). *An American Dilemma: The Negro Problem and Modern Democracy*. Harper & Brothers
National Association for the Advancement of Colored People Legal Defense and Educational Fund, New York, NY. (n.d.) "It's Not the Distance, 'It's the Niggers.' Comments on the Controversy over School Busing." https://eric.ed.gov/?id=ED063430.
Neustadt, R. (1990). *Presidential Power and Modern Presidents*. The Free Press.
Newlon, C. (1964). *L.B.J., the Man from Johnson City*. Dodd, Mead & Co.
Nichols, D. (2007). *A Matter of Justice: Eisenhower and the Beginning of the Civil Rights Revolution*. Simon & Schuste.
Nixon, R. (1967). *The Challenges We Face: Edited and Compiled from the Speeches and Papers of Richard M. Nixon*. Popular Books.
Nixon, R. (1970, March 24). "Statement about Desegregation of Elementary and Secondary Schools." Public papers of the Presidents: Richard M. Nixon. U.S. Government Printing Office
Nixon, R. M. (1962). *Six Crises*. Doubleday.
Nixon, R. M. (1978). *RN: The Memoirs of Richard Nixon*. Grosset & Dunlap.
Norris, M. L. (1989, January 24). "P.G. Sued over Teacher Transfers." *Washington Post*. https://www.washingtonpost.com/archive/politics/1989/01/24/pg-sued-over-teacher-transfers/65fc5cdf-ba47-43c8-a462-b91c9fa68233/.
Numan v. Bartley, *The Rise of Massive Resistance: Race and Politics in the South During the 1950s*, 77 (1969) LSU
O'Reilly, K. (1995). *Nixon's Piano: Presidents and Racial Politics from Washington to Clinton*. Free Press.

Office for Civil Rights. (2004). *Acting Diversity: Race-Neutral Alternatives in Education.* (DOE Publication No. OCR-00029). U.S. Department of Education. www.ed.gov/about/offices/list/ocr/edlite-raceneutralreport2.html

Ogletree, J. C., Jr. (2005). *All Deliberate Speed: Reflections on the First Half-Century of* Brown v. Board of Education. Norton and Company.

Orfield, G. (1969). *The Reconstruction of Southern Education: The Schools and the 1964 Civil Rights Act. 1969.* Wiley-Interscience.

Orfield, G. (1975). *Congressional Power: Congress and Social Change.* Harcourt Brace Jovanovich.

Orfield, G., & Eaton, S. E. (1996). *Dismantling Desegregation: The Quiet Reversal of* Brown v. Board of Education. The New Press.

Oudes, B. (Ed.). (1989). *From: The President: Richard Nixon's Secret Files.* Harper-Collins.

Panetta, L. E. and Gall, P. (1971). *Bring Us Together: The Nixon Team and the Civil Rights Retreat.* Lippincott.

Parents Involved in Community Schools v. Seattle School District, No. 1, 551 U.S. 701, (2007).

"Parents Try Anything to Stop Busing Children." (1971). *Las Vegas Review Journal.*

Pauley, G. (2005). "Remarks of Vice President Lyndon B. Johnson, Memorial Day, Gettysburg, Pennsylvania, May 30, 1963." In E. D. Rigsby & J.A. Aune (Eds.), *Civil Rights Rhetoric and the American Presidency* (pp. 155–197). Texas A&M University Press.

Perlstein, R. (2008). *Nixonland: The Rise of a President and the Fracturing of a Nation.* Scribner.

Peters, G., and Woolley, J. T. (2012). "Political Party Platforms." The American Presidency Project. http://www.presidency.ucsb.edu/ws/index.php?pid=25844

Plessy v. Ferguson, 163 U.S. 537, 16 S. Ct. 1138, 1896.

Plessy v. Ferguson, 163 U.S. 537, 548–57 (1896) Id.

Porambo, R. (2007). *No Cause for Indictment: An Autopsy of Newark.* Melville House.

"Public Papers of the President: Lyndon B Johnson." (1966). U.S. Government Printing Office.

"Public Papers of the Presidents: Gerald Ford." (1979). U.S. Government Printing Office.

Raffel, J. A. (1980). *The Politics of School Desegregation: The Metropolitan Remedy in Delaware.* Temple University Press.

Raffel, J. A. (1998). *A Historical Dictionary of School Segregation and Desegregation: The American Experience.* Greenwood.

Reagan, R. (1982, January 19). "The President's News Conference." http://www.presidency.ucsb.edu/ws/?pid=42476.

Reagan, R. (1983, November 10). "The President's News Conference." http://www.presidency.ucsb.edu/ws/?pid=43228.

Reagan, R. (1983, November 2). "Remarks on Signing the Bill Making the Birthday of Martin Luther King, Jr., a National Holiday." http://www.presidency.ucsb.edu/ws/?pid=40708.

Reagan, R. (1983, October 19). "The President's News Conference." http://www.presidency.ucsb.edu/ws/?pid=40666.

Reagan, R. (1986, May 21). "Remarks and a Question-and-Answer Session with High School Students from the Close Up Foundation." http://www.presidency.ucsb edu/ws/?pid=37314.

Reagan, R. (1986, October 2). "Statement on the Comprehensive Anti-Apartheid Act of 1986." http://www.presidency.ucsb.edu/ws/?pid=36537.

Reedy, G. (1982). *Lyndon B. Johnson: A Memoir*. Andrews McMeel Publishing

Reeves, R. (2001). *President Nixon: Alone in the White House*. Simon & Schuster.

Reichley, A. J. (1981). *Conservatives in an Age of Change: The Nixon and Ford Administrations*. The Brookings Institution.

Rodgers, H. R., Jr.. (1974). "The Supreme Court and School Desegregation Twenty Years Later." *Political Science Quarterly, 89*(4), 751–76

Roosevelt, F. D. (1937). Press Conference.

Rugh, J. S., & Massey, D. S. (2010). "Racial Segregation and the American Foreclosure Crisis." *American Sociological Review, 75*(5), 629–51.

Savage, C. (2007, November 6). "Maneuver Gave Bush a Conservative Rights Panel." *Boston Globe*.

Scammon, R., & Wattenberg, B. (1980). *The Real Majority: An Extraordinary Examination of the American Electorate*. Coward McCann.

"School Desegregation in Clark County, Nevada." (1973). University of Nevada Reno.

Schuman, H., Schuman, H., & Steeh, C. (1997). *Racial Attitudes in America: Trends and Interpretations* (revised edition). Harvard University Press.

Shesol, J (1998). *Mutual Contempt: Lyndon Johnson, Robert Kennedy, and the Feud That Defined a Decade*. W.W. Norton.

Shirbman, D. M. (2013, May 24). "L.B.J.'s Gettysburg Address." *New York Times*.

Shogan, R. (2001). *Bad News: Where the Press Goes Wrong in the Making of a President*. Ivan R. Dee.

Shull, S. A. (1999). *American Civil Rights Policy from Truman to Clinton: The Role of Presidential Leadership*. M.E. Sharpe.

Siddle Walker, V. (1996). *Their Highest Potential: An African American School Community in the Segregated South*. The University of North Carolina Press.

Siddle Walker, V. (2000). "Valued Segregated Schools For African American Children in the South 1935–1969: A Review of Common Characteristics." *Review of Educational Research, 70*, 235–85.

Sidey, H. (1968). *A Very Personal Presidency: Lyndon Johnson in the White House*. Andre Deutch.

Silber, Norman Isaac. (1984). *Reminiscences of Philip Elman: Oral History*. [Transcript]. Columbia Center for Oral History.

Sjoberg, G., Brymer, R., & Farris, B. (1994). *Transforming Urban Education*. Ed. J. Kretovics and E. Nussel (Eds.), pp. 99–108. Allyn and Bacon.

Smith, J. (2016). *Kennedy: The Nine of Us*. Harper.

Spear, A. (1967). *Black Chicago: The Making of a Negro Ghetto, 1890–1920*. University of Chicago Press.

"Special Message to Congress Concerning Federal Assistance to School Construction." (1955, February 8). Eisenhower, PPP, pp. 243–50.
Spitz, B. (1929). *Reagan: An American Journey*. Penguin Publishing Group.
St. John, J. (1976). *Jimmy Carter's Betrayal of the South*. Green Hill Publishers.
"Statement by the President (on H.R. 69)." (1974, August 21). David Lissy Files, Box 4, GRFPL, p.1.
Stern, M. (1992). *Calculating Visions: Kennedy, Johnson and Civil Rights*. Rutgers University Press.
Suburban Segregation from Gerald Ford to Bill Clinton, downloaded from Cambridge Books Online, dx.doi.org/10.1017/CBO978051164354.007.
Sullivan, C. Reporter, *Journal News*, Sunday, Jan. 13, 2013.
Sullivan, P. A., & Goldzwig, S. R. (2003). "Seven Lessons from President Clinton's Race Initiative: A Post-Mortem on the Politics of Desire." In R. E. Denton Jr. and R. L. Holloway (Eds.), *Images, Scandal, and Communication Strategies of the Clinton Presidency* (p. 143–72). Praeger.
Sunstein, C. (2004). "Did *Brown* Matter?" *The New Yorker*, 102–7.
Susan Eaton (Jace?) 2010/Vol 10, No. 4—educationnext.org
Swann v. Charlotte-Mecklenburg 402 U.S. 1, 91 S. Ct. 1267, 28 L. Ed. 2d 554, (1971).
T. Hartman Papers, House of Representatives Subject File, Box 44, GRFL.
Taeuber, K. E., Smock, P. J., & Taeuber, A. F. (1990). "Resignation of Public School Districts, 1968–1986." www.eric.ed.gov/contentdelivery/servlet/ERICServlet?accno=ED325575
The King Center. (2012). "Making of the King Holiday: A Chronology." http://www.thekingcenter.org/making-king-holiday.
The Letters of David Patrick Moynihan. (n.d.). "Daniel Patrick Moynihan: A Portrait in Letters of an American Visionary." (Public Affairs, $35)
The President's Initiative on Race, The Advisory Board's Report to the President. (1998). "One America in the 21st Century: Forging a New Future." Unpublished https://clintonwhitehouse4.archives.gov/media/pdf/PIR.pdf.
"The Prince George's School Case." (1989, January 29). *Washington Post*, D6. https://www.washingtonpost.com/archive/politics/1982/05/22/the-prince-georges-school-case/85b5cab9-a8b1-44e1-99ae-0f58f4fe7588/.
"The Year of the Great Decision." (1954). Report of the Executive Secretary, NAACP REPORT, 1954 C7CG 124 A2 B922 NAACP (1) EL. to NACCP Annual Convention, Jan. 3, 1955, CF/OF 142 A, B 73; Negro Males.
Thomas, Evan. (2016). *Being Nixon: A Man Divided*. Random House Trade.
Thompson, H. S. (1973). *Fear and Loathing on the Campaign Trail '72*. Everest Library.
Tillman, L. (2004). "(Un)intended Consequences? The Impact of the *Brown v. Board of Education* Decision on the Employment Status of Black Educators." *Education and Urban Society, 36*(3), 280–303.
"To Bus or Not to Bus: An Investigation Into the Sixth Grade Plan to Achieve Racial Integration." Clark County, Nevada (1972). S.1.

U.S. Commission on Civil Rights. (1966). "Hearings Before the United States Commission on Civil Rights: Hearings Held in Cleveland, Ohio, April 1–7, 1966." The Commission.
United States Congress. (1966). "Civil Rights, 1966: Hearings Before Subcommittee No. 5, Eighty-ninth Congress, Second Session." U.S. Government Printing Office.
United States Congress. (1966). "Civil Rights: Hearings Before a Subcommittee on the Judiciary United States Senate, Eighty-ninth Congress, Second Session, on S. 3296." U.S. Government Printing Office.
United States v. Brown, 494 F. Supp. 2d 440 (S.D. Miss 2007) (Feb. 17, 2005), aff'd 561 F.3d 420 (5th Cir. 2009).
Wade Henderson, President and CEO, Leadership Conference on Civil Rights et al., to the Honorable Michael B. Mukasey, Attorney Gen., U.S. Dep't of Justice, Rescind the OLC Opinion that Undermines the Credibility of the U.S. Commission on Civil Rights (Jan. 29, 2008), available at www.citizensforethics.org/node/.
Warren, E. (1977). *The Memoirs of Chief Justice Earl Warren.* Doubleday.
Whalen, C., & Whalen, B. (1985). *The Longest Debate: A Legislative History of the 1964 Civil Rights Act.* Seven Locks Press.
Wheeler, L. (1976). *Jimmy Who?: An Examination of Presidential Candidate Jimmy Carter the Man, His Career, His Stands on the Issues.* Barron's Woodbury.
White House Letters to John G. Hannah, Nov. 17, 1965
White, F. C., & Gill, W. J. (1981). *Why Reagan Won.* Regnery Gateway.
Wicker, T. (1991). *JFK and LBJ: The Influence of Personality upon Politics.* Ivan R. Dee.
Wicker, T. (1991). *One of Us: Richard Nixon and the American Dream.* Random House.
Wilkins, R., & Matthews, T. (1982). *Standing Fast: The Autobiography of Roy Wilkins.* Viking Press.
Wilkinson, J. H. (1979). *From Brown to Bakke: The Supreme Court and School Integration: 1954–1978.* Oxford University Press.
Witcover, J. (1977). *Marathon: The Pursuit of the Presidency, 1972–1976.* Viking Press.
Witcover, J. (2005). *The Making of an Ink-Stained Wretch: Half a Century Pounding the Political Beat.* Johns Hopkins University Press.
Woods v. Board of Education of the City of Highland Park, supra, note 2, before the Hon. John Feikens, District Judge at Detroit, Mich., on September 5 and 7, 1961, p. 67. Excerpts from proceedings: 6 Race Rel. L. Rep. 982 (1961)
Woodson, C. G. (2010 [1933]). *The Miseducation of the Negro.* Information Age Publishing.

Appendices

Each of these presidents were men of substance and compelled different peers to look at them in different ways. The following are selected peer perceptions illuminating the character of each man.

APPENDIX A

PRESIDENT DWIGHT D. EISENHOWER

Peer Perceptions

General Lucius Clay, Trusted Transition Team Member

"Resentment was out of character for Ike. He was the least vengeful man I ever knew." He also remarked, "Eisenhower agreed with *Brown* but viewed the ruling as a political burden not a blunder."

Herbert Brownell, Eisenhower's Attorney General

Brownell's commentary on the pressure to get Eisenhower to run for president and Ike's consideration was as follows, "Eisenhower enjoyed great fulfillment at this point in life. A poor boy who was now well off; a popular hero in this country and abroad, and a man with a wide network of friends."[2]

The basic problem of Little Rock was a defiance of federal authority. He took the same action that was enacted during the early days of the country in Shay's rebellion and Door's rebellion.[3] "Eisenhower's appointment to federal judgeship, especially to the 4th and 5th circuit constituted his greatest contribution to the cause of civil rights." He established a "beachhead in the Southern states for the enforcement of the Supreme Court's civil right decision; without it we would have faced a repeat of the Reconstruction period during which the courts played a major role in the undoing of the 14th Amendment."[4]

General Andrew Goodpaster, Supreme Commander of NATO and Superintendent of West Point

> One of the great assets Dwight Eisenhower had in any negotiation was his honesty and trustworthiness. In Eisenhower's own words, "it is essential in the geopolitical struggles that the world knows something about our good intentions, latent strengths, and respect for the rights of others."[5]

Emmet Hughes, Speechwriter

"Eisenhower was determined not to use federal power to push southern states towards dramatic social change. His political faith rested on the slow, gradual power of persuasion." He quotes Eisenhower as saying, "We can't demand perfection in these moral questions. All we can do is keep working towards a goal and keep it high. And the fellow who tells me that you can do these things by force is just plain nuts."[6]

Hughes commented on Eisenhower's perspective of communication between the White House and the public: "To Eisenhower, this communication should be discreet, distant and cool. He scanned the press carelessly and indifferent, he regarded most journalists as impudent inquisitors, he disliked public speeches and political rallies, and he distrusted reports or polls of public opinion. For this President, his office implied its privacy, and to be a President of all the people."[7]

Arthur Larson, Speechwriter

Larson reports that Eisenhower wanted no part of a "strong and unequivocal condemnation of racial discrimination." After working with Eisenhower and listening to his private view, Larson presented a damning conclusion about Eisenhower: "President Eisenhower, during his presidential tenure was neither emotionally nor intellectually in favor of combating segregation in general."[8]

Scotty Reston, Senior New York Times Correspondent

On musing as to why Ike was such a political phenom, Reston suggested, "After a generation of contention, of war, of Depression, of acrimonious divisions in the nation, he was urged to enter the arena precisely because he was an attractive mediator." Reston went on to observe that "Ike had calmed a turbulent [nation] and poured soothing balm on its abrasions."[9]

Earl Warren, Chief Justice of Supreme Court

In his memoir, Earl Warren denounced Eisenhower, as he saw it, for not embracing the *Brown* decision and publicly endorsing it from his bully pulpit. Warren wrote, "I have always believed that President Eisenhower resented our decision in *Brown v. Board of Education* and its progress."[10]

Warren discusses an incident at the White House: The chief justice was invited to one of Eisenhower's "stag dinners," informal gatherings of prominent officials, politicians, and personal friends of the president—at which the issue of the day could be discussed candidly and off the record. During the dinner, Warren relates that "the President went to considerable lengths to tell me what a great man John W. Davis was."

Warren further states that Eisenhower pulled him aside and said, "These are not bad people. All they are concerned about is to see that their sweet little girls are not required to sit in school alongside some big overgrown Negro."[11] Warren is the only source for this statement. Historian and political activists constantly use it.

Frederick Morrow, White House Administrative Officer for Special Projects

"On the whole, those of us who had the privilege of serving under President Eisenhower in the White House not only admired him without reservation, but were devoted to him."[12] Morrow goes on to surmise as to where the fault lay in his response to Ike's lukewarm positions on civil rights:

> For example, [the] President's lukewarm stand on civil rights make me heartsick. I could trust this man never to do anything that would jeopardize the civil rights or the personal dignity of the American Negro, but it was obvious that he would never take any positive giant step to prove that he unequivocally stood for the right of every American to walk this land in dignity and peace, clothed with every privilege—as well as every responsibility—accorded a citizen of our constitution. His failure to clearly and forthrightly respond to the Negro's plea for a strong position on civil rights was the greatest cross I had to bear in my eight years in Washington.[13]

APPENDIX B

PRESIDENT JOHN FITZGERALD KENNEDY

Peer Perceptions

George Smathers: Senator from Tennessee

Kennedy was "always greatly interested in civil rights. . . . Put it this way—not civil rights legislation so much, but civil rights because he was against discrimination. I think he felt that, as an Irishman, somewhere along the line he had been discriminated against. I don't know, but I did get the feeling that he felt that other Irishmen had felt the sting of prejudice."[14]

James A. Burke: U.S. Representative of Massachusetts

> I first started in politics in the state legislature, in 1937 and John F. Kennedy came along right after World War II. He was a very young man and he was a different type of a public figure. There was something about him, I don't know how to describe it, but he had a tremendous appeal to everyone; older people, young people, youngsters, children, everybody seemed to want to grasp his hand, and he had a tremendous effect on the body politic during those years. He was an idealist, and yet at the same time he was a realist in many ways.[15]

Simeon Booker: Jet Magazine Reporter Who Traveled as Part of the Press Corp

> What JFK managed to do was to keep the trust alive, in a way Eisenhower had failed to do. . . . He did it, in large part, by the force of his words and his own powerful personality, emphasizing time and again that he set a goal for himself, for which he expected to be accountable. Blacks saluted the President for appointing Negroes to high offices [and for] breaking down many barriers in informal ways.

Booker goes on to say, "Thus Kennedy captured the heart of Black Americans as many Blacks saw it. Lincoln freed us, FDR gave us jobs, and JFK gave us pride in ourselves."[16]

Walter Cronkite: Journalist and Broadcaster for CBS Evening News

The interviewer stated to Cronkite that Kennedy had a reputation for "having a particularly agile mind."

> "Did you think he was unusually smart, gifted, quick?" Cronkite responded, "He was particularly so. He had a great sense of humor, and he employed it frequently, very well. It was a very controlled sense of humor and he never got out of line with it . . .
> "And, of course he was extremely bright . . . he learned quickly in office, and he became presidential much more rapidly than might have been expected. Kennedy's problem, of course, throughout his too short term in office was there was this arrogance to run for office in the first place.
> "It almost required one-on-one relationships to build back the kind of confidence in the Senate that was going to aid him and put through his program. This was one of the things that delayed him, I think on the whole civil rights issue. He knew it was right, and he wanted to do what was right. But he couldn't bring the majority together."[17]

Jesse L. Jackson Sr.: Advisor to Martin Luther King Jr.

> The election of John F Kennedy felt like a euphoric moment for Black America. The Kennedys not just said segregation was illegal, they said it was immoral. It was the first time I ever heard a prominent White politician say that segregation was an abomination. That was a big deal.[18]

Nikita Sergei Khrushchev: First Secretary of the Communist Party of the Soviet Union (1953–1964)

In an interview with a *New York Times* reporter, Khrushchev commented, "The advantages Eisenhower had over Kennedy were that he was an older man, a hero of World War II who commanded great respect in the U.S. . . . President Kennedy is in a different position. Politically, he has a broader outlook. When I talked with him in Vienna, I found him a worthy partner."[19]

Walter Lippman: Columnist, New York Herald Tribune

> It has been truly impressive to see the precision of Mr. Kennedy's mind . . . his immense command of the facts, his instinct for the crucial point, his singular lack of demagoguery and sloganeering, his intense concern and interest in the subject itself, the stability and steadfastness of his nerves and his coolness and his courage, and through it all have transpired the recognizable marks of

Jacqueline B. Kennedy: First Lady of the United States

"History made him what he was. He sat and read history. This little boy in his bed, so much of the time. All the time he was in his bed, this little boy was reading history, was reading Marlborough. He devoured the Knights of the Round Table and he just loved that song." She goes on to say, "He was such a simple man. He was complex too. He had the hero, idealistic side, but then he had that other side, the pragmatic side. His friends were all his old friends. He loved his Irish Mafia."[21]

Louis E. Martin: Political Advisor to Presidents Kennedy, Johnson, and Carter; Founder of the Joint Center for Political and Economic Studies, Labeled "The Godfather of Black Politics"

I think that Kennedy was an exciting personality. This new spirit he brought with him symbolized by everything he did and said put the civil-rights issue in a perspective that we had never had it before. It became not only good Americanism, it was also a sophisticated thing. Everything . . . I mean he really excited people.

So I would say he helped build a kind of climate in the country at large for a greater tolerance and greater concern about the inequities of society and a greater receptivity to the forward movement. Although he didn't live to actually make the moves, I think he did help create a receptivity to them.[22]

Eleanor Roosevelt: First Lady and Wife of Franklin Roosevelt

On the occasion of Kennedy's visit with Mrs. Roosevelt just after the immediate death of a granddaughter, she remarked, "That young man behaved with such sensitivity and compassion throughout that whole day. He gave me more comfort than almost anyone around me, my family, or anybody else. The manner in which he treated me during the day of his visit won me—as did the many things he believed in and what he wanted to do."[23]

Arthur Schlesinger Jr.: American Historian

He was only six months older than I was, but he was the most spectacular, extraordinary man in my whole generation. He was an unfettered man. And I was caught by his charm, his concern for the country, his vision of the future, his irony, his humanness, his rational view of issues. His personal charm was enormous.[24]

Adlai E. Stevenson: Twice Democratic Candidate for President and U.S. Delegate to United Nations in the Kennedy Administration

> I still think that maybe this excitement of politics is a kind of fountain of youth. I like Jack. He's very bright, he has a full knowledge of contemporary affairs and problems—everything from housing to foreign affairs, he's very hardworking, energetic, does his homework. Whether he has a basic philosophy, I don't know. How deep he is, I don't know. It's a hard thing to measure in a man. He has this instinctive feel for politics that these Irish pols have, the Honey Fitzgerald instinct, and you should never underrate it.[25]

Robert C. Weaver: Administrator, Housing and Home Finance Agency (1961–1966)

> In response to a question by the interviewer of troubles during President Kennedy's time . . . Weaver responded, "Well, I think at times, I, as many people who worked in this administration, probably felt that there was over cautions on the part of the President. I for one never translated this into a feeling of lack of belief of his commitment to do what he had expressed as his views and his hopes but as a part of two things.
>
> "First of his own personality because this was a rather thoughtful and rather—I wouldn't say cautious—but certainly not a frivolous man: and of course the other thing which has been said so frequently is the fact that being a politically sophisticated person he was conscious of the fact that he did not come in by any landslide—he did not have any great mandate from the American people.
>
> "Kennedy was more a man of ideas and a man of concepts than a man of personal relationships in the sense of being able to work with people and adjust himself and adapt himself to what one has to do in order to, apparently, get legislation through in this country. I don't think he was ever as much at ease with the Congress as was Lyndon Johnson and other Presidents."[26]

Roy O. Wilkins: Twenty-Two-Year Executive Director of the National Association for Colored People (NAACP)

> When John F. Kennedy became President later that year, everyone expected him to come in and tear up the pea patch for civil rights. Through all the years I knew and watched Kennedy, I did not for a moment doubt his moral fervor and his sympathy for Black Americans was real enough as well, but getting him to turn those emotions into tangible political action was a matter of an entirely different order.

Until the last six months of his life he moved forward very, very cautiously on civil rights. One of the hardest problems the NAACP faced in those years was to complete his education on race to keep his feet to the fire on Capitol Hill.[27]

APPENDIX C

PRESIDENT LYNDON BAINES JOHNSON

Peer Perceptions

Carl B. Albert: Former House Majority Leader and Speaker of the House

He said to me that if there was anything he was going to do in his Administration, it was to give the Negro American his basic Constitutional rights, that he had been discriminated against ever since the country began, and that he thought he was man enough—or words to that effect—to put an end to it; and that he thought one man was just as good as another, and it didn't make any difference who he was.

We'd had certain forms of it up during my tenure in Congress several times. We'd always run up against two things. One was the civil-rights issue, and the other was the religious issue—so that one or the other would bog these things down every time, and it was never possible to get a bill on the President's desk ... and I would say that along with the 1964 Civil Rights Act was the great Elementary and Secondary Education Act.[28]

Stewart Alsop: Syndicated Columnist for Newsweek Magazine *and* The Saturday Evening Post

I think the story of Lyndon Johnson is a very sad story because in many ways he had great qualities, qualities of genuine greatness. He's a large-minded man, and he's a patriot in a kind of old-fashioned way, but in a way in which I admire. He had really enormous achievements in his first two or three years as president, and then he shot that albatross and then the whole road was down thereafter. He never could bring himself to realize what deep, deep trouble he was in until March 31, 1968. And suddenly the reality was right up in front of him.[29]

Joseph A. Califano: Domestic Policy Czar in the Johnson Administration and Former Secretary of Health, Education, and Welfare under President Jimmy Carter

He's a strong, powerful, highly intelligent, very articulate, good arguing man. He knew how to argue. You'd have a hell of an argument with him about a particular problem, and he might be annoyed at the moment, but that never lasted. That never lasted. And after you got to know him, my own judgment was that it wasn't really very important. If you couldn't take that kind of a thing from a man who was under the kind of pressure he was under, then you didn't belong in the White House.[30]

Elizabeth Carpenter: Aide to President Johnson, Secretary to First Lady Bird Johnson

I think that he's the man in whom you saw ambition, and ambition in the best sense of the word, not only for himself, but for you too. To me, that's one of the real qualities of the President. He extracts the best from the people around him. He thinks I can do something better than I can really do it, Joe; but because he thinks so, I try to do it better. To me that's a fantastic quality of leadership.[31]

Hodding Carter Jr.: Editor of the Delta Democrat-Times

Carter was seen as a gradualist on civil rights.

And I'll tell you a very interesting thing. This would be helpful to believe. He was a rough talking guy—is a rough talking guy. About eight years ago at the meeting of the American Society of Newspaper Editors, he spoke—he was then just Vice President—to the American Society on the space program.

After the meeting was over, then he said, "I'm going to name a few honorary Texans and take them into a meeting with me." And he said, "Hodding, I'm going to make you an honorary Texan for this because I'm going to say some things." And he did. He said, "You sons-of-bitches have got to find out that the world doesn't belong to all one group of people, that this is the Black man's world as well as the White man's world." . . . What I think about Lyndon Johnson is that he's a man of courage who believes implicitly in what he said he stood for.[32]

Reverend Theodore Hesburgh: President of the University of Notre Dame

It took a lot of sheer courage for a southerner to stand up before both houses of Congress and say, "We shall overcome." And I don't think he was doing it for play acting, I think he really meant it. I remember his voice quavering a little as he said it, and it took a lot of courage to say it because of all of the undertones of Martin Luther King and everything else that was behind that in the whole movement in the South.[33]

Hubert Humphry Jr.: Former Vice President with Lyndon Johnson 1965–1969

But the point is that whenever you had the leader with you, you knew that you were gaining some support. Because Johnson got votes by whispering in ears and pulling lapels, and nose-to-nose. You have just almost got to see the man. He'd get right up on you. He'd just lean right in on you, you know. Your nose would only be about—he was so big and tall he'd be kind of looking down on you, you see, and then he'd be pulling on your lapels and he'd be grabbing you and just literally.

Even if he wasn't asking you to vote for something, he'd be talking about the bills in such a way that you knew what he had in mind. Johnson always was able to take the measure of a man. He knew those that he could dominate, he knew those that he could outmaneuver. Right off the bat he sized you up. Johnson knew how to woo people. He was a born political lover. It's a most amazing thing.

Many people look upon Johnson as the heavy-handed man. That's not really true. He was sort of like a cowboy making love. He wasn't one of these Fifth Avenue, Madison Avenue penthouse lovers. He was from the ranch. But what I mean is he knew how to massage the senators. He knew which ones he could just push aside, he knew which ones he could threaten, and above all he knew which ones he'd have to spend time with and nourish along, to bring along, to make sure that they were coming along.

He was masterful at timing. He never wasted his shots. He reminded me of an army that had a limited amount of ammunition and had to meet a massive attack. And he saved his ammunition. Lots of people in politics keep shooting all the time, and first of all they run out of ammunition; secondly, they become such bad shots they don't hit anything because they've never learned how to conserve their ammunition.[34]

Russell B. Long: Senator from Louisiana 1948–1987

[My] first recollection of him was a very bright young man with a twinkle in his eye and a winning smile. He had a way of looking you in the eye and turning the personality on and making his point. He was a great salesman. He was the kind of fellow who sell ice boxes to Eskimos. I got to know him very intimately thereafter as the years went by, working with him on different things. We had common interests, for example, with regard to the Tidelands bill and various and sundry other bills where Louisiana and Texas had a community of interest.

On the 1957 Civil Rights Bill, Long recalled:

Here's how I recall that: when the matter came to final passage Lyndon felt that the South had been accommodated to the greatest extent that it could be accommodated, and he also thought that it was a meritorious bill. And in view of the fact that he was going to vote for it, coming from a state that was part of the old Confederacy, he was hoping that as many southern Democrats as conscientiously could go along with it could lean the extra mile and go along with that bill.[35]

Thurgood Marshall: Associate Supreme Justice of the U.S. Supreme Court

Honorable Justice Thurgood Marshall responded in an interview on Johnson's role on the elimination of Part III of Eisenhower's 1954 Civil Rights Act:

It was just barely progress because it had been a hundred years—eighty years—since we'd had one. The smallest slice was good rather than the whole loaf of bread. But it was understandable in my book because it was a strictly political move of getting something done. But when we'd been fighting since 1909 for something, it was good. Then when we looked at it, we had a different feeling.

We fought to the bitter end on that. Yet as you look back, it was great progress, it seems to me, to get them to move at all. I don't know, and I guess nobody would know, just what was sold in there and how it was sold. Whether we could have gotten more or not I don't know. Nobody will know except—well, Lyndon Johnson would know and those people that were running that inner corps of the Senate in those days.

You see, as I looked at him as a senator and leader, they always said he was a great compromiser, but I've always thought that he had the compromise in his pocket when the thing started each time. He just waited for the right time to take it out. He intended to wipe out as much of White discrimination out as he could. He intended to be to this century what Abraham Lincoln was to the last century, and he was going to do it.

I frankly believe if he had had four more years, he just about would have done it. I mean, he rebelled at the discrimination against women—women judges. He always did. He said he wanted to leave the presidency in a position that there was no government job with a race tag on it—none! That's what he was driving at. He would constantly saying, "If you've got any ideas, let me have them. If you don't want to bother with me, give them to Ramsey or Nick or somebody like that. But if there's any way we can break through, Let me know. I just think Lyndon Johnson, insofar as minorities, civil rights, people in general, the inherent dignity of the individual human being—I don't believe there has ever been a President to equal Lyndon Johnson—bar none!"[36]

George Reedy, Senate Staffer, Close Advisor and Press Secretary in the White House

Reedy portrayed Johnson's character as complicated.

> ... a magnificent, inspiring leader ... one minute and 'an insufferable bastard' the next. He goes on to say, "He was an example of what the Japanese call the contradiction of opposites. ... Driven, tyrannical, crude, insensitive, humorless ... he was also empathetic, shy, sophisticated, self-critical, witty and magnanimous.[37]

> The man had a remarkable capacity for persuading people to work together even when they didn't like each other very much. He was equally at home with conservative Richard B Russell of Georgia and liberal Stuart Symington of Missouri. Reedy posits as to Johnson's claim to be free from racial prejudice, "The man had less bigotry in him than anybody else I have ever met."[38]

Bayard Rustin: Civil Rights Leader and One of the Major Organizers of the 1963 March on Washington

Rustin responded that his first impression of Johnson in regard to his attitude toward civil rights or "the Negro" was weak:

> I felt that the Civil Rights Bill of 1957, in which Johnson was intensely involved was very weak, but a very important bill, largely because it was the first really important bill.
> Curiously enough, Johnson's behavior as vice president caused me to write an article two days after Kennedy's assassination, in which I said that I didn't think people ought to be fearful; that Truman had a fairly atrocious record as a senator, but that in fact Truman who began to open up, with the commission he appointed, a real federal concern in the civil-rights question; that under some pressure from Randolph he had integrated the Armed Forces, and that perhaps a southerner would be able to do more than a Yankee, particularly with a Boston accent, to get some things done in Congress that no one else had.[39]

Arthur Schlesinger: Historian, Advisor to Presidents Johnson and Kennedy, Pulitzer-Prize Winner for History in 1946, Pulitzer-Prize Winner for Biography in 1966

> For all his—his devastating instinct for the weaknesses of others, his unlimited capacity for self-pity, he was at the same time a man of brilliant intelligence, authentic social passions, and deep seriousness.[40]

Herman E. Talmadge: Former Governor of Georgia, Southern Conservative—from Georgia 1957–1981, Boycotted the 1964 Democratic National Convention after President Johnson Signed the Civil Rights Act of 1964

Johnson, I think, had the closest personal relations with members of the Senate of probably any President in the history of the country. Of course, he came up, you know, through the legislative branch. I think he was more legislative-oriented than any President perhaps in the history of the country. I think probably he was better trained for the presidency than any President in the history of this country.

He was a legislative wizard, as I've tried to point out in my previous remarks. I think his major strength was demonstrated as Majority Leader, when he could see the ebb and flow of a hundred strong personalities with different views, and this one pulling this way and the other one pulling the other way and this little group that way and this little group neutral, He could see what it would take to effect a compromise to achieve a given fact.

He was the greatest parliamentary tactician I ever saw; that was his greatest strength in my judgment. And what about his greatest personal weakness, again, as opposed to the political weakness? I would say his greatest personal weakness was fear of criticism, of not being loved, of being disliked.[41]

Strom Thurmond, Senator from South Carolina Elected in 1954, Introduced the "Southern Manifest" in 1966

His style was to gain all the power. He was chairman of just about every committee on the Democratic side that had power. A lot of senators didn't like that but they didn't say much because he was in the position to help them get better committees if they wanted them, or to help them in various other ways, such as getting bills through the Senate.

I cited Lyndon's Senate record and showed it was much more conservative than John Kennedy's Senate record, and the delegation decided to vote for Lyndon as I had recommended. But later when he became president, after President Kennedy was assassinated, he took a different turn and went further to the left. He was about the best I ever saw at maneuvering and carrying his point.

He just had unusual power, more than any leader has ever had while I have been in the Senate. Whether you liked it or not, that's the way he operated. The Southerners were the conservatives in the Democratic Party. They felt it was better to have a Southerner even if it were Lyndon than not to have a Southerner as majority leader.

A lot of the Southerners bickered and objected to the way he operated and objected to all the power he was accumulating under himself, but I think they still felt it would be better to have him. They thought if he got elected president, too, that it would be to the advantage of the South to have him. But, of course, after he got to be president he didn't show the South many favors.[42]

George Herbert Walker Bush: 41st President of the United States

He was the quintessence of Middle America, who touched deep chords of response in millions of our fellow citizens. As President, upholding what he termed "the silence majority" from Dallas to Davenport and Syracuse to Silver City, he loved America's good quiet, decent people and spoke for them.[43]

Roy Wilkins: Executive Director of NAACP 1965–1967, Active in NAACP Since 1931

In responding to the conventional talk of Johnson's credited role in the passage of Eisenhower's 1957 Civil Rights Act:

We feel that Mr. Johnson became convinced that the '57 Act which laid heavy emphasis on the right to vote was being consistent with his basic American position that every American ought to have access to the ballot box and we ought to make decisions by a majority of the vote. He believed basically in this. I feel that the '57 Act, he believed, with its emphasis on voting had the best chance of enactment and also was the kind of civil rights act for which he could vote without having to apologize for it in his home district.

In fact, Mr. Baker, I can't think of any more fitting way to bring this interview to a close than to say that in my own personal estimation, and I had the privilege of talking with the President on many occasions and of enjoying a relationship with him that I never expected to enjoy in the light of his allegiances and my own allegiances—say prior to 1957. But I grew to believe that the man is absolutely sincere on this question of opportunity and race. He has risen above his background.[44]

Robert Hardesty: Speechwriter, College President

His first state of the Union address in which he declares war on poverty, made it clear that he was not going to settle for the status quo. He had decided to rip the glittering cellophane wrap off our society and force us to look at what lay underneath—poverty, injustice, illiteracy, sickness, hunger.

To watch LBJ in action was to watch a master at work. When he was giving a speech, he didn't just speak to people, he didn't just address them. He courted them, he wooded them. He used every opportunity he had to sell his programs and to convert his critics. He believed, as Teddy Roosevelt did, that the Presidency is a "bully pulpit" and he never missed a chance to preach the gospel according to LBJ.[45]

APPENDIX D

PRESIDENT RICHARD MILHOUS NIXON

Peer Perceptions

Robert Finch: Secretary of Health, Education, and Welfare

Finch says of Nixon. "He was very conscious of his hard-scrabble background, and that marked him in (certain aspects of his political life) where it was 'me against the world.' He was proud of the fact that he earned his spurs."[46]

Gerald Ford: President of the United States

> Dick Nixon believed fundamentally in responsible civil-rights policy on the part of the Federal Government. I don't think that he favored mandatory busing. He didn't go as far as the liberals wanted. But he was more liberal than most conservatives.[47]

Theodore Hesburgh: Chairman of the U.S. Civil Rights Commission

Hesburgh wrote, "The President's posture . . . had not been such as to provide the clear affirmative policy direction necessary to assure that the full weight of the federal government will be behind the fight to secure equal rights for all minorities."[48]

H.R. Halderman

Halderman remarked,

> Coming out of his Quaker background, his view was that all people are equal—different, maybe, but equal. He clearly recognized the need for making progress in race relations, but he was adamant that it should not be made in a demographic show business way, but in a realistic way.
>
> He argued that—not on the integration of the schools—but the desegregation of schools.[49]

Richard Kleindienst: Deputy Attorney General

> He is one of the brightest, broad-gaged able man, who ever held that office. He was able to conceptualize foreign affairs and domestic problems. One of the

problems he had—and it might have been his great, limiting factors—was that he carried around in him grudge; He permitted himself to develop thoughts of retribution and revenge.[50]

Herbert Klein: Nixon's White House Communications Director

He didn't see a hatred of the easterners but rather, "a feeling of a poor boy from a small store in a small town" who kinda wished that he had "some of the trappings that go into being a Yale graduate."[51]

Eleanor Holmes Norton

There have been two civil-rights Nixons, neither of them ever particularly principled. The more benevolent has moved only with calculation, taking opposition when least seemed least likely but stopping short when challenged. The other seems to have enjoyed leading a popular retreat as the majority indicated those gains it could not stomach. Both these Nixons were beholden to the idea of the supremacy of majority preference.[52]

APPENDIX E

PRESIDENT GERALD RUDOLPH FORD

Peer Perceptions

William Coleman: Secretary of Transportation under Gerald Ford

In response to a question that probed whether the president overrode Coleman's office on anything, Coleman stated,

> No, I can't think of an instance, but I know of an instance where he wanted to override me. Ed Levi (Attorney General) came in one day to a cabinet meeting and his first issue was what to do with New York. Ford kind of passed over that, and the other issue was the busing in Boston. The attorney general said we should stay out of that and his solution was to file a brief on the side of the White parents . . . that it was illegal and everything, and I finally said you know this really amazes me. You talk about the first problem and you've got one mayor who is supposed to spend all the money and do everything, but yet when you

talk about a federal judge who is the only one trying to change the system, that you shouldn't let him do that and I went on and on.

President Ford finally said, "You know. Bill, I never believed in bussing. When I played football, even when I got hurt, I still walked to school." I said Mr. President, If you would go on television and say that's the reason why you're against it, I'll support you. He kind of laughed and we stayed out of the case.[53]

David Gergen: Counsel to Nixon, Ford, Reagan, and Clinton

In discussing the image popularized by journalist and selected press that Jerry Ford was inept, bumbling and clumsy Gergen points out in his book, "Those of us around him in government knew he was more intelligent and more physically graceful than the press said and we struggled to help people see the man we worked for each day, But in retrospect, most of us inside did not take the full measure of the man either. I wish I had."[54]

Congressman Alan Cranston: Liberal Democrat of California

Upon Ford's nomination for vice president, he said, "I doubt if there has ever been a time when integrity has so surpassed ideology in judging a man for high office."[55]

Congressman M. Griffith: Democrat of Michigan

> In all of the years I sat in the house, I never knew Mr. Ford to make a dishonest statement or a statement half-truth or half-false.[56]

Thomas Riley Jr. (Tip O'Neill): Speaker of the House

> God has been good to America, especially during difficult times. At the time of the civil war, he gave us Abraham Lincoln and at the time of Watergate, he gave us Geral—the right man at the right time who was able to put our nation back together again.[57]

David Broder: Washington Post *Columnist*

> In an odd, inexplicable way, the truth as begun to dawn on people in the final days of Gerald Ford's tenure that he was the kind of President that Americans wanted—and didn't know they had.[58]

Ron Messen: White House Press Secretary for Ford

> Unlike politicians who carefully calculate for decades how their every word and deed will sound and look when they eventually run for the White House, Ford moved into the oval office without having his persona distorted by lust for the presidency. The public sensed this genuineness. What a relief to have a regular person as president, particularly after the imperial presidencies of Nixon and Johnson, Ford was the "man next door."

Tom Brokaw: Journalist

> As a journalist I was especially grateful for his appreciation of our role, even when we challenged his policies and taxed his patience without constant presence and persistence. We could be adversaries but we were never his enemy, and that was a welcome change from his predecessor's time.[59]

APPENDIX F

PRESIDENT JIMMY CARTER

Peer Perceptions

Christopher Lasce

> The most intelligent politician who has risen to national prominence in a long time.[60]

Walter Mondale: Carter's Vice President

Mondale served in the US Senate from 1964–1976 through the Nixon and Ford years.

Carter says of his choice, "both geographically and politically, his knowledge and interest supplemented mine. . . . I trusted his judgment, honesty and frankness."[61]

Barack Obama: 44th President of the United States

Obama reflected that Carter had been misunderstood and that historically he should fare better. "He was mocked for the solar panels, but he was prescient and he brought environmental concerns out of the counterculture and directly into US policymaking. He introduced an explicit language around human rights and what had been and what had been an afterthought in foreign policy."

Obama goes on to say his successors learned from him that "it wasn't enough to talk about America as being a beacon for freedom as JFK or Ronald Reagan did but that it had to mean something."[62]

Andrew Young: Former U.S. Ambassador to the United Nations

> Carter understood better than anybody running the two major problems facing America, race and poverty.

Joseph A. Califano: Domestic Policy Czar in the Johnson Administration and Former Secretary of Health, Education, and Welfare under President Jimmy Carter

> It was nevertheless remarkable that a democratic president could go through almost all of his term without delivering a severent, ringing, major public address on civil rights. (Until his campaign attempt to brand Ronald Reagan as a racist) Carter dealt with civil rights issues when he had to. But he did not reach out with the kind of public energy and passion I thought was needed after the setbacks of the Nixon years to lead the nation or to break new ground.

Kenneth W. Stein: The First Permanent Director of a Carter Center

> Carter's strategic objectives were often more far-reaching than the short term policies to which the U.S government was inevitably limited. He knew where those policies ultimately had to go. Yet, he was often five years ahead of his time.[63]

APPENDIX G

PRESIDENT RONALD WILSON REAGAN

Peer Perceptions

Ralph David Abernathy: Civil Rights Leader and Lieutenant to Martin Luther King

In response to questioning of his support for candidate Ronald Reagan:

> Well I did it for the simple reason first. I did not believe that President Carter could lead the nation forward at that juncture. He is a good man but I just did not feel that you could run the country as he had run the state of Georgia and he did not have, around him, staff that was able to do that. Secondly, I supported Ronald Reagan because he was talking about jobs and income and I went on with that side of my political life and thirdly, I believe that young Black people should participate in both parties.[64]

Meg Greenfield: Editor of the Washington Post

> His leadership style, the long waiting out of the adversary, the immobility meanwhile, the refusal to give anything until the las moment, the willingness, nonetheless finally to yield to superior pressure or force in particular circumstances on almost everything, but only will something to show in return and only if the final deal can be interpreted as pitching the original. Reagan objected.[65]

Lyn Nofziger: Nixon's White House Counsel

> He is a very amiable person. There was, at the same time—and I always felt it—a kind of veil between him and the rest of the world; there was that final bit that you couldn't penetrate. Even Nancy mentioned this at one time. There was a protective mechanism, perhaps because of his father or mother . . . But I never felt that you got clear inside Ronald Reagan which maybe was fine. [66]

Martin Anderson: Senior Fellow at Hoover Institute

> The problem people have in understanding Reagan is that they compare him to something in their own lives. That doesn't work, because he was unique, he was different. He had a style I had never seen before and never seen since. He was the most warmly ruthless man I've ever seen. When he was going to get

something done he did not want to be in his way. He didn't take any pleasure in hurting people but you were gone if you were in his way.[67]

Jim Miller: Budget Director (1985–1984)

He was a man whose policies were so much in tune with what the country needed. He was very predictable. If you go back and look at his speech, the 1964 speech, it's all there.

He was an achiever from the very beginning . . . and had a great experience as governor of California. . . . But that time between his being governor of California and his doing all the circuit speeches gave him time to think about all these things. He wrote out all these scripts. . . . Some people in the media said 'oh he had writers etc' they were not writers . . . it was Ronald Reagan.

As Analise Anderson and Karen Skinner show in the book they edited, *In His Own hands*, he wrote those things and he thought through those things. And so when he became President he knew where he was going, he knew his philosophy, and he knew his direction.[68]

James Addison Baker III: United States Secretary of State

Like Jimmy Carter in 1976, Ronald Reagan had run as an outsider who criticized the Washington status quo. Unlike Carter, however, we needed to make plans to extend an immediate olive branch to Congress. I knew that President Reagan would have his hands full with a Democratic-controlled House that he had campaigned against vigorously. So it was even more essential to keep the lines of communication open and civil with Capitol Hill.[69]

Ron Reagan: Atheist Activist and Son of Ronald Reagan

Tenderhearted and sentimental in his personal dealings he could nevertheless have difficulty extending his sympathies to abstract classes of people—an obliviousness that was understandably taken for callousness.[70]

James Nuechterlein: Professor of American Studies, Valparaiso University

Reagan's leadership was above all a triumph of personality. His eloquence, charm, courage (recall his behavior after the assassination attempt) and remarkable sense of self-revived America's pride in the presidential office and by extension in the nation itself. No president in memory has displayed so healthy an ego and Reagan's most adamant political opponents concede his fundamental personal decency.[71]

George and Barbara Bush: 41st President and First lady

"Gotta tell ya, I really loved that guy. He's such a terrific fellow. Only one thing kinda bothered me, which I say, just never been able to understand—guy never seemed to need anybody."

"Except Nancy," says BB.

President-elect Bush continues, "off to Camp David every weekend, never took their kids with 'em! Bar and me, we'd go crazy if we found ourselves up there without a whole bunch of family running around."[72]

Gerald Ford: 38th President of the United States

Ford maintained a strained relationship with President Reagan. The animus occurred as a result of Reagan's behavior in the Carter-Ford contest. "His lack of campaigning was one of three or four reasons that resulted in my loss to Carter." It's not his (Reagan's) nature to help someone else. He believed in winning on his own.

> Totally off the record he was not what I would call a technically competent President. You know his knowledge of the budget, his knowledge of foreign policy—it was not up to the standards of either Republican or Democrat Presidents. .But he had a helluva of a flair. He could sell himself probably better than any president since FDR and maybe JFK. So I praise his assets, but I have reservations about his technical ability.[73]

APPENDIX H

May 30, 1963, Lyndon Johnson's Remarks at Gettysburg on Civil Rights:

> On this hallowed ground, heroic deeds were performed and eloquent words were spoken a century ago.
>
> We, the living, have not forgotten—and the world will never forget—the deeds or the words of Gettysburg. We honor them now as we join on this Memorial Day of 1963 in a prayer for permanent peace of the world and fulfillment of our hopes for universal freedom and justice.
>
> We are called to honor our own words of reverent prayer with resolution in the deeds we must perform to preserve peace and the hope of freedom.
>
> We keep a vigil of peace around the world.
>
> Until the world knows no aggressors, until the arms of tyranny have been laid down, until freedom has risen up in every land, we shall maintain our vigil to make sure our sons who died on foreign fields shall not have died in vain.
>
> As we maintain the vigil of peace, we must remember that justice is a vigil, too—a vigil we must keep in our own streets and schools and among the lives

of all our people—so that those who died here on their native soil shall not have died in vain.

One hundred years ago, the slave was freed.

One hundred years later, the Negro remains in bondage to the color of his skin.

The Negro today asks justice.

We do not answer him—we do not answer those who lie beneath this soil—when we reply to the Negro by asking, "Patience."

It is empty to plead that the solution to the dilemmas of the present rests on the hands of the clock. The solution is in our hands. Unless we are willing to yield up our destiny of greatness among the civilizations of history, Americans—White and Negro together—must be about the business of resolving the challenge which confronts us now.

Our nation found its soul in honor on these fields of Gettysburg 100 years ago. We must not lose that soul in dishonor now on the fields of hate.

To ask for patience from the Negro is to ask him to give more of what he has already given enough. But to fail to ask of him—and of all Americans—perseverance within the processes of a free and responsible society would be to fail to ask what the national interest requires of all its citizens.

The law cannot save those who deny it but neither can the law serve any who do not use it. The history of injustice and inequality is a history of disuse of the law. Law has not failed—and is not failing. We as a nation have failed ourselves by not trusting the law and by not using the law to gain sooner the ends of justice which law alone serves.

If the White over-estimates what he has done for the Negro without the law, the Negro may under-estimate what he is doing and can do for himself with the law.

If it is empty to ask Negro or White for patience, it is not empty—it is merely honest—to ask perseverance. Men may build barricades—and others may hurl themselves against those barricades—but what would happen at the barricades would yield no answers. The answers will only be wrought by our perseverance together. It is deceit to promise more as it would be cowardice to demand less.

In this hour, it is not our respective races which are at stake—it is our nation. Let those who care for their country come forward, North and South, White and Negro, to lead the way through this moment of challenge and decision.

The Negro says, "Now." Others say, "Never." The voice of responsible Americans—the voice of those who died here and the great man who spoke here—their voices say, "Together." There is no other way.

Until justice is blind to color, until education is unaware of race, until opportunity is unconcerned with the color of men's skins, emancipation will be a proclamation but not a fact. To the extent that the proclamation of emancipation is not fulfilled in fact, to that extent we shall have fallen short of assuring freedom to the free.[74]

NOTES

1. David Eisenhower and Julie Nixon Eisenhower (2011), *Going Home to Glory: A Memoir of Life with Dwight D. Eisenhower* (Simon & Schuster), 104.
2. Herbert Brownell and John P. Burke (1993), *Advising Ike: The Memoirs of Attorney General Herbert Brownell* (University of Press Kansas), 300.
3. Brownell and Burke (1993), *Advising Ike*, 103.
4. Brownell and Burke (1993), *Advising Ike*, 182, 89–113.
5. Susan Eisenhower (2020), Essay, in *How Ike Led: The Principles behind Eisenhower's Biggest Decisions* (Thomas Dunne Books), 305.
6. Emmet John Hughes (1981), *The Ordeal of Power: A Political Memoir of the Eisenhower Years* (Atheneum), 200–201.
7. Emmet John Hughes (1972), *The Living Presidency* (McCann and Geoghegan), 140.
8. Arthur Larson (1968), *Eisenhower: The President Nobody Knew* (Scribner's), 124.
9. James Reston (1956), "The Eisenhower Touch," *New York Times*.
10. Earl Warren (1977), *The Memoirs of Earl Warren* (Doubleday), 291–92.
11. Earl Warren (1977), *The Memoirs of Earl Warren*, 291–92.
12. Frederic E. Morrow (1963), *Black Man in the White House: A Diary of the Eisenhower Years by the Administrative Officer for Special Projects, the White House, 1955–1961* (Coward-McCann), 11–13.
13. Morrow (1963), *Black Man in the White House*, 11–13.
14. Chris Matthews, "Charm," in *Jack Kennedy: Elusive Hero* (Simon & Schuster), 230.
15. Excerpts from James Burke, recorded interview by Bill Hartigan, April 14, 1976. Washington DC, John F, Kennedy Library, Oral History Program.
16. Steven Levingston (2017), *Kennedy and King, the President, the Pastor and the Battle over Civil Rights* (Hachette Books), 226.
17. Excerpts from Walter Cronkite, recorded interview by Steven Fagan and Vicki Daitch, April 14, 2004. John F. Kennedy Library Oral History Program.
18. Jared Cohen (2020), Recorded conversation with Jesse Jackson, June 21, 2017, Cannes, France in *Accidental Presidents: Eight Men Who Changed America (*Simon & Schuster)..
19. Ralph G. Martin (1984), *A Hero for Our Time: An Intimate Story of the Kennedy Years* (Fawcett Crest), 502.
20. Barbara Leaming (2006), *Jack Kennedy: The Education of a Statesman* (W.W. Norton and Company), 255.
21. Raw notes of Ted White as cited in Chris Matthews, *Jack Kennedy: Elusive Hero* (Simon & Schuster), 400–01.
22. Excerpts from recorded interview by Ronald J. Grele. May 11, 1966, John F Kennedy Library Oral history Program.
23. Martin (1984), *A Hero for Our Time*, 220.
24. Martin (1984), *A Hero for Our Time*, 262.
25. Martin (1984), *A Hero for Our Time*, 143.

26. Excerpts from a recorded interview by Daniel Patrick Moynihan, July 8,1964, John F Kennedy Library, Old History Program.

27. Roy Wilkins and Tom Matthews (1983), *Standing Fast: The Autobiography of Roy Wilkins* (The Viking Press), 27.

28. Oral History Transcript. Lyndon B. Johnson Library Oral Histories [NAID 24617781], http://www lbjlibrary.org.

29. Lyndon B Johnson Library Oral Histories, http://www.lbjlibrary.org.

30. Lyndon B Johnson Library, interview by Paige Mulholan and Joseph B. Frantz.

31. Oral histories of Elizabeth Carpenter interview, 12/3/1968- Joe B Frantz.

32. Lyndon B. Johnson, interview with Carter. Library Oral Histories. http://www .lbjlibrary.org.

33. Paige and Mull. Interview, 2/1/1971.NAID 24617781.

34. Michael L. Gillette (1977, June 21), Hubert H. Humphrey, interview 3 (III), www.discoverlbj.org/item/oh-humphreyh-19770621-3-79-43.

35. Michael L. Gillette (1997, February 22), interview, www.discoverlbj.org/item/ ohlongr-19770222-1-89-17.

36. T. H. Baker (1969, July 10), interview, www.discoverlbj.org/item/oh-marshallT -1969-07-10-1-74-216.

37. Robert Dallek (1991), *Lone Star Rising: Lyndon Johnson and His Times: 1908–1960* (Oxford University Press), 352.

38. George Reedy (1982), *Lyndon B Johnson: A Memoir* (Andrews McMeel Pub), 12.

39. T. H. Baker, interview of Bayrd Rustin. Tape #1, www.discoverlbj.org/item/oh rustinb-1969061761-74-65.

40. Robert A. Caro (2012), *The Passage to Power: The Years of Lyndon Johnson* (Vintage Books), 589.

41. T. H. Baker (1989, January 17), interview, Www.discoverlbj.org/item/ ohTalmadge-196907-7-1-78-13.

42. Michael Gillette, oral history transcript Lyndon B Johnson Library (NAID 24617781).

43. Jonathan Aitkin (1993), *Nixon: The Life* (Regency Publishing).

44. Interview with T. H. Baker, April 1, 1969.

45. Robert Hardesty (1983, August 27), "The LBJ the Nation Seldom Saw."

46. Deborah Hart Strober and Gerald S. Strober (1994), *H. R. Halderman in Nixon: An Ural History of His Presidency* (Harper Collins), 115.

47. Strober and Strober (1994), *H. R. Halderman in Nixon*, 115.

48. Michael A. Genovese (2001), *The Power of the American Presidency: 1789–2000* (Oxford University Press).

49. Strober and Strober (1994), *H. R. Halderman in Nixon*, 113.

50. Dallek (1991), *Lone Star Rising*, 352.

51. Strober and Strober (1994), *H. R. Halderman in Nixon*, 113.

52. Genovese (2001), *The Power of the American Presidency*.

53. Interviewed by Richard Norton Smith, December 15, 2001. http:// geraldfordfoundation.org/centenial/oralhistory/bill-coleman.

54. David Gergen (2000), *Eyewitness to Power* (Simon & Schuster), 109.

55. Jim Kratsas (2013, summer), "A Providential President: Gerald Ford at 100, the Story of an Unexpected National Leader," archives.gov/files/publications/prologue/2013/summer/ford.pdf.

56. Kratsas (2013, summer), "A Providential President."

57. Kratsas (2013, summer), "A Providential President."

58. Krapsas (2013, summer), "A Providential President," 45. Prologue.

59. The funeral of Gerald Ford [YouTube].

60. Kevin Mattson (2009), *"What the Heck Are You Up to, Mr. President?": Jimmy Carter, America's "Malaise" and the Speech That Should Have Changed the Country* (Bloomsberry), 45.

61. Jimmy Carter (2010), *White House Diary* (Farrar, Straus and Giroux), 87.

62. Jonathan Alter (2020), *His Very Best: Jimmy Carter a Life* (Simon & Schuster), 669.

63. Peter G. Bourne (1997), *Jimmy Carter* (Scriber's), 495.

64. Interviewed by Brian Lamb, C-Span Book notes, October 29, 1989.

65. Martin Anderson and Annelise Anderson (2010), "Reagan the Man," in *Reagan's Secret War: The Untold Story of His Fight to Save the World from Nuclear Disaster* (Penguin Random House), 11.

66. Deborah Hart Strober and Gerald S. Strober (1998), *Reagan: The Man and His Presidency* (Houghton Miflin), 44.

67. Strober and Strober (1998), *Reagan*, 45.

68. Reagan Retrospective, Ep 5. Season 2, October3, 2016, Jim Miller [YouTube].

69. Chris Matthews (2013), *Tip and the Gipper* (Simon & Schuster), 35.

70. Matthews (2013), *Tip and the Gipper*, 127.

71. Stephen E. Ambrose, M. E. Bradford, Alonzo L. Hamby, Forrest McDonald, George H. Nash, James Nuechterlein, and Karl O'Lessker (1986, April 1), "How Great Was Ronald Reagan? Our 40th president's place in history," *Hoover Institute Policy Review*, https://www.hoover.org/research/how-great-was-ronald-reagan.

72. Edmund Dutch Morris (1999), *A Memoir of Ronald Reagan*, 638.

73. Thomas M. DeFrank (2007), *Write It When I'm Gone* (GP Putnam's Sons), 109–10.

74. Lyndon B. Johnson (2017, April 28), "May 30, 1963: Remarks at Gettysburg on Civil Rights," Miller Center, https://millercenter.org/the-presidency/presidential-speeches/may-30-1963-remarks-gettysburg-civil-rights.